PRAISE FOR **IRON IN THE BLOOD**

"One of America's great writers tackles one of America's great rivalries; a combination as perfect as Denny Chimes and Toomer's Corner. Auburn–Alabama is more than a football game. It's a cultural phenomenon, equal parts colorful and historic, fascinating and fun. If you love it—all of it—you'll love this book."

—Dan Wetzel, *New York Times* Bestselling Author and ESPN National Columnist

"College football isn't religion in the Deep South, but if it were a faith anywhere, it would be on the banks of Black Warrior River in Tuscaloosa, Alabama and on The Plains of Auburn, Alabama. And when these two schools meet every autumn right after Thanksgiving, life stops in the Yellowhammer State and the prayers for victory begin in this rivalry that is unlike any other in the history of sports. I've lived in Alabama for two decades, written cover stories and books about Alabama and Auburn, but no one has done a better job of capturing the essence, the melodrama, and flat-out craziness of the Iron Bowl than Jay Busbee in *Iron in the Blood*. Deeply reported, lyrical, moving, poignant, and at times side-splitting funny, Busbee has delivered the authoritative book on the only rivalry in the world that people plan weddings around, delay funerals for, and once upon time, killed some sacred trees over. A masterful account."

—Lars Anderson, *New York Times* Bestselling Author, *Chasing The Bear* and *The Storm and The Tide*

"From Bear and Bo to Shug and Saban to the rise of Cam Newton and the fall of the Confederacy, Busbee looks under every scrap of iron in the yard to discover the roots of college football's most ridiculously passionate rivalry."
—Ryan McGee, *New York Times* Bestselling Author and ESPN College Football Reporter

"*Iron in the Blood* is a wonderful tribute to one of college football's most storied rivalries. Jay Busbee brings the passion, history, and electric atmosphere that define the annual clash to the page in a way that kept me from putting it down. A must-read for anybody who loves college football and its history."
—Tom Fornelli, CBS Sports College Football Reporter

"The definitive history of *the* definitive rivalry in college football. Jay Busbee has brought the rich history, tradition, and passion of Alabama–Auburn to life in this book—from the early days to their biggest moments, their larger than life coaches, rivalry-defining plays, and everything in between. If you love college football, read this book!"
—Andrea Adelson, ESPN College Football Reporter

"*Iron in the Blood* takes us into one of the most hate-filled rivalries in college football. Jay gives us readers a fascinating, detailed look into the longtime football war between Auburn and Alabama. With so many colorful coaches, rabid fans, and involved politicians, Jay brings to light why the Iron Bowl is so much more than just a series of games."
—Ross Dellenger, Yahoo Sports College Football Reporter

IRON IN THE BLOOD

Also by Jay Busbee

Earnhardt Nation: The Full-Throttle Saga of NASCAR's First Family

IRON IN THE BLOOD

How the **ALABAMA** vs. **AUBURN** Rivalry Shaped the Soul of the South

JAY BUSBEE

Matt Holt Books
An Imprint of BenBella Books, Inc.
Dallas, TX

Iron in the Blood copyright © 2025 by Jay Busbee

All rights reserved. Except in the case of brief quotations embodied in critical articles or reviews, no part of this book may be used or reproduced, stored, transmitted, or used in any manner whatsoever, including for training artificial intelligence (AI) technologies or for automated text and data mining, without prior written permission from the publisher.

Matt Holt is an imprint of BenBella Books, Inc.
8080 N. Central Expressway
Suite 1700
Dallas, TX 75206
benbellabooks.com
Send feedback to feedback@benbellabooks.com

BenBella and *Matt Holt* are federally registered trademarks.

Printed in the United States of America
10 9 8 7 6 5 4 3 2 1

Library of Congress Control Number: 2025007185
ISBN 9781637747162 (hardcover)
ISBN 9781637747179 (electronic)

Editing by Lydia Choi
Copyediting by Kelly Brillhart
Proofreading by Ashley Casteel and Cheryl Beacham
Text design and composition by Jordan Koluch
Cover design by Brigid Pearson
Cover image © Getty Images / Kevin C. Cox
Printed by Lake Book Manufacturing

**Special discounts for bulk sales are available.
Please contact bulkorders@benbellabooks.com.**

For Stephen, Andrew, Brian, and Stacey

Have courage and stay happy, y'all.

CONTENTS

Introduction: **The Most Important Turf in Alabama**   1

Chapter 1: **The West Point of the South**   5
Chapter 2: **Born Fighting**   11

    Iron Bowl 1893: The First One   17

Chapter 3: **Separate Ways**   22
Chapter 4: **The Game that Changed Southern Football**   28

    Timeout: "Yea Alabama" and "Rammer Jammer"   35

Chapter 5: **The Tide Rises**   37

    Iron Bowl 1948: A Resumption of Hostilities   41

Chapter 6: **It's Pronounced "Jerr-dn"**   44

    Timeout: The Auburn Creed   51

Chapter 7: **A Starr Falls on T-Town**   52
Chapter 8: **A Graveyard for Coaches**   59
Chapter 9: **The Man from Moro Bottom**   68
Chapter 10: **Champion Tigers**   82
Chapter 11: **Faith Rewarded**   87
Chapter 12: **When the Chain Hit the Pipe**   96

Timeout: War Eagle	101
Chapter 13: **The Tarnished Crown**	103
Chapter 14: **Bigger Than Ball**	110
Chapter 15: **Falling Off the Pace**	117
Chapter 16: **The Bear vs. the Snake**	123
Iron Bowl 1967: The Run in the Mud	132
Chapter 17: **The Pat Sullivan Experience**	136
Timeout: Roll Tide	144
Chapter 18: **The Game That Changed the South**	145
Iron Bowl 1972: Punt Bama Punt	155
Chapter 19: **The Last Days of Shug Jordan**	159
Chapter 20: **The Sign of the Wolf**	166
Iron Bowl 1981: The Record	172
Chapter 21: **Bo**	177
Iron Bowl 1982: Bo Over the Top	185
Chapter 22: **The Lord Gets His Football Coach**	190
Chapter 23: **Bo Does Anything, Not Everything**	195
Iron Bowl 1985: The Kick	204
Iron Bowl 1989: The Final Brick	209
Chapter 24: **The Sun Sets on The Plains**	214
Timeout: Aubie, Big Al, and the Bands	220
Chapter 25: **Junction Boy Made Good**	223
Chapter 26: **The Most Auburn Year Ever**	228
Chapter 27: **The Tide Recedes**	234

Chapter 28: **The Man from Monongah** 239
Chapter 29: **Fear the Thumb** 248
Chapter 30: **The Process Comes to Tuscaloosa** 256
Chapter 31: **Superman on The Plains** 264

    Iron Bowl 2010: The Camback 273

Chapter 32: **The Man with Too Much Bama in Him** 278
Chapter 33: **Tragedy and Healing** 290

    Iron Bowl 2013: Kick Six 299

Chapter 34: **Joyless Murderball** 306
Chapter 35: **Chaos on The Plains** 313
Chapter 36: **Make Bama Great Again** 319
Chapter 37: **Senator Coach Tuberville** 330

    Iron Bowl 2023: Gravedigger 334

Chapter 38: **The End of an Era** 339

Epilogue 345
Bibliography 351
Acknowledgments 381

"Nothing matters more than beating that cow college on the other side of the state."
>Bear Bryant, head coach,
>University of Alabama, 1958–1982

"Wait until you whip their ass. You ain't seen nothing yet. It will be a different world."
>Pat Dye, head coach,
>Auburn University, 1981–1992

Introduction

THE MOST IMPORTANT TURF IN ALABAMA

There's a small square of turf in the north corner of Auburn's Jordan-Hare Stadium that's some of the most hallowed ground in recent college football history. That stretch of grass has raised hopes and shattered dreams, inspired celebrations and broken hearts. Europe has cathedrals; America has college football stadiums. And that little swatch of green in a tiny town in eastern Alabama is one of the most sanctified spots of them all.

In November 2013, Auburn's Chris Davis stood about 109 yards away from that particular stretch of grass, in the opposite end zone, his feet right on the *E* in TIGERS. The sun had gone down an hour before, and with it Auburn's apparent hopes for a national championship. There was one second remaining on the clock, one second standing between Auburn and oblivion.

Alabama—dreaded, feared, loathed Alabama—was lining up for a long field goal to break a 28–28 tie. Kicking is always dicey business in college football. Kicking has probably caused more heart attacks in the South than smoking and fried foods combined. Kicking is salvation or damnation, no middle ground.

With that 0:01 showing on Jordan-Hare's dated scoreboard, foot met leather. The ball flew into the Alabama night, and it was clear from the moment of impact that this kick wouldn't fly far enough. This was the Alabama–Auburn rivalry in microcosm: Alabama unable to escape the gravitational pull of Auburn; Auburn hanging on by its fingernails until a miracle occurred. As the ball traced an arc that would fall short of the crossbar, Auburn fans sighed with relief and Alabama fans grumbled; the game would go to overtime and they'd settle it there.

Only . . . the ball was still in the air. And Davis was still back there, waiting for it to fall. He caught the short field goal attempt, his heels nearly out of bounds . . . and he ran from that end zone straight into college football history and Auburn legend. Kick Six, they called it then, and they will forever.

Ten years later almost to the day, Alabama's Jalen Milroe looked out on that same corner of the end zone. Milroe, a cannon-armed quarterback from Katy, Texas, faced even more dire circumstances than Auburn had. Alabama, a national championship dark horse, was losing 24–20 with just over 40 seconds remaining in the game. Down to his last snap, 31 yards from the end zone, Milroe had only one option: heave it north and pray.

He threw it deep—nearly half the length of the football field—and there, waiting in the end zone, almost exactly where Davis had crossed the goal line, stood Alabama receiver Isaiah Bond. The play was known internally as Gravedigger—because it would bury the opponent—and on this night, it worked to perfection for Alabama. Bond caught the ball, struck a James Bond–style pose—Bond, get it?—and Alabama won a most improbable Iron Bowl.

When you're making a list of college football's greatest plays, Kick Six ranks right there at the top. And although no one knew it at the time, Gravedigger would turn college football upside down, locking marquee programs out of the College Football Playoff and leading—directly or indirectly—to hundreds of major and minor coaching changes, and the total upheaval of several blue-chip programs.

Two plays. Endless ripples throughout college football. All from one corner of one end zone.

This is a book about two programs that took very different paths to arrive at the same destination, programs that are both nurturing mother and stern father to their fans—fans who, especially in the case of Alabama, may not have come anywhere near attending either school. It's a century-plus-long tale of loyalty and love, faith and perseverance.

"It's in the DNA," ESPN journalist Ryan McGee says. "With these Alabama and Auburn people, the granddad went there. The grandma went there. Their great-uncle played football there. Their cousin was on the softball team. The difference is that it is a literal strand of your DNA. It's not just, your family has had Red Sox tickets since 1945."

"If you're an Auburn fan, you probably have some sort of tie to Auburn. You either went to school here, or you have family that went to school here, or you live close by," says *Auburn Observer* writer Justin Ferguson. "Whereas if you're an Alabama fan and you don't have a tie to the school, you're probably also a Dallas Cowboys fan and a New England Patriots fan."

"There's no denying who the two teams' archrival is," says ESPN national columnist Dan Wetzel. "Alabama's archrival is Auburn, Auburn's archrival is Alabama. Oklahoma will say, 'Well, we care more about Texas than Oklahoma State,' Michigan will say, 'We care more about Ohio State than Michigan State.' An out-of-state rival can be intense, but you're not on top of each other all day long."

This is a tale of two warring families—patricians and underdogs, an elite institution and an everyman one. This is a tale of two schools that embody the best—and, at times, the worst—of a beautiful state ravaged by its own basest instincts.

This is a story about national championships won and lost, icons who rose and fell, legends born and dynasties crumbled. It's a story of one-name giants who walked the earth: *Bear. Shug. Bo. Nick.* It's a forever war with battles as memorable as family members' names: *The Kick. Punt Bama Punt. The Run in the Mud. The Camback.* But more than that, it's a story of how these two universities shaped the history of their state, how they pushed Alabama ahead—and, at some points, held it back—in a century-plus of societal upheaval. Sports reflect society, and the ways in which these two programs reflect the Yellowhammer State are to their credit... mostly.

"In the state of Alabama, people are told over and over again how terrible they are at so many different things," says John Talty, author of multiple books on Alabama and college football. *"You're toward the bottom three in obesity, bottom three in poverty, bottom three in education.* The thing that they can really beat their chest about is football. You can't talk trash to the state of Alabama or the people within it about football. I do think it gives the people in this state a tremendous source of pride and joy, knowing that football is Alabama's number one product to the world. That really permeates so much of the culture and how people act day-to-day."

Fundamentally, this is a story for the people who invest in this game and these institutions with holy reverence, the fans who head to T-Town or The Plains every fall Saturday, rolling down Interstate 85 or Highway 280 or Interstate 20 or Highway 82 or any of a hundred back roads that lead down from the mountains, through the Alabama pines, up from the Gulf. People live and die with the Tide and the Tigers, and that is in no way a literary conceit. They love these programs with their whole blessed hearts. Much like religion, in Alabama you get baptized into the crimson or orange fold at birth, and also much like religion, if you decide to break away from the family orthodoxy, you risk the wrath of generations of loved ones.

This is the story of the players on the field and the coaches on the sidelines, yes, but it's also a story for the people in the stands, the fans who wait all their lives for a moment like Kick Six or Gravedigger, and then rise as one to cheer both their team and their own good luck to be there to witness that moment. And if you're not one of those people, allow us to introduce you to this whole glorious, mad, crimson-and-white, blue-and-burnt-orange circus.

There are more important things than football in Alabama, but we'll be damned if we can think of them right now. Here's why.

Chapter 1

THE WEST POINT OF THE SOUTH

The campus burned.

Union soldiers arrived at the University of Alabama in April 1865 hell-bent on torching what had become a symbolic wellspring of the Confederacy, the capstone of the Yellowhammer State, and a training ground for Confederate soldiers. In the waning days of the Civil War, when the conflict's outcome was clear and all that remained was a final tally of the dead, Union soldiers put the torch to the university.

Tuscaloosa sits roughly 60 miles west of Birmingham and far from most sites of Civil War conflict. For the most part, its role during the war was to provide support—specifically, manpower—to Confederate war efforts. When Alabama seceded from the Union, the university transitioned into a military institution—some even dubbed it "The West Point of the South"—and an array of generals, colonels, majors, and other Confederate officers spread forth from Tuscaloosa.

The city also hosted some of the Civil War's first POWs, thanks to its location deep within the Confederacy. Union soldiers captured at Bull Run were shipped to Tuscaloosa and imprisoned in buildings on University Avenue about a mile west of campus. Confederate soldiers were hospitalized in buildings around the city. Cannon, cloth, and explosives were manufactured all over Tuscaloosa, even on the grounds of the university itself.

Like much of the South during the war, Tuscaloosa saw its fortunes rise quickly and crash even faster. The optimism of the early days of the war faded to grim realization that the Union army would soon crush the rebellion, and Tuscaloosa knew its geographic distance from the theaters of war would not save it from Union forces.

"If the enemy ever reach this place," University of Alabama president Landon C. Garland wrote Governor John Gill Shorter in 1863, "they would not leave at this University one brick standing upon the other."

Two years later, the Union proved him correct. Union General John T. Croxton left Birmingham on March 30, 1865, with 1,500 cavalrymen and orders to travel to Tuscaloosa "to destroy the bridge, factories, mills, university, and whatever else may be of benefit to the rebel cause." Within a week, General Robert E. Lee would surrender to General Ulysses S. Grant at Appomattox, but before then, there was still a rebellion to quell.

On the evening of April 3, Croxton's troops looped around Tuscaloosa to approach from the north. Confederate forces attempted to sabotage the bridge across the Black Warrior River from Northport into Tuscaloosa, but the Union reconstructed the bridge and began marching into the city in the early hours of April 4.

The attack on Tuscaloosa came so swiftly that much of the city was caught by surprise—Union troops even interrupted a wedding in progress, arresting the groom, a Confederate officer. A small skirmish at the intersection of University Boulevard and Greensboro Avenue ended quickly when the Union troops overwhelmed the city's last line of defense: the university's young cadets.

"The cadets averaged fifteen or sixteen years of age and were equipped with muskets of poor quality," historical records indicate, "while the Federal troops were using Spencer repeating carbines which were the best type of gun used in the war." The overmatched cadets were ordered to retreat, and the Union now had Tuscaloosa at its mercy.

Union soldiers proceeded to torch the university and surrounding factories, sending plumes of black smoke curling high into the skies above

Tuscaloosa. A small roundhouse near what is now Gorgas Library weathered the attack, as did two other academic and residential structures. The President's Mansion and its surrounding buildings survived the fire too, thanks to—if legend is to be believed—the actions of Louisa Frances Garland, the university president's wife. Spotting flames near the campus, Louisa Garland rushed from a nearby hospital where she had hidden, found Union soldiers lighting her parlor on fire, and demanded they extinguish the flames.

True or not, the message embedded in the story is clear: *Bring your fire and your fury to Alabama. We'll stomp it out. And one day, we'll have our revenge.*

———

As long as it's existed, Alabama has been a state at war with itself. In the early 19th century, Alabama Fever—a lust for land on which to grow cotton—lured both workers and capital from all over the South. That set up a familiar dynamic that would define the state for decades to come: the ongoing struggle between the land's owners and its farmers.

"For the yeoman farmers, the driving concern was maintaining their personal independence, remaining free from control by anyone else," wrote Edwin C. Bridges in *Alabama: The Making of an American State*. "The planters' lifestyle and aspirations seem almost designed to provoke the yeoman farmers' fears. Not only were the planters wealthier and better educated, they also did not depend on the labor of their own hands." The conflict runs through the state's DNA, and it would surface on the football field soon enough.

Alabama in its earliest decades was a mass of contradictions, opposites living side by side with shared lives. Throughout its history, Alabama has made room for, in the words of former University of Alabama dean E. Culpepper Clark, "hillbillies and industrial workers, small farmers and big planters, a large Black population concentrated in its Black Belt (named for its rich alluvial soil) . . . rocket scientists and rednecks, aristocrats and populists, a politically influential KKK and a politically active NAACP, lintheads and longshoremen, bankers and shopkeepers." A state of opposites, then, with little in common to bind them together . . . with one major exception.

The University of Alabama's origins predate the state itself. The Alabama territory was admitted to the Union on December 14, 1819, but the US Congress had already directed the territory to set aside property for a designated "seminary of learning." That "seminary"—the University of the State of Alabama—was officially created by the state's General Assembly on December 18, 1820, even though it didn't actually have a home.

Early on, Tuscaloosa was the capital of Alabama, and it won the right to host the university in 1827. Four years later, on April 18, 1831, the University of Alabama's first four professors began educating its first 52 students.

Designed by Scottish architects, built by enslaved workers, constructed with sandstone and lumber from the university's own holdings, the University of Alabama immediately sought to establish itself as the epicenter of higher learning and elite preparedness in the state. Tuition, including room and board, ran $80 a year.

Right from the start, though, the university's high-minded aspirations posed a significant problem for a state still largely under the control of multiple Native American tribes. The university expected incoming students to read classical Greek and Latin, but the state of Alabama wasn't prepared to educate its young students up to that level. The university lowered its standards for entry, and ended up enrolling a vast range of unqualified and unprepared students—for instance, only eight of the 105 students who enrolled in 1835 actually graduated.

The university struggled to develop its identity; plans to establish it as a seminary failed early on, and Garland reoriented the school as a military academy just prior to the Civil War. That helped fuel the school's growth ... and also made it a prime target for Union forces in the final days of the Civil War.

After Union forces burned most of the campus, the school was rebuilt and reopened in 1871, ditching the military school ethos. Over the next 30 years, with the aid of compensation from Congress for war losses, the university constructed many of the Classical Revival academic buildings that populate the campus today.

College football had established a foothold in northern colleges, but it wasn't until 1892 that the sport made its way to the University of Alabama, courtesy of a student by the name of William G. Little. He'd played the sport at Phillips Exeter Academy, and arrived at Alabama "carrying his uniform and a great bag of enthusiasm for the game," in the words of the *Crimson White*, Alabama's student newspaper.

"Football is the game of the future in college life," Little declared. "Players will be forced to live a most ascetic life, on a diet of rare beef and pork, to say nothing of rice pudding for dessert, for additional courage and fortitude, to stand the bumps and injuries."

Little organized a team of fellow students, and the university's Athletic Association hired a gentleman with the magnificent name of Eugene Beauharnais Beaumont Jr. to coach the team, apparently only because he hailed from the University of Pennsylvania in the hallowed Ivy League.

The University of Alabama's football dynasty began by, appropriately enough, beating the hell out of an overmatched opponent. On Friday, November 11, 1892, the Cadets—the Crimson Tide nickname was still years in the future—stomped a group of Birmingham-area high schoolers, 56–0.

Led by "Big" Little, and wearing white sweaters with UA stitched on the front, red stockings, and absolutely no pads or helmets, the Cadets employed the so-called flying wedge to devastating effect. One of the "mass momentum" plays of college football's earliest days, the flying wedge involved players charging down the field in a tight V shape, splitting the skin and splintering the unprotected bones of anyone unlucky enough to be in their path. (Mass momentum plays were literally deadly; in the first three years of the 1890s, 71 players died as a result of injuries suffered on the field, according to the *New York Times*. At the dawn of the 20th century, college football came within a hairsbreadth of being outlawed entirely.)

The team would go on to lose the next day to a tougher opponent, Birmingham Athletic Club, by a score of 5–4, when—according to news reports of the day—a BAC kicker drilled a 65-yard field goal. (This was via dropkick. The NCAA recognizes the longest placekicked field goal in college history at 69 yards, achieved by Abilene Christian's Ove Johansson in 1976.)

Football caught on rapidly at Alabama—so rapidly that administrators briefly barred athletic teams from playing off campus, and even considered banning the sport entirely. Alabama students turned out in raucous, rowdy numbers to cheer on their men in crimson ... and nowhere was Alabama's pride and exuberance more in evidence than when they played a certain agricultural school on the other side of the state.

Chapter 2

BORN FIGHTING

The train rumbled southwest from Atlanta, carrying a crew of football-mad young men. They were students at Georgia Tech, yes, but they were also football players from the big city, and they were headed to some little backwater Alabama town to throw around the locals. This was 1896, a decade before they would become known as the Yellow Jackets, so they went by the name Blacksmiths.

Anticipation was high; even in its earliest days, college football had the ability to stir the blood of players and fans alike. Just three years before, the Blacksmiths had walloped their in-state rivals, the Georgia Bulldogs, resulting in a postgame rock fight that created one of the South's most enduring college football rivalries. Today, though, they would be facing off against the students of the Agricultural and Mechanical College of Alabama.

As they approached the small town of Auburn, however, they realized that they weren't stopping. They could hear the brakes of the train, but the landscape kept blowing by. What was going on?

Blame the students of Auburn's tiny agricultural college. In exultation at their first on-campus game ever, they'd spent the night before slicking up the tracks with a mixture of wagon-axle grease, soap, and lard. They greased up 400 yards of track on either side of the Auburn train station, and when the train hit the greasy mess, it skidded for miles, almost to nearby Loachapoka. The Blacksmiths had to walk all the way back to Auburn, carrying their bags and gear with them in a grim small-hours walk.

The fact that Auburn beat Georgia Tech 45–0 in that game is an enduring Auburn legend. For decades afterward, pajama-clad students would commemorate the moment in a "Wreck Tech" march from the campus to the nearby train depot.

Also part of the Auburn legend: The school immediately lost its next game to Georgia, 12–6, giving the Bulldogs the title in the Southern Intercollegiate Athletic Association, the forerunner of the SEC. At Auburn, chaos rules, and nothing goes quite as you'd expect.

It's somehow fitting that Auburn University was born fighting. It's also appropriate that one of Auburn's creation stories is an incident of glorious, chaotic vandalism that would probably be classified as domestic terrorism today.

The school that would one day become Auburn began as an idea, an idea that both the town of Auburn, in eastern Alabama, and the town of Greensboro, in the western half of the state, wanted to claim for their own. In 1854, both towns appealed to the Alabama Conference of the Methodist Church, seeking to host a men's college. Greensboro, located in Alabama's fertile Black Belt, had the edge, and in January 1856, the state legislature established there a Methodist school it named Southern University. In the process, though, the legislature riled up the town of Auburn by, in effect, dismissing the entire region as poverty-stricken and irredeemable.

Just one month after creating Southern University, the legislature established East Alabama Male College in the town of Auburn. At that point, the town comprised a bank, a post office, a railroad stop, and a handful of churches; the college only added to its growth, from wide spot in the road to legitimate town.

East Alabama Male College opened its doors in 1859, with six professors teaching moral philosophy, natural science, mathematics, and ancient languages. Students admitted to the small Methodist college were required to know Latin and Greek and, once on campus, attend prayer services twice daily. State lawmakers prohibited the sale of alcoholic beverages within the town of Auburn and five miles outside its boundaries, with a first offense carrying a massive $100 fine and each subsequent offense adding three months in prison. This law has since been repealed.

Within two years of the college's opening, the young state of Alabama withdrew from the Union. College students and faculty members alike enlisted in the Confederate army, and the college served as a Confederate hospital. The town of Auburn remained untouched during the war until July 1864, when Major General Lovell H. Rousseau's Union forces torched a few buildings and tore up some railroad tracks, but left the town and the college largely intact.

Shortly after the war ended, East Alabama Male College found itself the centerpiece of a fundamental philosophical battle between two opposing forces. For decades, Southern colleges had followed the lead of their Northeastern forebears—a heavy emphasis on classical literature and ancient languages, the better to develop educated elites to run the nation. Such was the case over in Tuscaloosa and, early on, in Auburn too.

After a resounding defeat in the Civil War, however, many educators in the postwar South believed the region had failed to develop students who were ready to compete, whether on the battlefield or in modern society. The region needed schools that could educate students in applied science, agriculture, and other immediately useful disciplines.

East Alabama Male College never recovered its footing after the war; a combination of financial troubles and logistical ones, like a leaking roof, outstripped the community's ability to fund the school. In 1871, the college's trustees donated the entire property to the state of Alabama, which used Civil War-era federal legislation to breathe new life into the school.

The Morrill Act, first proposed in the 1850s and named for a congressman from Vermont, granted federal money to states for the express purpose of creating colleges designed to teach agriculture, mechanics, and military tactics. In sharp contrast to the more elite-minded education of classical antiquity—which favored the children of the upper class—Morrill Act universities were intended to open up higher education to a broader base of Americans. (Southern states had opposed the Morrill Act prior to departing the Union, reasoning that it would hasten the end of their slavery-based agricultural economy. The Civil War handled that matter effectively enough.)

Alabama applied for a Morrill Act land grant, and received permission to use 240,000 acres of public land for a college . . . with an undetermined location. Again, the town of Auburn found itself in a fight with a western Alabama town for the right to host a college, but this time, the opponent was far more fearsome: Tuscaloosa, home of the University of Alabama.

Tuscaloosa's argument was simple: bring all the state's higher learning into one location. The future T-Town also didn't relish the thought of a federally backed university elsewhere in the state, cutting into its established success and presence. But Tuscaloosa's success was a beacon to Auburn, which wanted its own version of the estimated $100,000 a year that the University of Alabama pumped into the local economy.

Auburn won this battle—in one sense, its most important Iron Bowl victory ever—and on February 26, 1872, the Alabama legislature established the Agricultural and Mechanical College of Alabama on the campus of the old East Alabama Male College. With a heavy emphasis on agriculture, the college served a significant need in Alabama—without its traditional system of unpaid labor, the state's agricultural framework was in disarray. The college helped train students in both the theory and practice of agriculture, even as an entire new labor force—sharecropping—replaced the old form of enslaved labor.

The college admitted only male students, classified them as cadets, and expected them to participate in military-style drills every weekday. Gambling and other tomfoolery were forbidden, and cadets were not permitted to use firearms, foul language, or alcohol. The school was serious about its rules: one student who was caught abandoning his duties for the sin of participating in a baseball game was confined to chapel for two Saturdays and forced to walk the "punishment post"—marching back and forth while carrying a chunk of wood that could weigh as much as 10 pounds.

More than two decades before their first matchup on the football field, Alabama and Auburn began hurling insults at each other. Isaac Taylor Tichenor, the first president of the Agricultural and Mechanical College, contended that the University of Alabama "prepared only a relative few for the learned professions," wrote Dwayne Cox in *The Village on the Plain*, a history of Auburn. "An institution such as the Agricultural and Mechanical College at Auburn, which brought vocational training to the masses, deserved more state patronage than the elitist University of Alabama."

Tichenor didn't stop there. He contended that the University of Alabama, in Cox's words, "produced politicians who could hold forth on theories of constitutional law, but it failed to prepare the region for modern warfare. He believed that the New South needed experts trained in applied science, . . . not polished socialites steeped in ancient lore." This may be the first recorded instance of Auburn calling out Alabama, and it had the desired effect of riling up the blue bloods over in Tuscaloosa.

Soon enough, though, administrators at universities throughout Alabama had a more pressing problem to deal with: the incursion of a malicious influence, one that threatened discipline, drew the interest of the student body, and aroused ungentlemanly passion.

Its name: football.

Begun in the Northeast in the years after the Civil War, football soon made its way south. In Auburn, a history and Latin professor by the name of George Petrie fell in love with the game and introduced it to the Agricultural and Mechanical College campus. Naturally, it was an immediate hit, and also naturally, the college expressed concern about its pernicious influence.

"President [William LeRoy] Broun appreciated the manly qualities instilled by intercollegiate athletics, but he wanted to keep sports subordinate to the school's educational mission," Cox wrote. "In addition, football contests became occasions for overindulgence in alcoholic beverages." As it was in the beginning, is now, and ever shall be.

Petrie, a graduate of the University of Virginia, imported his alma mater's blue and orange color scheme to The Plains, giving the school an identity it retains to this day. The Agricultural and Mechanical College played its first intercollegiate football game in 1892, in Atlanta's Piedmont Park against the University of Georgia.

One year later, attention turned to that university over in Tuscaloosa.

IRON BOWL 1893: THE FIRST ONE

They rolled into town from both sides of the state, ready to drink, fight, and watch football. They sported crimson and white, or blue and orange, and oh, did they love their boys on the field. They cheered every score, and cursed the referees, and grew salty about the game's conclusion, and left one hell of a mess behind, overwhelming hotel rooms and restaurants, their laughter and whoops of delirium carrying well into the night.

This was not the 21st century. This was the first-ever meeting between Auburn and Alabama in 1893, and it set the tone for the next century-plus to come.

The date: February 22, 1893. The place: Lakeview Park in Birmingham. The site: Base Ball Park, a restriped ballfield inside the park in Birmingham's southern reaches. That afternoon—a Wednesday, oddly enough—marked the first football game between the University of Alabama and the Agricultural and Mechanical College of Alabama. (This book will refer to the latter institution as Auburn for simplicity's sake, even though the school didn't officially take that name until 1960. Likewise, we're calling this rivalry game the Iron Bowl, although that moniker wouldn't come around for several more decades.)

Fans began to arrive at Lakeview Park around 2:00 p.m., traveling in everything from private cars to taxicabs to horse-drawn carriages. Steam-engine trains from both Tuscaloosa and Auburn added more cars in order to bring hundreds more fans for the mass pilgrimage to Base Ball Park. The mood in the air was jubilant—everyone there to see "the manly sport of foot ball [sic]," as the *Daily News*—later to become the *Birmingham News*—put it in a substantial Page 3 story right next to a notice about the impending inauguration of President Grover Cleveland.

"Men and women who heretofore have jeered at such exhibitions of brawn and muscle were eager to see the contest," some unnamed poet at the *News* continued. "Little children just beginning to toddle about were anxious to see the big boys fight."

The crowd—estimated at as many as 5,000 fans—overwhelmed the poor ticket taker, who nonetheless tabulated gate receipts of $1,200 to $1,500. Once inside, men and boys rushed to the sidelines, standing at the roped-off edges of the field. (The *News* helpfully but unnecessarily points out that these men were "unaccompanied by ladies.") Brilliantly decorated carriages lined the east side of the field, marking the spot of what was effectively the first tailgate in Auburn–Alabama history.

Members of the local Birmingham Police Department attempted to keep the crowds in order, putting up rope lines to maintain some semblance of order. It proved as difficult then as it is now to get football fans in the state of Alabama to calm down.

What's fascinating about the first Auburn–Alabama matchup is just how familiar it seems, how many of the elements still present today were baked into the game's DNA from the very first day. An Auburn or Alabama fan from the 21st century, transported back to Lakeview Park, would have no trouble picking out their team.

The players from "Tuskaloosa," as it was then spelled, wore red stockings and white sweaters with a large *U* and *A* stitched onto their chests. This was before the term *Crimson Tide* existed, but the crimson of their uniforms—and of the fans' flags—was evident everywhere. Meanwhile, the boys from Auburn wore white pants, blue stockings, and blue sweaters with an orange *A* sewn onto the front.

Naturally, even in this first iteration of the game, there were disputes.

Alabama considered the February 22 game to be the end of its first season playing football. On the other hand, Auburn considered this game the start of their 1893 season. The "football in the fall" tradition was still years in the future.

Alabama took the field first, just before 3 p.m., and every crimson-wearing fan rose and cheered their arrival. Auburn followed, and their fans shouted every bit as loudly. The fever pitch overwhelmed many in attendance, including the *News* writer, who gushed that the players' "handsome faces, broad shoulders, strong little limbs, and powerful arms were the admiration of the young and old of each sex." Two Yale football veterans, J. W. Taylor and E. L. Simons, served as officials for the game, sporting very un-referee-like derby hats and walking sticks. (They apparently did their job well, receiving no complaints or threats from the crowd, a rarity then as now.)

From the start of the game, which began shortly before 3:30 p.m., it was an out-and-out dogfight. There was little punting and, for that matter, little defense. The game bore some resemblance to the football of today, but there were some significant differences too. Touchdowns were worth four points, and a kick after the touchdown was worth two. Field goals were worth five points. Players wore no safety equipment, and everyone played both offense and defense unless they were injured. Not only that, but the players ranged in age from a 16-year-old to a college professor.

"As the boys would pile up on one another," the *News* wrote, "the ladies would get alarmed, fearing that they would have their bones broken, but their gentlemen friends would kindly assure the timid sympathetic women that the athletic youths could be dropped from the top of the grand stand [*sic*] to the ground without sustaining any injury." This was manifestly untrue, but on-the-fly mythmaking is an essential element of college football.

The biggest play of the first half came when Auburn captain Tom Daniels ripped off a 65-yard gain to set up a touchdown; delirious Auburn fans stormed the field to celebrate with him. (In the first recruiting controversy of the Alabama–Auburn rivalry, Daniels enrolled at Auburn for just one semester after playing for four years at what was then called Trinity College, now Duke University.)

The teams traded touchdowns, and at halftime, the score stood at 14–12. Both teams used a series of wedge plays—the flying wedge, the turtleback wedge, the revolving wedge—to varying degrees of success. (The passing game, like much of what is familiar to modern fans, did not yet exist.) One notable picture from the game taken by John Horgan Jr. depicts the flying wedge in action. The crowds along the sidelines are clearly visible, as is the mass of players in the center of the field.

The game included plenty of scoring, an actual controversy—whether Alabama had truly scored on its final possession—and, when the final whistle blew, a 32–22 victory for Auburn. It was a defiant, definitive blow struck by the blue-collar lads and ladies of Auburn—the school began admitting women in 1892—and a poke in the eye of the well-bred elitists of Alabama. Neither side would forget how that moment felt, and the feeling would run through the blood of their children, grandchildren, and great-grandchildren.

After the game, the victorious Auburn lads gathered around a carriage where a young socialite by the name of Delma Wilson presented a cup to the winning team and captain Daniels. In her moment in the spotlight, Miss Wilson rose to her feet and proclaimed, "Gallant and victorious captain, in the name of the city of Birmingham, I present this cup. Drink from it and remember the victory hat. You have won this day. May you and your team live to see many more victories."

"We feel proud of the honor," Daniels replied, "and assure you it is a great pleasure to receive this cup from the city of Birmingham and through your hands."

Cheers rippled across the park, and both teams—and their fans—barreled into Birmingham to keep the party going. The Alabama team commandeered most of the 100 rooms of the Caldwell Hotel, a magnificent six-story French Renaissance edifice in downtown Birmingham bedecked with crimson and white for the occasion.

That evening, Alabama fans drowned their sorrows in a special menu featuring "Consommé a la Tuscaloosa" and "Potage a l'Auburn" as a first course, with "University Salad," "Baked Kikoph Lamb," "Right Guard Cornbread with Left Tackle Buttermilk," "Left Flank of Beef," "Braized Quarter Back of Tennessee Lamb," and other courses, with a dessert of "One-team-out-in-the-cold Sherbet."

Meanwhile, the victorious Auburn squad and their fans claimed the Florence Hotel, a brick-and-wrought-iron castle not far from the Caldwell. No record exists of their menu, but the joy of beating an in-state rival surely tasted better than any beef or lamb. (The Caldwell burned almost to the ground less than two years later, while the Florence was demolished in 1916 and is now the site of an IMAX theater.)

The first-ever gridiron battle between the two rivals was an absolute, unqualified success. The *Birmingham News* breathlessly called it "the day on which the greatest foot ball [sic] game was ever played in Alabama." Correction: the greatest game *so far*.

Something had come to life on a tiny field in Birmingham on February 22, 1893, and no one present that day in Lakeview Park could have possibly imagined how far it would reach, and how powerful it would become.

1893 IRON BOWL

Final Score: Auburn 32, Alabama 22

Chapter 3

SEPARATE WAYS

From the earliest days of Alabama football, one mantra became clear: *Beat Auburn*. All other sins can be excused, but not losing to that agricultural school. E. B. Beaumont, Alabama's first coach, learned that hard lesson quickly; he was dismissed after just one season leading the Cadets and posting a record of 2–2. In eulogizing the Beaumont "era," Alabama's college yearbook, the *Corolla*, was brutal: "We were unfortunate in securing a coach. After keeping him for a short time, we found that his knowledge of the game was very limited. We therefore got rid of him."

Despite the school's enthusiasm for the sport, Alabama's actual football players weren't exactly covering themselves in glory. Dubbed "The Thin Red Line," Alabama struggled in almost every game; in 1895, Auburn waxed them 48–0. After that game, Hill Ferguson, a player and future university trustee, sighed, "Nobody seemed to have enough interest to take a picture of the team."

The early Auburn–Alabama matchups were loosely organized. From the start, when the two schools couldn't even agree to which season the game belonged, there was strife.

Early on, Auburn held a decided edge, winning six of the first seven matchups between 1893 and 1902. In one four-game stretch, Auburn outscored Alabama 141–5. Auburn cycled through a series of head coaches—including John Heisman, for whom the trophy is named—in the first decade of the program's existence before settling on Mike Donahue. A Yale-educated Irishman, Donahue was a wee gentleman—standing 5 foot 4, he was not yet 30 when he took over coaching duties at Auburn. Fuzzy Woodruff, the esteemed Southern sportswriter, called Donahue "a mouse-like little man with little to say, save when aroused, on which he was capable of utterances of great fire and fervor." Some of that spittle and fury was directed at Alabama, particularly in regard to the 1907 Iron Bowl.

That game ended in a 6–6 tie, but it also ended—for four decades—the schools' budding rivalry. Popular mythology sprang up that the two schools fought so much during the game, both on the field and in the stands, that officials terminated the whole affair, but the truth was a lot more mundane. Auburn and Alabama couldn't agree on a per diem for players, or on where the referees would hail from, or even when to schedule the game during the season. (Except for that initial 1893 Iron Bowl held in February, and two in 1902 and 1903 held in October, the game has kicked off at the end of November or the start of December every year it's been played.)

In 1907, 17 players from each team received $2 apiece—around $70 in current dollars—for food and lodging. Early in 1908, Auburn asked Alabama to increase the per diem to $3.50 for 22 players per team. Alabama countered with an offer of $3 per day for 20 players. That proved to be the breaking point, although the ongoing hostility between the two schools was certainly a significant factor. The seemingly minor issues nonetheless proved insurmountable, and both sides decided to walk away from the fight until 1948.

Each school flourished on its own. Auburn found significant success under Donahue, who guided the team to undefeated seasons in 1913 and 1914. A key component of those teams: halfback Kirk Newell, who inspired flights of literary fancy like this fawning passage in the *Glomerata*, Auburn's official yearbook: "At all times heady and ready to take advantage of any slip by the opposing team, his directing of the attack was all that could be desired, and it would be useless to comment further on his skill in carrying the ball, so unanimous is the opinion that he was the best in the South." Newell would go on to serve in World War I, and was severely injured when a grenade exploded near him.

Fielding stars with evocative names like Fatty Warren, Baby Taylor, and Moon Ducote, Auburn traded blows with the toughest programs of the era, including Heisman-coached Georgia Tech. Retroactive analyses have awarded Auburn national championships for their 1910 and 1913 seasons, although—unlike its rival across the state—the school does not formally claim these post hoc titles as championships.

It was in this era that fate—which so often seems to punch Auburn in the face—swung a heavy fist in the direction of The Plains. In 1920, incoming Auburn president Spright Dowell declared football an unnecessary distraction for the university's students, and vowed to weaken "the unnatural and exaggerated position which [football] occupies in the eyes of the students and the public."

In an attempt to reduce football to the standing of an intramural activity, Dowell wrestled control of the sport away from the Auburn Athletic Association, a consortium of coaches, alumni, and boosters. He required coaches to teach classes, denied university funding for the football program, allowed intramural teams to play on the football team's field, constricted the recruiting pipeline, and—horrors!—forced the team to use only provably amateur and scandal-free student-athletes. (For as long as there's been college football, boosters have provided athletes with under-the-table payments, no-show jobs, and "scholarships" that required no actual classwork. It's the cost of doing business.)

Dowell's anti-football stance put him firmly on the opposite side of the field from more progressive-minded Southern college presidents, including the leaders of Vanderbilt, Georgia, Georgia Tech, Florida, and

Arkansas. Most notably, President George H. Denny at Alabama took the exact opposite tack of Dowell, emphasizing football as both the university's brand and identity long before such concepts even had names. The results would pay dividends for Alabama for decades to come.

The administrative meddling disgusted Donahue enough that he left Auburn after the 1922 season with a record of 106–35–5, a winning percentage better than Shug Jordan, Pat Dye, Tommy Tuberville, or Terry Bowden. His name now graces the street beside Jordan-Hare Stadium where Auburn's players enter the stadium via the famed "Tiger Walk" today.

As for Dowell? He sowed the seeds of his own professional demise by kicking out player after player for academic struggles or misbehavior. The final straw came when he took decisive action against star quarterback Frank Tuxworth for the crime of sneaking into the women's dormitory following a night of revelry. Irate at a "most unwholesome fraternization between the sexes," Dowell booted Tuxworth off the team and briefly expelled him from the university. With Tuxworth went the last of Dowell's goodwill. "To Hell With Spright Dowell" signs popped up all over campus—a stunning-for-the-time defiance of authority—and soon afterward, Dowell was fired by Alabama Governor Bibb Graves.

"Dowell's supporters tended to be more pious, to dislike intercollegiate football or at least want to curb the excesses associated with it, and to value the traditional mores of the agrarian South," wrote professor Andrew Doyle. "His opponents were mostly urban businessmen who valued football as both commercial entertainment and as a symbol of modernity and inclusion in the national cultural mainstream."

Dowell certainly believed he had Auburn's best interests at heart by deemphasizing football in favor of the school's educational mission, but he deeply misjudged how the former could immeasurably enhance the latter. He unquestionably transformed Auburn into a more efficient, more well-funded institution of higher learning. But he also presided over the university in an era when the football team plummeted from competitive in the 1910s to winless in 1927 . . . a year that, not coincidentally, marked his final days in office. At Auburn, keeping the university functioning was nice; keeping the football team winning was essential.

At the same time Auburn was floundering, Alabama established itself as a national football power, getting out to a head start that Auburn has never closed. After Dowell departed, it would be years before Auburn would win more than three games in a season, and decades before the football program regained a mindset of sustained dominance. And oh, would there be a whole lot of losing in between.

The early years of the 20th century were brutal days in college football, in large part because there was almost no protection for the players and no regard for safety. Consider this observation in 1913 from Tennessee's Bull Bayer, watching Alabama's first All-American, Bully Van de Graaff, in action:

"His ear had a real nasty cut, and it was dangling from his head, bleeding badly," Bayer said. "He grabbed his own ear and tried to yank it from his head. His teammates stopped him, and the managers bandaged him. Man, was that guy a tough one. He wanted to tear off his own ear so he could keep playing."

One of the most significant factors in the broadening appeal of football came when public high schools—as opposed to only private prep schools—began playing the sport. That allowed a wider range of fans across the country to become invested in the game, which led naturally to regional fandom. "When football diffuses down to the local level and local boys are playing football at every county high school across the state, and their sons go on to play for Alabama and Auburn, that builds the bonds of attachment between the plain folk," says Doyle. "Maybe they're poor, maybe they're somewhere north of the poverty level, but they really didn't have that much interest in the rich boys' games until their boys started playing."

The fever for football spread across the country, but the nation remained divided along regional lines. Northern, Midwestern, and West Coast teams played each other, but the South stayed isolated, disregarded in football as it was in every other facet of American life. The region wasn't invited to the football party it could see happening in the rest of the country, and that only fed the burning resentment that still coursed through the Southern character from the Civil War era.

Like many schools, Alabama didn't field a team in 1918 because of World War I. But once students returned to campus and American life returned to normal, President Denny initiated a significant expansion of the university's offerings—and that included a major boost to the football program. Within a few years, new Alabama head coach Xen Scott built the foundation for what would become a truly fearsome squad.

Scott led the Tide to its first great victory: a 9–7 win in 1922 over Penn before 20,000 fans at famed Franklin Field in Philadelphia. Knocking off one of the Ivy League's big guns on its home field, in what the *Brooklyn Daily Eagle* called "the hardest fought battle seen on the famous Quaker gridiron in seven years," burnished the pride and ego of the "savage Southerners" from Alabama.

In what would become a refrain for the coming years, the *New York Times* noted that Penn "had looked upon today's game as just a little more than a practice contest. That is where Penn made its big mistake. Alabama fought all the way and presented a well-balanced team." (For a sense of perspective, Alabama historian Kirk McNair says the victory was the equivalent of Penn rolling into Tuscaloosa and defeating Alabama today.)

Scott wouldn't get to enjoy the fruits of his labor; cancer forced him into retirement after the 1922 season, and he died at age 41 just two years later. Wallace Wade took over, transforming Alabama into a national power that would earn six Rose Bowl visits, win five national championships before World War II, and produce a bona fide Hollywood movie star. Under Wade, Alabama football would carry forth the banner for an entire region.

And it all began with one trip west.

Chapter 4

THE GAME THAT CHANGED SOUTHERN FOOTBALL

The locker room was silent. Outside, the first sun of the new year shone on the San Gabriel Mountains, heralding promise and hope. In here, though, in this tiny locker room deep inside the Rose Bowl in Pasadena, California, pain and desolation hung in the air.

These boys, these men, they'd come all this way, traveled 2,000 miles of railway, the farthest from home most had ever been. They carried with them the hopes and dreams not just of their families, not just of their university, but of their whole region. They were the University of Alabama, they were a long way from home, and they were getting their crimson tails handed to them.

No one in the entire country outside the state of Alabama believed the Tide belonged in the 1926 Rose Bowl, and through the first half, the team had proven them right. Alabama trailed the mighty University of Washington 12–0, and in the gloom it felt like 120–0.

Then Wallace Wade, the legendary Alabama coach, came in and looked around at his despondent crew. The disgust in his voice was evident.

"And they told me that boys from the South would fight."

That was all he said, and all he needed to say.

By 1926, the South had been playing football for several decades, but it wasn't enough to impress the gridiron A-listers elsewhere in the United States. College football's ruling cartel and blue-blood programs looked down on the South as a misbegotten, unruly child, and Southerners' feeble attempts to play football weren't any more worthy of respect than their attempts to make war or create industry.

Even in the 1920s, the Civil War remained within the living memory of thousands of Southerners, and the sting of that loss still rankled the pride of much of the white population. The region as a whole craved self-respect and self-esteem, and football provided an easy boost to their collective ego.

"There's this deeply embedded cultural sentiment that the Civil War wasn't lost because of the toughness of the soldiers," says author Lars Anderson. "There's this belief in the South that it would take two Union soldiers to take down one Confederate." That mentality carried over neatly to the football field.

Wade's 1925 squad posted a 9–0 record and allowed only a single touchdown. There were no playoffs in those days, no bowls or other postseason opportunities—nothing except the Rose Bowl, the Granddaddy of Them All, played in Pasadena every New Year's Day, then as now.

The game pitted regular-season champions from both coasts against one another. At that point, there were few more fearsome programs than Washington. Then known as the Purple Tornado, the Huskies dominated their competition in the Pacific Coast Conference—the predecessor of the Pac-12—and once posted *nine* undefeated seasons in a row, from 1908 to 1916. In the 1926 game, Washington would face whatever sacrificial lamb the East could serve up.

Despite its own unblemished record, Alabama suffered under the same biases that enveloped the rest of the South in those days—too poor, too dumb, too weak to compete with the mighty Northern schools. Schools from the South still carried the stain of the Civil War, and other institutions were all too happy to dismiss them out of hand over long-standing, still-simmering regional animosities. The Rose Bowl committee invited four other teams ahead of Alabama—Dartmouth, Michigan, Colgate, and Princeton—but all declined, attempting to sidestep yet another "college-football-is-too-professional" controversy that had welled up during the season.

Weeks before the game, the Rose Bowl committee received a telegram from the office of Alabama Governor William Brandon that read, "If you are interested in a real opponent for your West Coast football team, then give Alabama serious consideration." The telegram had been the idea of Champ Pickens, the first true Alabama booster, a manager of the 1896 team, and the originator of the Million Dollar Band's nickname.

With no options, the committee gritted its teeth and reached out to the fourth-ranked Tide. Even then, the Rose Bowl committee held its nose at the idea of inviting a horde of Southern scalawags to the party. "I've never heard of Alabama as a football team," one committee member sniffed, "and I can't take a chance on mixing a lemon with a rose."

"In those days, Alabama, or the Southern teams, weren't noted for great football potential," Alabama halfback and future cowboy movie star Johnny Mack Brown would say in 1969. "But it seems like they thought perhaps we were lazy, full of hookworms or something of that sort."

Southern teams that had trekked north often found the going rough. Princeton beat Virginia 116–0—yes, by three figures—in 1890. But Georgia Tech had managed to win a national title in 1917. Centre College from Kentucky took down Harvard in 1921. Alabama had beaten Penn, yes, but the general feeling was that these were quirks and upsets, and Southerners needed to know their place and stay in it.

The biases ran deep. Will Rogers, the most famous humorist of the day, slagged Alabama's hometown as "Tusca-loser." A Los Angeles columnist dubbed Alabama's players "Swamp Students." One sportswriter predicted Washington would win by 51 points. Another colorfully speculated that the Purple Tornado would "blow the Crimson Tide back across the continent as a pale pink stream."

There was ample reason to love Washington. Led by All-American running back George "Wildcat" Wilson, the Purple Tornado had manhandled its foes all season, shutting out 6 of 10, allowing no more than 14 points to any opponent. Washington had won its first three games by a combined score of 223–0. So when Washington came into the championship game a 2–1 favorite, no one was particularly surprised. The team didn't even bother to show up in Pasadena until the day before the game—"the Huskies play better when they have not been exposed to the enervating Southern breezes for any length of time," according to Washington officials.

But the rest of the nation wasn't reckoning with the formidable power of white Southern memory. Pickens organized a telegram campaign beseeching the Tide to carry on the honor of their region. Tuscaloosa civic leaders had no problem loading the entire emotional weight of the Civil War on the backs of the Alabama team, and implored the Tide to avenge the South's loss in the War of Northern Aggression.

"What the un-Dixie part of the planet didn't realize was that football, like practically everything else in the South, had taken on the imprint of the Civil War: Us versus them," writes Diane Roberts in *Tribal: College Football and the Secret Heart of America*. "The war was 60 years ago; 20th-century America had moved on; the South had not. Veterans of the Army of Northern Virginia or the Magnolia Rifles, their butternut caps tattered, still marched on Confederate Memorial Day and the United Daughters of the Confederacy dedicated monuments in every county seat from the Blue Ridge to the bayous."

Wade knew all this, and used it to his advantage. "Southern football is not recognized or respected," he said in his pregame speech. "Boys, here's your chance to change that forever."

The Tide botched their first chance. Washington ran up 12 unanswered points in the first half, containing Alabama on both sides of the ball. The boys who represented Alabama's finest hopes plodded into the locker room, heads down.

"We were dejected country boys," Alabama punter Grant Gillis would later recall to the *Birmingham News*. "We had our lip out. Wade came in after everybody was sitting down. He said, 'And they told me that boys from the South would fight.' And he walked out. That's all he said."

Roused by a love of their homeland and a sense of wounded pride, Alabama scored three touchdowns in seven minutes, the go-ahead score a 30-yard pass from Allison "Pooley" Hubert to Johnny Mack Brown.

"The third period will go down as the greatest chapter Alabama has ever written in the Book of Football," *Birmingham News* reporter Zipp Newman wrote in the typically florid style of the day. "A beaten team came back via the road of determination and cold grid tactics. Alabama threw the Huskies into hysterics. They were helpless to stop the outburst of the Tide that hurled giants like splinters into the air."

Washington would cut the score to 20–19, but Alabama held strong. Washington head coach Enoch Bagshaw was so incensed, he left the field without shaking Wade's hand. The crowd of 45,000—less than half the Rose Bowl's current capacity—cheered the underdog Tide.

"That 45,000 was close to capacity then," Brown said in 1962, "because the Rose Bowl wasn't really a bowl; it was more of a horseshoe. One end wasn't closed. Alabama closed it for them."

The *Birmingham News* called the shocking win "a tidal wave brought on by a vicious tornado," mixing meteorological metaphors in its joy. The Tide celebrated all the way back to Alabama, stopping to enjoy the adulation of delirious crowds all over the South. Red and white flags accompanied the Tide all the way back home to Tuscaloosa—"Tusca-loser" no more.

"It was the first time [Southerners] were like, 'We're better than you. You guys can make fun of us for everything, but there's one thing we can do better, and that's play football,'" Lars Anderson says. (Important caveat: this was decades before Alabama, Washington, or any other major college football team would integrate.)

"Football is, at its core, a sport for rough, hard-nosed, strong, stubborn people, and Southerners fit that bill better than anybody," says journalist Tommy Tomlinson. "The game they were playing back in the '20s, everybody just ran the ball all the time and beat up on each other. That sort of blood sport was made for Southern boys."

Wallace Wade got himself a statue out of the championship, the first coach to earn one at Alabama. But perhaps the greatest individual benefit from the game accrued to Johnny Mack Brown, who parlayed his Rose Bowl heroism into what would become a four-decade-long, 160-plus-movie Hollywood film career.

It's too much to say that the 1926 Rose Bowl helped the South move forward and leave behind the scars of the Civil War. It's not too much to say that the 1926 Rose Bowl helped the South in the eyes of the rest of the country, elevating their reputation from hillbillies and lowlifes to ... well, troublemakers with the potential to cause real damage, at the very least.

Southern newspapers had little issue with conflating the Rose Bowl victory with a Civil War do-over. The *Atlanta Georgian* called Alabama's win over Washington "the greatest victory for the South since the first Battle of Bull Run."

Even other Southern institutions of higher learning got in on the act. "Alabama was our representative in fighting for us against the world," said Vanderbilt coach Dan McGugin. "I fought, bled, died and was resurrected with the Crimson Tide."

It's worth considering what might have happened had Alabama lost the Rose Bowl. "Suppose Alabama had lost badly in 1926," said Auburn historian Wayne Flynt in the documentary *Roses of Crimson*. "Suppose they had been defeated by 40 points. Would football have then become the sort of important, defining experience for Southerners that it is going to become over the next five decades? And my answer to that is, no it would not have. Because the South would have just been proved yet again to be inferior in some other dimension of life, and what would have happened is, the South would have found something else in which to excel. It would have invested this kind of emotional energy and physical commitment into something else."

The university's triumph helped Alabama fans back home start to stand a little straighter. There was no question that many viewed Alabama's win as a form of redemption for the South's loss in the Civil War. Alabama's victory was, in the words of Flynt in his book *Alabama in the Twentieth Century*, "a decisive rebuttal to negative northern publicity that depicted Southerners as overly pious Bible Belters, hookworm-sapped weaklings, lazy slaggards, or incest-prone defectives."

"It was really the first time the South had gained national superiority in something since, basically, the Civil War," says author Keith Dunnavant. "It was a bellwether moment in terms of overcoming the cloak of inferiority. And it was in front of the entire country, too. The Rose Bowl was one of the signature events already in sports."

The very next year, when Alabama was on its way to face Stanford in the Rose Bowl, Governor Brandon made sure that everyone on the team knew exactly whom they were playing for. "Alabama's glory is in your hands," Brandon told them. "May each member of your team turn his face to the sun-kissed hills of Alabama and fight like hell as did your sires in bygone days."

Brandon did not rally the troops: Alabama and Stanford tied 7–7. But the South had established a beachhead in Pasadena, and 14 of the next 21 Rose Bowls included Southern schools. Southern football was here to stay.

TIMEOUT:
"YEA ALABAMA" AND "RAMMER JAMMER"

Now a century old, Alabama's fight song carries elements of the program's long history tucked within its lyrics, and when performed by Alabama's Million Dollar Band, it can bring a tear to the eye of any Tide fan.

For the initial few decades of its existence, Alabama inspired stately tunes like "The Alabama University March: Composed and Respectfully Dedicated to the Faculty of the University of Alabama," composed by A. P. Pfister in 1839—an evocative title, but not exactly a sing-along. Varsity sports began to stir the blood of Alabama students in the early 20th century, and they craved their own fight song.

Dr. George H. Denny brought the melody of Washington and Lee University's fight song to campus when he became president in 1912 to create "The Alabama Swing," but students rejected the secondhand tune, along with "Glory, Glory Alabama," new lyrics atop the somber notes of "The Battle Hymn of the Republic."

The *Crimson White*, Alabama's student newspaper, pushed for a new, unique song, and by 1925, as the school was piling up intercollegiate championships, the demand grew insistent: "Along with a championship team we should have a championship song," the editors wrote. "We want a new song and we want it now!"

Campus humor magazine *Rammer Jammer* upped the ante with a $50 prize—roughly $900 in 2025 dollars—for the best song. And when the Alabama football team pulled off its dramatic 1926 Rose Bowl victory, well, inspiration struck.

A student named Ethelred "Epp" Sykes won, and used his $50 prize to help create a musical arrangement so the Million Dollar Band could play along with the lyrics. "Yea, Alabama!" the song begins. "Drown 'em, Tide!"

"Yea Alabama" is packed with references to the 1925 season and the Rose Bowl—"Remember the Rose Bowl, we'll win then!"—where Alabama first burst into the nation's consciousness. "Go teach the Bulldogs to behave," the song gloats, "Send the Yellow Jackets to a watery grave!" Alabama certainly got Georgia to "behave" that year, beating the Bulldogs 27–0, and the Tide beat then-rival Georgia Tech 7–0 on a rainy day. At the time of the song's writing, Alabama hadn't played Auburn for nearly 20 years, and wouldn't play the Tigers again for another 22, hence Auburn's absence. It's safe to say that a "Yea Alabama" written today would have very different lyrics ... but the same attitude.

Incidentally, *Rammer Jammer*—which was published from 1924 through 1956—was the source material for one of Alabama's more recent cheers, along with Alabama's state bird, the yellowhammer. Adapted from Ole Miss's "Hotty Toddy" chant in the 1980s, it's chanted after every victory, and conveniently enough, it's applicable to any opponent:

> *Hey [opposing team]*
> *Hey [opposing team]*
> *Hey [opposing team]*
> *We just beat the hell out of you!*
> *Rammer Jammer, Yellowhammer*
> *Give 'em hell Alabama!*

Banned on two occasions, "Rammer Jammer" returned in 2005 after an Alabama Student Government Association vote found 98 percent in favor of the chant. And it's been a fixture of Alabama victories ever since.

Chapter 5

THE TIDE RISES

How many championships does Alabama have? Well, it depends on whom you ask. According to the Crimson Tide recordkeepers, Alabama claims 18 national titles as of 2025. According to contemporary pollsters, the Tide won somewhat fewer than that. Retroactive scrutiny, free from contemporary bias, by historians capable of assessing all of a season's games without deadline pressures, has awarded Alabama several debatable national titles ... starting with their second one.

Flush with the glow of a national championship, Alabama returned only 10 lettermen from the instant-legend 1926 Rose Bowl–winning squad. Gone were stars like Brown and Hubert. But Wade guided the team to a 9–0 regular season that included six shutouts, and no team scored more than seven points against Alabama all season. Unfortunately for the Tide, Alabama could manage only seven points against Stanford in the Rose Bowl, and the season ended with that 7–7 tie.

Even so, Stanford was named the national champion—a title it still claims today—under the then-standard Dickinson System of rating opponents by their strength of schedule, while the Tide was ranked a lowly ninth. The system, designed by Frank G. Dickinson, an economics professor at the University of Illinois, dinged Alabama for the weakness of the Southern Conference. Moreover, Dickinson noted that under his system, Dartmouth would have won the title the previous year, not Alabama. However, five retroactive analyses named Alabama either champion or co-champion, and that's good enough for Alabama to add the 1926 season to its titles.

The Tide turned out to sea in 1927, losing four games, more than in the previous four seasons combined. Two straight 6–3 seasons followed, and in the what-have-you-done-for-me-lately style that has become an Alabama trademark, fans began grumbling that Wade had lost a step.

Wade, incensed, delivered one of the all-time great you'll-miss-me-when-I'm-gone kiss-offs in 1930, leading Alabama to a perfect 10–0 record and a thorough dismantling of Washington in the Rose Bowl. Alabama posted eight shutouts—including a 64–0 pasting of Ole Miss—and outscored its opponents by a total of 271–13. No retroactive analysis was needed this time around: Alabama was the national champion in the moment. And then Wade was gone, off to Duke.

Wade's replacement, Frank Thomas, took another four seasons to win his first title. The Tide fought its way to another undefeated season in 1934, and won the Rose Bowl on the talent of players like quarterback Dixie Howell, wide receiver Don Hutson, and a feisty end from Arkansas by the name of Bryant.

George Denny, who served as president of Alabama from 1912 to 1936, possessed a keen understanding of the way football could be used as a promotional vehicle to attract valuable out-of-state tuition dollars. He began running advertisements in New York and New Jersey newspapers, touting Alabama's warm climate and the school's low tuition; the revenue from out-of-state students helped Alabama negotiate the Depression better than many universities of its day.

Denny also presided over an era of relaxed rule enforcement and progressive social codes at Alabama. "Denny was relatively tolerant by the standards of the day, and Alabama acquired a reputation as a 'party school' during his tenure. The university aggressively recruited female students and permitted unchaperoned dating," Andrew Doyle wrote in 2004. "Denny also adopted a see-no-evil approach to Prohibition violations."

Perhaps coincidentally, perhaps not, this put Alabama starkly at odds with the moral crusade underway at Spright Dowell's Auburn. Alabama was playing better than Auburn on the football field, and celebrating better afterward too.

Alabama would tack on another championship in 1941 just before World War II halted football across the country . . . but this one was considerably less justifiable. Alabama finished the season ranked third in the SEC and 20th overall, with a record of 9–2 and shutout losses to Mississippi State and Vanderbilt. Only a single poll—the Houlgate System—deemed Alabama co-champions alongside Minnesota, and that was good enough for a 1983 Alabama reassessment to claim that title. Alabama has many world-beating teams in its long, illustrious history. The 1941 "national champions" are not one of them.

"Lots of teams have gone back and claimed old titles, most of them probably inspired by the Tide," wrote Jason Kirk in 2018. "Kentucky, Minnesota, Oklahoma State, Texas A&M, and USC are a few who've treated themselves to retroactive crowns. Many of those are actually defensible . . . and most of Bama's revisionist histories are fine. But nobody else has claimed anything quite as egregious as 1941."

Auburn, meanwhile, suffered through a swoon even as Alabama thrived. The high points were few—Jimmy Hitchcock was the school's first All-American, in 1932, and Auburn played in its first bowl game in 1937. (Trivia: Auburn's first bowl game took place in Havana, Cuba, at the Bacardi Bowl, where the Tigers battled Villanova to a 7–7 tie.)

The major off-field news for both schools came in 1932. The Southern Conference had grown too bloated, boasting 23 teams. Granted, it's a number not far off from the current iteration of the Big Ten, but back in the early

'30s, it was deemed unmanageable. In 1932, for instance, Tennessee, LSU, and Auburn all played a different number of conference games . . . and all claimed they were entitled to the conference championship. So several Southern Conference teams decided to break off and form their own conference. At the end of the 1932 season, the Southeastern Conference was chartered to include 12 institutions: Alabama, Auburn, Georgia, Georgia Tech, Kentucky, LSU, Mississippi State, Ole Miss, Sewanee (which later became the University of the South), Tennessee, Tulane, and Vanderbilt. Sewanee left in 1940, and Georgia Tech and Tulane in the 1960s; the rest have remained in what has proven to be a landmark, and highly lucrative, partnership.

Alabama's first post-World War II star was an undersized 160-pound dual threat who had trouble keeping his feet on the ground. Harry Gilmer's specialty was a jump pass, where he'd leap into the air to hurl the ball downfield. It's the kind of thing that drives coaches insane, then and now, but Gilmer pulled it off so effectively and efficiently that he kept doing it.

"If I was going to throw on the run, I would jump to throw, the reason being I could turn my hips downfield, and you need to get up in the air and throw to do that," he once said. "You can't do that if your feet are on the ground and you have to step to throw."

Alabama was one of the first schools to field a team in 1944, giving Gilmer and his teammates an advantage rolling into the all-out 1945 season. Along with his fellow "war babies," Gilmer led the Tide to an undefeated season in 1945 that prompted another Rose Bowl invitation, this time against mighty USC. The team traveled west from Tuscaloosa on four sleeper cars, but took nearly four days to reach California since they had to wait for troop-laden trains from the West Coast to pass through.

Thomas's pregame locker room speech was just three words—"Block and tackle"—repeated over and over, at an increasingly loud and frenetic volume. Inspired, Gilmer rushed for 116 yards and one touchdown, threw for another, and was named the game's MVP in the 34–14 victory. Although Alabama finished that year undefeated and untied, the Tide was ranked third in the AP polls behind Army and Navy.

IRON BOWL 1948:
A RESUMPTION OF HOSTILITIES

By 1948, college football had firmly established itself as one of America's premier sports. Baseball's appeal was intense but limited; in huge swaths of the country—the South, for instance—there was no major league team within hundreds of miles. Professional football was an afterthought at best. So fans poured their hopes, their dreams, their energies into their college football teams ... and, in Alabama, fans started wondering why exactly the state's two marquee universities still weren't playing each other.

Fandom, like nature, abhors a vacuum, so in the absence of a head-to-head matchup, Auburn and Alabama fans stoked rivalries that remain hot to this day—Alabama with Tennessee, Auburn with Georgia. Even so, there was a growing demand that the Tigers and Tide get their acts together, drop whatever petty differences kept them apart, and start playing some damn football again.

Alabama understood that it had little to gain from playing Auburn, which had struggled for years in the new Southeastern Conference. (This was a complete reversal of the early years of the century, when Auburn was by far the more dominant force.) The school even prepared a report to cloak its objections in a veneer of civility, claiming that rivalry games in other states, like Georgia, South Carolina, Louisiana, and Tennessee, had led to lawless behavior.

"We hazard nothing in saying that the game would not make a single constructive contribution to education in the state," Alabama's Committee on Physical Education and Athletics declared.

"The fundamental question is," the report concluded, "Do the people of Alabama need a tranquil, sane kind of athletics in their two major institutions, or an irrational rabid kind?" Never in Alabama history has there been a question less in need of an answer.

Alabama state legislators had attempted everything from resolutions to appeals to charity to reunite the schools, but the divide remained strong. Only when the state began threatening the funding for both schools did their presidents agree to resume the game. Pride is one thing; allowing state legislators to tinker with university finances is another matter entirely.

In another of those what-if moments, the schools briefly toyed with the idea of holding the game on their respective campuses 50 years before that would actually happen. But that idea was short-lived, and Auburn and Alabama agreed to play in Birmingham on December 4, 1948.

At a pregame pep rally at Woodrow Wilson Park, students from both schools buried a symbolic "hatchet." (Overseeing that rally: Birmingham's public safety commissioner, Eugene "Bull" Connor.) The *Birmingham News* fawned over the impending "scraperoo," where tickets "are as tight as a pair of mail-order shoes" and "harder to find than a Dixiecrat on the federal payroll."

"You can feel it in your bones," the *News* reported. "You can hear it with your own ears. You can see it with your own eyes. All Alabama is talking and singing of Saturday's first tussle in 41 years between the state's two top institutions of higher learning."

Reality didn't match up to the anticipation, at least for Auburn fans. Before 46,000 fans, Alabama destroyed the Tigers by a score of 55–0, still the widest margin of victory in an Iron Bowl. Auburn managed an upset win the next year, knocking off Alabama 14–13, but that was only a brief moment of joy before the brutality that was to come. In 1950, Auburn went 0–10, and The Plains were sorrowful indeed.

They needed a savior, badly. Fortunately, one was already waiting.

1948 IRON BOWL

Final Score: Alabama 55, Auburn 0

Chapter 6

IT'S PRONOUNCED "JERR-DN"

Under a blanket of moonless darkness, five thousand ships crossed the choppy, turbulent English Channel toward Normandy. Within Force U, destined for Utah Beach, men from the Army Corps of Engineers huddled close against the chill. They'd been riding across the murky water for hours. The smell of piss and vomit was everywhere. The date was June 6, 1944, and the worst was very much yet to come.

At H hour, 0630, the ground assault would begin. The 8th Infantry would lead the beach assault, and soon afterward, combat engineers would follow to handle the grinding, necessary work of clearing entrances to and exits from the beach and assisting combat infantry in claiming, stabilizing, and organizing the beach. It would be dangerous, deadly work for these engineers, and as they sat in their carrier, they understood that they might well be living the final minutes of their lives.

Some of the men thought about what awaited them on the beaches of Normandy, the German gun emplacements in the hills ready to rain down hell upon them. Some thought of wives and girlfriends back home. One remembered the creed he carried with him, in a printed newspaper clipping, and thought of his beloved Auburn University.

His name was Ralph Jordan. His men called him Lieutenant. Everyone back home just called him Shug.

Decades before John Lewis, Hosea Williams, and others would march across the Edmund Pettus Bridge and make Selma famous as the scene of a decisive moment in the Civil Rights Movement, the city was a thriving cotton metropolis. Built atop a steep bluff overlooking the Alabama River, Selma was the largest cotton market in central Alabama. The town boasted two cotton compresses, four large cotton warehouses, four cottonseed oil mills, a brick plant, an iron foundry, and an ice plant. Selma's quiet paved roads drifted past massive live oaks. The railroad that ran through town was a key artery, not just for Alabama but for the South as a whole.

It was here, on September 25, 1910, that James Ralph Jordan was born, just a few years before the boll weevil would devastate Selma. Left-handed at birth, young Ralph got his knuckles rapped every time he wrote with that hand, and so he became ambidextrous. Later in life, he could show off quite the party trick: the ability to write his name with both hands simultaneously, backward with the right, forward with the left.

A dominant high school athlete, Jordan played football with teammates who sported names like Boots Chambless, Sleepy Molpus, and Gump Ariail. And speaking of distinctive names—it was in high school where Jordan picked up his famous nickname. A classmate named Billy Lapsley asked him where he was from, and Jordan replied, "I've been living in Whatley."

"Oh, down there where the sugar cane grows," Billy replied. "We're going to call you Sugar Cane. We're going to call you Shug."

Jordan liked the idea, and initially sported a sweatshirt with the nickname, spelled "SUG," as in the first three letters of *sugar*. But that didn't sound quite right when spoken, so somewhere along the line an *h* got dropped in just to alleviate all doubt.

Young Shug's athletic feats were enough to attract the attention of Alabama's Wade, now a few years removed from his first, massive Rose Bowl triumph. Granted, the thought of a future Auburn legend nearly going to Alabama still sends shudders through the souls of Tigers everywhere. But much like another famous Alabama local 50 years later, Jordan passed on Alabama... or, more specifically, Alabama passed on him.

"I had what is now known as the deadly combination," Jordan later recalled. "I was too little and too slow."

So Jordan instead attended Auburn and made postgraduate plans to teach high school and coach football in north Alabama. But a heavy Klan presence in the area convinced Jordan—who was raised Catholic—to consider another career path. In 1933, he began recruiting for Auburn, cruising the two-lanes of Alabama in a blue V-8 Ford that cost the Auburn athletic department $350. He spent long hours trying to recruit high schoolers to come play at tiny Drake Field—seating capacity 700, as long as someone bothered to construct the grandstands.

Jordan loved his school and loved the opportunity it gave him to grow, to learn under crusty veteran football coaches. And then the war came.

Jordan signed on as a lieutenant in the Army Corps of Engineers in 1942. He reported to Camp Edwards in Massachusetts, and sailed in August to Scotland to await further orders for the American–British invasion of North Africa. He was part of the 1st Engineer Special Brigade, an amphibious assault force tasked with easing the path of their fellow soldiers.

Jordan helped design roads, docks, and bridges in French North Africa, and wrote home in February 1943 that "I have been made to feel very much at home by the sight of basketball courts in the small towns in the region." Upon the completion of one successful invasion, he connected with several other Auburn men, and cries of "War Eagle!" rang out in the North African night.

Still, Jordan ached for more. He wrote Billy Lapsley, his old classmate, that he had played in one "bowl game"—the invasion of North Africa—and now wanted to play in the "Rose Bowl"—the invasion of mainland Europe. Soon he would get his chance.

In January 1943, Jordan began working on advance plans to invade Sicily under none other than General George Patton. The invasion would commence in July 1943. "God, I loved that Patton's style," Jordan would later say. "I still remember him coming over with a radio message to the effect that he was taking command of the newly-born 7th Army, which would have its baptism of blood on the beaches of Sicily the next morning."

Early in 1944, the 33-year-old Jordan was among the million and a half US troops gathered in the United Kingdom for an imminent move across the English Channel and the invasion of Normandy. Rehearsals were held during April and May. Jordan was in charge of a landing boat outfit, and ran practice for the amphibious landing near the Isle of Wight.

The days grew long. But the men knew the moment was near when they were told, "Pack all your personal possessions in your footlockers, and write the address of your next of kin on the top."

They boarded their boats and prepared to set off across the channel. Bad weather delayed the operation, and Jordan remained aboard the ship. The sour stench of seasick men, the pungent vapors of gasoline, and the foul odor of backed-up toilets were burned into his mind.

June 6 was predicted to be good weather, and Eisenhower declared, "OK. We'll go."

Jordan's ship headed toward France. He thought of his wife, Evelyn, and their seventh wedding anniversary, just two days away. He thought of his daughters. He thought of his life growing up in Selma. And he thought of Auburn.

On his person, he carried a copy of the Auburn Creed, written just a few months before by George Petrie and printed in the January 21, 1944, edition of the *Auburn Plainsman*. He would look at it often, drawing comfort from its words, then refolding it once again.

Then there was no more time to reminisce.

Loaded down with 40-pound bags of wire cutters, gas masks, canteens, rations, and other essentials, Jordan and his men headed for Utah Beach. Once upon a time, it was a pleasant recreational beach, where families in northern France would while away long summer days. On this day, a gray morning, steel crosses—the so-called Czech hedgehogs—dotted the waves. The beach was a gentle slope down to the water, with low sand dunes and 100 yards of open space between the shoreline and cover.

The Germans were estimated to have more than 110 guns defending Utah Beach, ranging from 75mm to 170mm, and they rained down fire on the American-led landing force. The first wave of troops touched down at 0630, men wading through 100 yards of water to face that wide-open beach.

"There had been a lot of carrying on the night before," Jordan would later recall. "It was silent in the landing craft. I never saw an atheist or an agnostic when it came time to hit the beach."

Just over two hours after the first men came ashore, Jordan's craft reached the beach. His boat had drifted south of the designated landing point, since the offshore current had been stronger than expected and smoke from the overhead bombardment had obscured landmarks.

As he came ashore, shrapnel from a German 88 ripped through his shoulder and upper arm. But he kept at his post, rallying his men . . . and thinking of football.

"If it hadn't been for football and having participated," he later said, "not only as a player but also having watched many a fine football player, or just an ordinary football player, give it everything he got, I don't know whether I'd have gotten any further on that day."

As part of the 1st Engineer Special Brigade, Jordan was responsible for organizing the movement of troops inland. Engineers contacted the

Airborne Division, tapped the French telephone system for communications, blew holes in the concrete seawall, repaired roads, and cleared mines. Theirs was the necessary grunt work, the logistical heavy lifting required for the mission to succeed.

And it did. By nightfall, more than 21,000 troops, 1,700 vehicles, and 1,700 tons of supplies had landed on Utah Beach. By June 10, Jordan had helped orchestrate the arrival of more than 62,000 troops, 41,000 vehicles, and 10,000 tons of supplies, building walls, clearing mines, and blasting holes in seawalls. Only after that work was done did he get serious treatment for his wounds.

Jordan's bravery in the face of injury drew the notice of his superiors, many of whom were happy to sing his praises afterward. In an extensive letter to Auburn University president Hanly Funderburk after Jordan's death, Captain Henry McHarg showered the man from Selma with praise:

"He basically asked to be stitched up so he could stay with his troops during the initial phase of the invasion," McHarg wrote. "It hurt him like hell, but he knew he wasn't going to die. After awhile he couldn't use his arm and he broke out in a tremendous fever. It was a fine thing to have done to stay on the beach."

Jordan made it as far as Paris, but didn't get to go into Germany. He instead was sent to Okinawa in 1945. He was promoted to the rank of major and honorably discharged.

Jordan rarely went into detail about his World War II experiences. "I don't think it affected my personality at all," he once said. "It made me appreciate being here. I saw [bodies] stacked up like cordwood. I could easily have been one of them ... I had been scared before I went over there and I was damn sure scared over there."

"We would travel together, and one thing we didn't talk about was Normandy," recalls Terry Henley, one of Jordan's finest and most vocal players. "He refused to talk about that, ever. I mentioned it one time, and he said, 'We just don't talk about that.'"

It's impossible to put Jordan's experiences in a modern context. College coaches now operate in the tiniest bubble possible; they often go straight from their own playing days into a graduate-school apprenticeship, and then work their way up the career ladder, rarely leaving the coaching ranks. It's a tough life, but it's not a truly terrifying one, not in the way that riding in a small ship across the choppy North Atlantic into a hailstorm of enemy fire would be.

Jordan may have claimed that the war didn't affect his personality, but it damn sure shaped it. When you've already stared into the face of hell, how hard could it be to stare across the field at Bear Bryant?

TIMEOUT: THE AUBURN CREED

George Petrie (1866–1947) was Auburn's first football coach, organizing the inaugural game between Auburn and Georgia on February 20, 1892. (Auburn won 10–0.) Petrie worked as a professor and administrator at Auburn for more than 50 years, and in 1943, he summed up his feelings for his beloved school and its alumni in this creed.

I believe that this is a practical world and that I can count only on what I earn. Therefore, I believe in work, hard work.

I believe in education, which gives me the knowledge to work wisely and trains my mind and my hands to work skillfully.

I believe in honesty and truthfulness, without which I cannot win the respect and confidence of my fellow men.

I believe in a sound mind, in a sound body and a spirit that is not afraid, and in clean sports that develop these qualities.

I believe in obedience to law because it protects the rights of all.

I believe in the human touch, which cultivates sympathy with my fellow men and mutual helpfulness and brings happiness for all.

I believe in my Country, because it is a land of freedom and because it is my own home, and that I can best serve that country by "doing justly, loving mercy, and walking humbly with my God."

And because Auburn men and women believe in these things, I believe in Auburn and love it.

Chapter 7

A STARR FALLS ON T-TOWN

It's impossible to overstate the love Alabama fans have for their Tide. They set wedding dates well outside football season. They take out mortgage-sized loans on RVs for tailgating. They wrap their children in houndstooth-checked onesies. They invest in paintings by Daniel Moore, who depicts memorable moments in Tide history on canvas. Funeral homes stock custom-made caskets featuring the logo of the Crimson Tide. Alabama fans' devotion to their team is all-encompassing and eternal, and players like Bart Starr are the reason why.

Bryan Bartlett Starr was born in Montgomery, Alabama, on January 9, 1934, the child of Ben and Lula Starr. Young Bart's father was a mechanic and a blacksmith with an imposing demeanor; Starr was one of many Alabama boys who grew up revering and fearing their father in equal measure.

As a lad living in Montgomery, Starr idolized Alabama quarterback Harry Gilmer, who pioneered that theatrical but risky passing style—leaping into the air and hurling the ball downfield. Bart and his brother, Bubba, played tackle football long into the Alabama evenings, connecting with their father through sports.

But heart-wrenching tragedy struck the Starr family in 1947. While running barefoot, Bubba stepped on a dog bone and shrieked in pain. His mother cleaned the wound but didn't get him the then-new tetanus shot. Bubba died three days later of tetanus poisoning, and the family nearly splintered. Lula Starr blamed herself, and Ben Starr grew cold and distant from his surviving son, lashing him with callous insults like "Your brother would have..."

Starr resolved to live his life in honor of his brother and in defiance of his father's cruelty. He joined the football team at Sidney Lanier High, but found the game deeply challenging. When he was assigned to junior varsity, he came home and told his father he would be quitting the team.

"All right, it's your decision," Ben Starr replied. "I'm glad you'll be home in the afternoons. I want you to weed the garden and cut the cornstalks. I want the garden cleaned up for fall."

The threat of pulling weeds was enough to convince Starr to give football another try. He stuck with the team, made the varsity squad in his junior year, and when the school's starting quarterback went down with an injury in an October game against Tuscaloosa High School, Starr got his chance. He stepped into the huddle, shocking his teammates with his confident vibe and his clear-eyed leadership. Lanier would upset favored Tuscaloosa 13–0, and Starr claimed the starting quarterback job from then on.

After a summer spent learning the position from Kentucky starting quarterback Vito "Babe" Parilli, Starr came very close to attending the University of Kentucky to play under that school's coach, an imposing tyrant by the name of Paul Bryant. But he'd committed a cardinal sin for a football player: he'd fallen in love. The object of his affections, Cherry Morton, would be attending Auburn in the fall... and that was a long drive from Lexington. So Starr opted to attend nearby Alabama... and nothing would be the same, for him or for the Crimson Tide.

When Starr arrived on Alabama's campus in 1952, about 6,000 undergrads attended the school. Denny Stadium, built at a cost of $100,000 with early Rose Bowl revenues, was simply two disconnected grandstands with a seating capacity—often unfilled—of 31,000. Alabama offered only a handful of sports for men, and none for women. Every coach in every sport helped coach the football team in the fall.

Those were violent days in college football, and at the University of Alabama in particular. In his biography of Starr, Keith Dunnavant recounts many incidents of player-on-player, player-on-coach, and coach-on-player violence that would get people suspended and run out of town in the modern era. For instance, one of Alabama's 1930s-era All-American linemen, a beast by the name of Arthur "Tarzan" White, once grew so angry at Hank Crisp—a crusty, one-handed assistant coach who instilled toughness in the entire program over several decades—that he threw Crisp over the fence surrounding the practice field. Crisp walked back around the fence, straight up to White, belted him a couple times, and practice resumed.

Crisp bloodied his players in "bull-in-the-ring" one-on-one battles. Players clotheslined opponents, threatened other teams with unspeakable violence, broke jaws. And looming over it all was the specter of the Korean War, then ramping up, with a draft threatening to pluck players off the field and send them to Asia.

January 1, 1953, marked the first time fans across the country could view all four major bowls—Orange, Rose, Sugar, and Cotton—live on television. In the Orange Bowl, Alabama beat Syracuse so badly—and so thoroughly—that several Tide players walked off the field celebrating when the clock hit zero, with their team leading 41–6. As it turned out, that wasn't the end of the game—just the end of the third quarter. Final score: 61–6, Alabama. Starr played the second half—the war forced the NCAA to allow freshmen to play—and at one point, he fired five straight passes to receiver Joe Curtis, attempting to give him the Orange Bowl record for receptions. Curtis missed the first four but finally caught the fifth.

Alabama's quarterback is always the third-most-famous person in the state—behind the coaches of Alabama and Auburn, ahead of the governor—but Starr resolutely refused to change with his new fame. "A life splattered with tales of womanizing, drunken escapades, and felony rampages certainly would make a biographer's job more colorful," wrote Dunnavant, "but Starr was who he was: a little dull perhaps, compared to many of his contemporaries, but always authentic."

The next year Starr led the Tide to a 6–2–3 record; in the decimated offensive year of 1953, that was enough to claim an SEC title. Alabama went on to play Rice in the Cotton Bowl, and that led to one of the strangest plays ever seen on a college football field.

Rice was leading 7–6 in the second quarter when Owls halfback Dicky Maegle cut around the right side of the Alabama line and found daylight. He had a wide-open field ahead of him—Starr, on defense, had been blocked—and it appeared Maegle was about to break off a 95-yard run.

On the Alabama sideline, fullback Tommy Lewis watched and seethed. And then he acted, leaping off the sideline and blindsiding Maegle right there in the middle of the field. The sellout crowd booed, and the officials ruled that Maegle's 95-yard touchdown would stand.

Lewis sat on the bench, cradling his head in his hands as his teammates surrounded him to ward off prying eyes. Later, he would try to explain himself with words that would resonate through the decades.

"I'm too emotional," Lewis said. "Too full of Bama."

Starr eloped out of the public view. He and Cherry drove just across the Alabama border into Columbus, Mississippi, to find a justice of the peace and close the deal. Starr kept the marriage from his narrow-focus coaches, lest he lose his scholarship.

Starr suffered back pain throughout his junior season in 1954, which he said at the time was the result of a punting incident while practicing. The pain was so severe that doctors put him in traction for part of the season, and the team fell apart in his absence. Head coach Red Drew was fired; his replacement, J. B. "Ears" Whitworth, arrived on campus just as newspapers around the country were collating the most successful programs of the last quarter century. Alabama ranked third behind Notre Dame and Tennessee, but the Alabama of 1955 was a long way from the Alabama that had put up all those wins.

Of all his many sins, misfires, mistakes, and misjudgments, one of Whitworth's worst was sidelining Starr. The former All-SEC freshman, and future NFL Hall of Famer, spent most of his senior year on the bench as Alabama turned in the only winless season in modern history. Fortunately for Starr, Alabama's head basketball coach, Johnny Dee, believed in him, and Dee made a call to a colleague at the Green Bay Packers. The rest, for Starr, was NFL history.

Starr's senior year of 1956 happened to coincide with another momentous event at the University of Alabama: the arrival of Autherine Lucy, the first Black student to attend the school. Lucy had spent years attempting to gain admission; her first enrollment was rescinded when the university learned she wasn't white. An NAACP court challenge overturned the university's decision, and Lucy was admitted on the condition that she could not enter any dormitories or dining halls.

On Friday, February 3, 1956, a gray and rainy Tuscaloosa morning, Lucy walked onto campus, a graduate student in library science, and stepped into history. She entered Eugene Smith Hall for her first class, and then walked diagonally across the Quad toward Graves Hall—a building that would one day bear her name. Later that night, a crowd gathered along University Boulevard to protest Lucy's enrollment. Chanting "Keep Bama white!" and "To hell with Autherine!" the crowd marched to the intersection of Greensboro and University—the site of Tuscaloosa's one brief Civil War battle. On Saturday night, a virulently anti-Autherine crowd gathered at Denny Chimes. Nearby, someone burned a cross. Speakers urged nonviolence... but also made sure to note where and when Lucy's Monday classes would take place.

On Monday, riots broke out on campus and a mob of thousands—made up not just of students, but also of local Klansmen—burned crosses, threw eggs, and attacked the car that drove Lucy from class to class. As she sat in her children's literature class, Lucy could hear the mob chanting, "Hey, hey, ho, where in the hell did Autherine go? Hey, hey, ho, where in the hell did that n—r go?" Soon afterward, Alabama officials suspended her for what they claimed was her own safety.

"Yes, there was peace on the campus, but it was peace at a great price," Martin Luther King Jr. would say weeks later from the pulpit at Dexter Avenue Baptist Church in Montgomery. "It was peace that had been purchased at the exorbitant price of an inept trustee board succumbing to the whims and caprices of a vicious mob. It was peace that had been purchased at the price of allowing mobocracy to reign supreme over democracy."

Lucy and the NAACP filed suit against an array of individuals at Alabama, and a federal court in Birmingham ruled that she be reinstated. But the University of Alabama wasn't much interested in following the dictates of a federal court, and expelled Lucy for alleged slander of the university. Weary of the struggle, she walked away and did not return for decades. Not until 1988 did the university rescind the expulsion; Lucy returned and completed her master's degree in 1992.

Decades later, the truth about Starr's back injury would come out. He wasn't injured in punting exercises. In 2016, Cherry told AL.com that Starr was brutally beaten with a paddle during initiations into the A-Club, Alabama's lettermen's association.

"His whole back all the way up to his rib cage looked like a piece of raw meat," Cherry Starr told reporter Joseph Goodman. "The bruising went all the way up his back. It was red and black and awful looking. It was so brutal." Starr kept the incident quiet, Cherry said, because he believed that confessing it "would make him look bad."

The back injury haunted Starr for the rest of his career, and rendered him unfit for military service; he failed his Air Force physical after his rookie season at Green Bay. He would go on to play 16 seasons with the Packers, winning five NFL championship titles, including the first two Super Bowls.

As for Whitworth, his three-year tenure at Alabama ended with a record of 4–24–2, numbers so woeful they seem like a misprint. Everyone piled on Whitworth—alumni, other coaches, fans, opposing teams, even his own players—and thus, it was time for a change.

After he was ousted, Whitworth ran into a couple of his players in downtown Tuscaloosa. He was tearful and regretful, and tried in some small way to make amends. "I'd have given anything in the world to see you guys succeed as football players," he said. "I apologize."

It would be the last time an Alabama head coach apologized for anything for a long, long time.

Chapter 8

A GRAVEYARD FOR COACHES

Not for the first time and not for the last, Shug Jordan sat and accepted the judgmental eyes of faculty and administrators uncertain of the relevance and purpose of football. He was back in Auburn, back on The Plains, enduring yet another interview for yet another position. But this was the one he truly wanted—head football coach of the Auburn Tigers. The school's formal name may have been Alabama Polytechnic Institute—it had changed from Agricultural and Mechanical College of Alabama in 1899—but this was *Auburn*, forever and ever, amen.

Like many agricultural and mechanical institutions in the Deep South, Auburn was meant for the students who didn't come from big cities, children of blue-collar families, a generation not destined for the elite white-columned schools of higher learning where a future in the upper reaches of Yellowhammer State society was virtually assured. At agricultural and mechanical colleges, you weren't there for a coronation; you were there for job training. This was the world Jordan loved, the world where he belonged.

Jordan, in 1951, looked every member of the search committee in the eyes and delivered a rousing closing argument: "If you can't put your faith in an Auburn man," he declared, "who can you put your faith in?"

Auburn man or not, the years immediately after the war were rough ones for Jordan. Thanks to a changeover in athletic administrations, he wasn't welcome back at Auburn, deemed a relic of a prior era. Jordan spent his days talking with an old and solitary Auburn man by the name of Cliff Hare. In those quiet days together, two men sharing confidences and company, they couldn't possibly have imagined their names would grace a stadium together in the decades to come.

Hare was an Auburn legend, a member of the school's earliest football teams, a professor and dean deeply invested in Tiger athletics, and the former president of the Southern Conference. But even legends get lonely. He told Jordan how he and Dr. Steadman Sanford—whose name also adorns a stadium, the one in Athens, Georgia—would get together every year at Hare's house to divide up the gate receipts from that year's Georgia–Auburn game. They'd take the money out of its boxes, lay it out right there on the dining room table, and split it evenly.

Jordan was suffering through the aimless, drifting ennui common to soldiers after World War II. Their mission accomplished, they now lacked purpose and direction. In 1946, for instance, Jordan attempted to catch on with an ill-fated pro football franchise, the Miami Seahawks of the All-America Football Conference. He bailed on the ramshackle Seahawks after just a few weeks, opting to take a more stable job: assistant football coach and head basketball coach at the University of Georgia. (The Seahawks went bankrupt after one season, relocated to Baltimore, and were reconstituted as the Baltimore Colts.)

Jordan signed on with the Dawgs three games into the 1946 season. Coaching under Georgia legend Wally Butts, Jordan learned how to run a coaching staff, dispensing praise when necessary and getting out of their way when he wasn't necessary. But he also learned what not to do: Butts's tyrannical methods of player motivation and discipline didn't make their way into Jordan's repertoire.

That year, Jordan also got his first true taste of anti-Southern bias in the world of college football. Georgia finished the regular season 10–0, winning the SEC along the way. The Bulldogs then beat North Carolina in the Sugar Bowl, 20–10. But Georgia ended the year ranked third, behind Notre Dame and Army, neither of which played in a bowl game, even though they had battled to a tie in Yankee Stadium earlier in the season. Retroactive analyses have deemed Georgia the best team in the country in 1946, but that did Butts and crew no good in the moment, and the Bulldogs don't claim 1946 as one of their national championships.

Meanwhile, over on The Plains, matters were dire indeed. The school dismissed Carl Voyles, who had pushed out Jordan but struggled to a 15–22 record over four seasons. Newspaper reports of the day listed Jordan as a potential new coach, alongside men with evocative names like Scabs Scarborough, Red Sanders, Slick Morton, and future Alabama coach Ears Whitworth. But once again, Auburn passed over Jordan . . . and the slide continued.

The 1950 team, coached by Earl Brown, lost all 10 of its games, and failed to even score in seven of them. Auburn's 10-year-old stadium, with a capacity of 21,500, was now named for Cliff Hare, but few fans bothered to show up to it.

In the state of Alabama, everyone picks a side in the Auburn–Alabama rivalry—it's just a matter of when and where loyalties come to the surface. On January 17, 1951, just two days after being sworn in to office, Alabama Governor Gordon Persons swan-dived into the Auburn fray by announcing that Alabama Polytechnic Institute needed a new football coach and staff. Not even the boldest politicians today would dare order a wholesale athletic department overhaul; football coaches earn more than governors by an order of magnitude.

University president Ralph Draughon wasn't exactly thrilled to find his employment decisions being scrutinized by the governor, but he didn't really have a choice; Persons was a longtime Auburn supporter and declared himself a highly interested party. Persons held a meeting with nearly two dozen Auburn alumni and faculty in Montgomery that January, a meeting interrupted by two Auburn players who carried a petition signed by 62 members of the 1950 team. "We, the Auburn football players, disagree with your action taken with our head coach, Earl Brown," the petition read. "We want you to know we have full confidence in Coach Brown and know that you have made a grave mistake."

Persons reversed course, giving Brown another season to right the ship. But Auburn boosters—in a move that would characterize them for the rest of their long history—began meddling with the process. "The record of Coach Brown is marked with a sense of dismal failures on the football field," more than 70 alumni wrote Persons. "We believe that the degree of alumni loyalty which has been unparalleled throughout the nation heretofore will be seriously strained if Coach Earl Brown is retained during the present year." On February 11, the university's faculty athletic subcommittee voted to buy out Brown and pay for the final year of his contract: a mighty $9,000.

Brown didn't hold back as he left. "Auburn is a graveyard for coaches," he said as he left. "God have pity on the man who comes here."

Jordan, having been burned by the school multiple times before, was reluctant to apply again, despite encouragement from friends in the Auburn community. Finally, he got fed up enough to write an application, which read in its entirety, "I hereby apply for the head coaching job at Auburn. Sincerely, Ralph Jordan."

More than 220 applications flowed in for the Auburn job. In the end, the search committee was swayed by Jordan's appeal as "an Auburn man," and offered him the job just after midnight on February 26, 1951. Jordan insisted on, and got, a five-year contract for $12,500 per year, a princely sum for the day.

Jordan was facing tough odds. The *Montgomery Advertiser* noted that he "has been chosen to bring the Tiger gridiron sport out of the wilderness," and the *Birmingham News* wrote that he would be taking over "in the Tigers' darkest hour," and was "charged with the toughest job in the SEC. He is expected to restore the Tigers to their old gridiron glory." No pressure there.

Jordan had to figure out what to do with a team that had won just three games in the last three years, and he did that by running his team through a spring gauntlet that ground them to the bone. "Our practices that spring were rough," he'd say later. "It was nothing fancy, just hammer-and-tong, dog-eat-dog football. We worked every day until we just had to quit. We lost a lot of people. In a way, that was the idea. We wanted to see who would submit to discipline, and we didn't try to deter anyone from leaving."

Jordan's fall class featured 11 seniors, 19 juniors, 29 sophomores, and 90 freshmen. One of the players who survived that grueling spring was a sophomore from Mobile attempting to fight his way into the quarterback and safety positions. His name was Vince Dooley, and while he had some success at Auburn, he would go on to bigger things later in life. He first made his mark in Jordan's head coaching debut, a 24–14 win over Vanderbilt. Auburn ran the ball a stunning 86 times that game, and Dooley clinched the win with a late interception.

The Tigers started the 1951 season 3–0, and enthusiasm ran high. But then reality set in: Auburn closed out its first season under Jordan getting pasted in four straight games—by Ole Miss, Georgia, Clemson, and hated Alabama. The team took a step back in 1952, going 2–8 on the year. Jordan spent the offseason glad-handing booster groups on the rubber-chicken circuit, assuring them that all was well, and the team was very much on track. But privately, he was starting to lose his curly hair in chunks. How could it all go so wrong, and what could he do to get Auburn headed in the right direction?

As it turned out, salvation came from both within and without. A combination of tighter substitution rules and the improvement of Auburn's young players began to work to Jordan's advantage, starting with the 1953 season. And Jordan's love of defense began to pay dividends.

To help sculpt his Auburn team, Jordan brought in Hal Herring, who had played under the legendary Paul Brown in Cleveland, and turned him loose on the defense. Herring was a film-study obsessive decades before such grinding was commonplace, and he was one of the first defensive coordinators to call in plays from the sidelines.

On the offensive side of the ball, Jordan and offensive coordinator—then called the offensive coach—Charlie Waller implemented a split-T formation, which spread out the guards, tackles, and ends in order to break apart the defense. The intention was to give the Tigers' ballcarriers—including Dooley, their option quarterback—room to create even in tight situations.

Working in Jordan's favor was the new NCAA rule that prohibited unlimited substitutions. Previously (and, obviously, today), teams could swap in new players on every play. But in 1953, the NCAA dropped a bomb on coaches and teams alike.

Every generation thinks it's tougher than the one following it, but in the case of the earliest college football players, they may have been right. For most of the game's first few decades, players competed on both offense and defense; a player substituted out in the first half couldn't return until the second half, and a player who left the field in the second half couldn't return to the game.

However, the drawbacks of this limited substitution became obvious. Schools in the game's earliest days placed no restrictions on roster size, so larger schools with deeper rosters could simply pound smaller schools with multiple rounds of substitution.

Beginning in the 1933 season, the NCAA permitted players to leave and return once per quarter, giving starters a chance to rest and heal up. During World War II, a player shortage forced a further change—players could now substitute in and out freely, and savvy coaches quickly picked up on the fact that their players could specialize on offense *or* defense.

Michigan's Fritz Crisler deployed positional specialization for the first time against Army in 1945, using eight players for offense, eight for defense, and three on both sides of the ball. The Wolverines lost 28–7, but the move impressed Army head coach Red Blaik, who termed the offensive and defensive teams "platoons," and rode them to substantial success in the late 1940s.

In January 1953, the NCAA mandated a sudden change: the end of the two-platoon system and the return of the "iron man" football player, effective immediately. Reports of the day insisted that unlimited-substitution rules had ended college football at as many as 50 smaller schools.

Alabama's then head coach Red Drew raged that the new rules returned college football to "the horse and buggy days," and Mississippi State's Murray Warmath claimed the change set the game back 15 years. Smaller schools, meanwhile, were grateful for a move that reduced larger schools' manpower edge. Michigan's Crisler, who had used the platoon system to such effect a few years before, said that the NCAA was "gravely concerned about those schools that have had to abandon football."

The NCAA would reinstate unlimited substitution in the 1965 season, and it's remained in effect to this day. For forward-thinking coaches in 1953, though, the NCAA's new rule would prove to be an unexpected gift. The rule meant players who could handle the game on both sides of the ball were at a premium, and Auburn, which had spent grueling springs molding exactly that kind of player, suddenly found itself holding two rosters' worth of assets.

Jordan developed "X" and "Y" teams—he knew that terming one "A" and one "B" would create an inaccurate perception that one was better than the other—and ran them out in waves, each playing 10-minute stretches of football. It worked to near perfection: the 1953 squad went

7–2–1 and led the SEC in scoring at 25.7 points per game, up more than 10 points from 1952. A late-season loss to Alabama cost Auburn a shot at the Cotton Bowl, but the team begrudgingly accepted an invitation to the Gator Bowl.

"We were all down. The coaches kind of talked us into going," Dooley later recalled. "They said, 'Well, they're going to give you watches and jackets.' So we said, 'We'll go.'"

The 1954 team notched Jordan's first win against Alabama, and the 1955 team broke Auburn's 13-game losing streak to mighty Georgia Tech. But that season taught Jordan another hard lesson about the vagaries and whims of college football. Even though Auburn and Tech finished with the same record, and even though Auburn had beaten Tech, the Yellow Jackets got the coveted Sugar Bowl bid that year. College football is a game, yes, but it's also a beauty contest, and Jordan's Tigers weren't yet the belle of the ball.

Still, the sun was shining on The Plains once again. In just four years, Jordan had transformed Auburn into a legitimate national top-20 team. Cliff Hare Stadium added another 13,000 seats to increase its capacity to 34,500. Everything was coming up orange and blue, and it was about to get even better . . . and so, so much worse.

The NCAA and the SEC frequently sniffed around Jordan's program, and after a few years, dogged investigators latched onto a bone. On December 15, 1955, the *Birmingham News* wrote that the SEC was investigating a report that an Auburn recruiter paid $1,000 to Robert and Harry Beaube, twin running backs from Gadsden, Alabama. Their father, a reverend, said he wished the boys "would just forget about football." The Beaube twins reported the Auburn payment to their father, who returned the money the next day. But the hammer fell on Auburn all the same.

The SEC fined the school $2,000 for the violation, and Auburn opted not to appeal. Investigators found that Herring, Jordan's defensive coach, had paid the twins $500 apiece, apparently acting on behalf of a booster.

Auburn president Draughon acknowledged the violation, but noted that Auburn wasn't alone. He hinted that "another institution" had implied it would supply the twins with a furnished apartment. Without mentioning names, Draughon was clearly pointing directly at Alabama, which was the only other school to have recruited the Beaubes. Auburn officials also hinted that Alabama officials had ratted out Auburn. "To penalize one institution and not the other can only result in sharpening the rivalry," Draughon said.

Jordan and Jeff Beard, Auburn's athletic director, then drove to the home of Hueytown High School quarterback Richard Rush, their new signal caller. There, they gathered up evidence of gifts they said Alabama had sent Rush to entice him—a TV, clothes, a coat, and, strangely, $28.47 in cash. The SEC fined Alabama $1,000 for the violation, which school officials blamed on enthusiastic alumni.

In May 1956, the NCAA instituted a three-year probationary period—"rough stuff," Draughon called it—barring Auburn from bowl games for two years. (The NCAA was known for draconian penalties in those days. At the same time Auburn was hit with its penalties, Louisville and Florida were both blindsided by two-year probations. One Louisville official called the penalty "a little bit heavy for the violation we committed," while a Florida official said the school learned it was under investigation only when the probation was handed down.)

The NCAA also issued a warning, according to the AP: "Any violation of the probation might lead to a recommendation for expulsion from the NCAA." Jordan raged, but there was little he could do about the monolithic, dictatorial mandates of the NCAA. And very soon, he would have a much more immediate challenge to his kingdom on The Plains.

Chapter 9

THE MAN FROM MORO BOTTOM

The carnival rolled into Fordyce, Arkansas, with a simple plan: entertain the rubes, yes, but separate them from their money too. And if one of the locals got knocked around along the way, well, those were the breaks. Carnival life isn't for everyone.

In the late 1920s, the Depression was still a couple years off. The South was still finding its footing after the Civil War, scratching out a meager living from the soil. Days were long and nights were too brief, so when a carnival came through town—with its collection of clowns, jugglers, knife throwers, freaks, and animals—there was reason to celebrate.

Bear wrestling had been around in some form or fashion in America since 1877, when a man grappled with a bear before a cheering crowd in New York City, and by the 1920s, men all over the country were wrestling bears who'd had their claws removed and their jaws muzzled shut. Wrestlers as famous as "Rowdy" Roddy Piper and Bobby "The Brain" Heenan would one day wrestle bears in less-than-prestige bouts. All too often, bear wrestling was a grim affair; the bears were malnourished and mistreated.

This particular Arkansas carnival had a bear ready to rumble with a simple proposition: wrestle the bear, and win a dollar for every minute you can stay upright. Even in the late 1920s, a dollar wasn't a whole lot of money—worth less than $20 in today's currency—but the challenge proved too enticing for one local youngster to resist.

Maybe he was trying to impress a young woman, maybe he wanted to show off to his buddies, maybe he needed to prove that he was more than just a boy from the tiny town of Moro Bottom, Arkansas. Whatever the reason, the boy was going to wrestle that damn bear.

Once the kid took the bait, the carnival's master of ceremonies marched through town, proclaiming that the lad "WILL WRESTLE A BEAR TONIGHT AT THE LYRIC THEATER." That was enough to fill the theater, half the crowd rooting for the boy, half for the bear.

The boy was a well-known figure about town; he played football at nearby Fordyce High School, and even at 13 years old, he stood 6 foot 1 and weighed 180 pounds. The muzzled bear wasn't exactly a full-grown grizzly—closer to "scraggly," as the boy would later describe him—but hey, a bear is a bear no matter how small.

So the boy knew he needed a plan to survive in the ring. Wisely or not, he opted for a strategy born on the football field: Treat the bear like an opposing ballcarrier. Charge him and hold him down. And that's exactly what he did. The audience roared its approval, and the boy kept the tired old bear pinned.

The promoter, keenly aware that a boy pinning a bear didn't make for a good performance—and didn't exactly reflect well on the bear either—began whispering, "Let him up. Let him up." The boy didn't care. Hell, for a dollar a minute, the boy figured, he'd hold that ol' bear till the beast died.

Scraggly or not, the bear was still a bear, and it managed to wriggle its way free of the boy's grip. And that's when the boy realized two extremely unpleasant facts: One, the bear's muzzle had come off, and its teeth were free. And two, in the midst of the grappling, the bear had managed to strike a pretty solid blow to his head, which began to bleed.

The boy understood that he'd made his point and a strategic retreat was now the wisest course of action. He leaped off the stage, into the empty seats that lined the front row, and ran up the aisle to get away from the bear.

Later on, the boy, bandaged and sore, came back around to collect his winnings for wrestling the bear. But naturally, the carnival was gone, vanished down the road. There would be no financial reward for wrestling a bear.

All Paul Bryant got out of the deal were some scars and the greatest nickname in college football history. It ended up being a pretty fair trade after all.

Paul Bryant was born on September 11, 1913, in Moro Bottom, Arkansas, and were it not for football, that's where he likely would have lived out the rest of his days. Many an opposing fan, player, and coach surely wished he'd never found his way out of the Arkansas cotton fields.

Moro Bottom was barely a wide spot in the road, a two-mile stretch of timberland alongside Moro Creek where just six families lived, tilled the soil, and kept a watchful eye out for roaming packs of wild hogs. Bryant, the 11th of 12 children born to Ida Kilgore and Wilson Monroe Bryant, fought for life from the moment of his birth. Three of his siblings had died in infancy. The rest toiled on and around the 260-acre family farm, working the land to raise cotton and vegetables.

Paul learned to lift heavy loads, plow the earth, and haul water for the livestock. He was up every morning at four o'clock, preparing for the day's work. Almost every day, he would load up vegetables in the family's mule-drawn wagon to make the seven-mile trek along gravel-strewn, rutted trails to Fordyce alongside his mother.

Even by Depression-era standards, Paul was poor as dirt; decades later, he could still remember the names of boys who had mocked him or his aged mules as they clomped into town. Girls laughed at his clothes, and one of his teachers once moved him away from the front of the classroom because of his stench.

Although his mother wanted him to become a preacher, young Paul all too often fell prey to the devil's influence. He once got paddled hard enough to raise blisters for the crime of putting a turtle in a female classmate's desk. He earned another paddling for tossing a cat through an open church window into the lap of another female classmate.

Still, Paul had been raised in the Church of God, and he was pious if not outwardly religious. In the years to come, he had little patience for those who described him in messianic, walk-on-water terms, another lingering wisp of his mother's influence. He knew such comparisons were overstepping theological bounds, even if his disciples didn't.

The family moved to Fordyce proper when Paul was around 13 years old, and that opened up an entire new world for him: football. After he was asked to join the Fordyce High School Redbugs, he had a cobbler nail cleats onto his regular shoes. He had little skill, but he had drive and determination, and for rural Arkansas high school football, that was more than enough.

Ike Murry, a Redbugs teammate, once recalled that Bryant "was a showman, even in those days. Crowds loved him. He never caught many passes. His best play was when he went downfield to block a halfback... Bear would rumble down and put a rolling block at that halfback. I don't think he ever blocked him, but he'd always raise a cloud of dirt, kicking and scrambling around the guy's feet. The crowd would roar. People loved it."

"All I had was football," Bryant would later say. "I hung on as though it were life or death, which it was."

As a senior, Paul was big enough to draw attention from colleges. He was working as a butcher's helper when Alabama's Hank Crisp arrived in town. Crisp had lost his right hand at age 13 while cutting corn, but still had enough talent to play running back at Virginia Tech. He joined Alabama's coaching staff in 1921, and wouldn't leave for 46 years.

So when the already-legendary Crisp made his pitch—"Would you like to go to Alabama?"—Bryant instantly agreed: "I sure would." He first crossed the Black Warrior River and rode onto the campus of the University of Alabama in Crisp's Model A Ford. Bryant wore a pair of green pants—"knickers," he called them—and carried a small satchel with little more inside than another pair of pants.

Because he wasn't quite prepared for Alabama, Paul spent a year earning math and Spanish credits at Tuscaloosa High School. It was a tough go for the country lad from Arkansas. At one point, he wrote a letter to his cousin, Collins Kilgore, suggesting that he might want to quit this school business and go work in the Texas oil fields.

Kilgore fired off what might have been the most consequential telegram of Bryant's life:

GO AHEAD AND QUIT. JUST LIKE EVERYBODY SAID YOU WOULD.

Bryant would experience doubts in his life, moments of indecision or insecurity. But never again would he be farther than arm's length from football.

Just 17 when he formally enrolled at Alabama in the fall of 1931, Paul felt out of place and ill at ease among the more educated, more well-bred students there. He created his trademark slow, stately walk and deliberate speech patterns at this point in his life, a way of projecting confidence he didn't actually feel.

On the field, Bryant was the definition of a solid-but-unspectacular end, not just because of his talent but because of his teammate. At Alabama, he lined up alongside Don Hutson, a fellow Arkansas high schooler who would go on to a Hall of Fame career with the Green Bay Packers. Dubbed "the Alabama Antelope," Hutson, a more talented receiver than Bryant by orders of magnitude, was one of the earliest practitioners of route running, showing discipline and speed unseen in most other players of his era.

"Don had the most fluid motion you had ever seen when he was running," Bryant would later recall. "It looked like he was going just as fast as possible when all of a sudden he would put on an extra burst of speed and be gone."

Alabama during these days was undergoing a transition. Wallace Wade had left the team to take a job at Duke literally the day before Bryant arrived on campus. So coaching the team fell to Frank Thomas, who would prove to be a useful role model for Bryant in the years ahead.

Bryant was good enough to see playing time in several notable games, including Alabama's 29–13 Rose Bowl victory over Stanford on New Year's Day 1935. He was also too tough to know exactly when to quit. Against Mississippi State one year, he injured his leg in the first quarter, returned to the game, and found out two days later that he'd fractured his fibula. Even then, he attempted to play against Tennessee, and ended up having one of his finest statistical games, catching one touchdown pass and lateraling to teammate Riley Smith—a future No. 2 overall NFL draft pick—for another.

Atlanta sportswriter Ralph McGill, who would go on to much greater fame as a Pulitzer Prize–winning columnist railing against segregation, was highly, and rightly, skeptical of the whole "broken leg" tale. Sportswriting in those days tended to be more mythmaking than factual. But McGill traveled to Tuscaloosa, looked at the X-rays himself, and came away convinced that Bryant was both telling the truth and an incredibly tough human being.

"It was just," Bryant later said, "one little old bone."

Five months almost to the day after that Rose Bowl win—June 2, 1935—Bryant ended his bachelorhood when he married Mary Harmon Black. (He would call her "Mary Harmon" throughout their marriage.) He hadn't drawn much interest from pro football scouts—not that there were many pro scouts to show interest in the first place—so he opted to stay in Tuscaloosa, learning coaching under Thomas.

After four years, Bryant moved north to take an assistant job at Vanderbilt. He thrived at Vandy, but assistants aren't supposed to "thrive," and he got kicked to the curb. He then began the itinerant assistant coach's journey, interviewing all over the South for jobs. He managed to land an interview for the head coaching slot at Arkansas. The interview went well, and Bryant left Fayetteville thinking the job was his.

There was just one problem. The date was December 7, 1941, and the Japanese were attacking Pearl Harbor. The Arkansas job—and pretty much everything else in American life—would have to wait.

The next day, Bryant reported to Washington, D.C., to join the Navy. He was commissioned in 1942, and served aboard the USS *Uruguay*, a ship tasked with ferrying troops to North Africa and other ports of call. After 13 months at sea, he was deployed to the football field; he trained recruits and coached the North Carolina Navy Pre-Flight football team—a.k.a. the Cloudbusters—at the University of North Carolina at Chapel Hill. One of his players: Otto Graham, the legendary Cleveland Browns Hall of Fame quarterback.

When the Navy dropped the program in 1945, Bryant needed a job. In Chicago, watching Hutson and the rest of the Packers take on a team of college all-stars—imagine a game like that happening now—he ran into a friend, George Preston Marshall, the owner of the NFL's Washington Redskins. Marshall offered him a job as an assistant coach in the NFL; Bryant responded that he was seeking a head coaching job.

"Why the hell didn't you say so?" Marshall replied. He told Bryant to go wait for a call in his hotel room. When the call came, it was from Harry Clifton "Curley" Byrd, president of the University of Maryland, offering him the job as head football coach sight unseen, as long as he could get from Chicago to Maryland by eight o'clock the next morning.

The postwar chaos in college football was not unlike the chaos of the 2020 COVID season: everyone was making up rules on the fly and discarding long-standing "tradition" as irrelevant or useless. Bryant signed his deal to coach Maryland on September 7, 1945, before he was even officially discharged from the Navy. He flew to Chapel Hill and handpicked 17 Cloudbusters to join him at Maryland. As one player later recalled, they were discharged on the 18th, enrolled at Maryland on the 19th, and played the first game of the season on the 27th.

Bryant's first game as head coach was against Guilford College, and Hutson traveled to Maryland to lend support. Bryant was terrified, and spent most of the night before throwing up.

"Paul," Hutson said, "if you're this nervous about playing Guilford, you're in the wrong business."

Maryland won, 60–6.

Even at the relatively youthful—for a coach—age of 32, Bryant skewed old school in his coaching philosophies. He spent the first hour of his first practice at Maryland preaching the paramount importance of blocking and tackling. He kept the playbook tight, teaching his players barely a handful of plays. And, not all that far removed from his own playing days, he was as likely to get in and mix it up with his players as he was to whistle commands from afar. The theory Bryant embodied, consciously or unconsciously, was simple: if you feared disappointing your coach more than you feared the opponent, you'd make quick work of that opponent.

Bryant was on the leading edge of a revolution in American culture, with a tidal wave of World War II veterans attempting to rejoin society. The demand for small, affordable one-family homes mushroomed, driven by a desire for ownership and a need for escape from the crowded conditions of America's cities. Bryant was part of the creation of suburbia—backyards, patios, evening baseball games, and cookouts—and deeply tied to educational institutions at the exact moment the G.I. Bill was swelling enrollments all over the country. Working-class Americans who had been locked out of universities just a few years before were now able to afford entry, and that changed the complexion of higher education for decades to come.

However, Bryant's time at Maryland didn't last long. In what would become a recurring theme in his life, he clashed with the administration and decided to seek employment elsewhere. His quick turnaround at Maryland—the team went 6–2–1 during his only season at the helm—had given him options, and a telegram from Dr. Herman Donovan, the president of the University of Kentucky, helped him find his new path:

IF YOU WANT TO BE HEAD COACH AT KENTUCKY CALL ME COLLECT.

Bryant took the job, with its generous starting salary of $8,500 a year.

Horse country suited him. Kentucky was where the Bear Bryant Alabama fans would come to know flowered into full bloom. He didn't just push the envelope—he shredded the envelope and told you to pick it up. He was aggressive, unapologetic, and ruthless in his treatment of his players, but he'd defend them against the armies of heaven itself if need be. He was so utterly indifferent to the slings and arrows of academics and athletics officials, they might as well have been a gentle breeze on his skin. He was Paul Bryant, and he did what he damn well pleased. You followed along or you stepped aside, but you didn't get in his way.

Bryant began each season with what he termed a "retreat" to a farm near Lexington. It was legal for players to attend summer camps in those days, as long as they didn't take a football with them. (Sure. Whatever.) Bryant would put his players to work on conditioning, and if they were late to practice, he'd send them out into a nearby field to shovel cow chips for an hour.

Bryant promised Kentucky he'd bring the school a championship within five years, and in 1950, he delivered on that promise. That season, Kentucky won its first 10 games, and didn't allow a single point in the first four. In their 10th game, the Wildcats beat North Dakota 83–0, a whipping so severe and so thorough that Bryant pulled his first three squads at the half and sent them to a nearby practice field to scrimmage against each other.

In the next game, the third-ranked Wildcats lost to No. 9 Tennessee 7–0, one in a long line of Knoxville frustrations for Bryant. But Kentucky claimed the SEC championship by virtue of one more conference win than the Vols, and Bryant used that to successfully lobby for a Sugar Bowl berth against Oklahoma. In those days, national championship polls were taken before the bowls, and Oklahoma won both the AP and UPI polls.

The Sooners had won 31 straight games and were the year's undisputed No. 1 team, but Bryant and his coaches studied film to prepare—an anomaly in those days—and knocked off the mighty Sooners 13–7. Kentucky claims the 1950 national championship to this day.

After the Sugar Bowl, Oklahoma coach Bud Wilkinson made a gesture that impressed Bryant deeply, so much so that he would imitate it in later years. Wilkinson, still feeling the sting of defeat, came over to the Kentucky locker room to shake the hands of Bryant and his players.

"He showed me the class I wish I had," Bryant later said, and in years to come he would make the same gesture himself, even when it pained his soul to do so.

Those were good days in Kentucky, and Bryant wanted to enjoy them. But when he got back to his desk from the victorious New Orleans trip, he found 64 Sugar Bowl tickets he'd paid for out of his own pocket, unused. And he realized that no matter what he did on the football field, it wouldn't matter. He now understood what ruled Kentucky: basketball.

One of the few men to face down the Bear and live to tell the tale was Adolph Rupp, the legendary basketball coach who effectively owned the entire state of Kentucky. Bryant, many years his junior, simply didn't have the juice to compete with Rupp, who was in the process of building a career that would include six Final Four appearances and four national championships. Basketball was Kentucky's first love, and football would always be a bridesmaid. As Bryant would later put it, he received cigarette lighters for winning seasons, while Rupp got Cadillacs.

But Rupp had troubles of his own: a 1951 point-shaving scandal and several NCAA eligibility violations on his watch staining the program so badly that Kentucky's entire 1952–53 basketball season was canceled. In Bryant's eyes, that kind of bone-deep corruption harmed his own recruiting efforts by association. Despite the scandals, Kentucky gave Rupp a contract extension in February 1954, and just like that, Bryant decided he was gone. There was a pecking order at Kentucky, and Bryant wouldn't ever rise higher than No. 2.

The move shocked Kentucky administrators and Bryant's own players, in part because it was some exceptionally bad timing on his part. By February, schools had locked in their coaches for the coming year. Bryant was looking at a barren hiring landscape.

The only school to even interview him: Texas A&M. Bryant accepted the job, to the gleeful delight of alumni and students. At a delirious rally during his first appearance, he stripped off his jacket, stomped on it, and declared, "Boys, it's time to win some damn football games!"

Bryant took a good look at his first Aggies team and declared, "We're 10 percent silk and 90 percent sow's ear. Half the team is smaller than a monkey's cojones. The other half is slower than smoke off shit." He also saw the boosters, alumni, and media massing along the edges of his program, and he knew he had only one option to get this crew into game shape: get the hell out of town.

The Bryant legend truly begins in the tiny town of Junction, Texas, population 2,400 then and now. Bryant hauled his A&M team out there to train in 1954. This was the first time he did that, and the only time—the very next year, the NCAA made the practice illegal.

A&M had acquired an old Army base near Junction that had been used as a summer training facility for the school's physics and geology majors. "Housing," such as it was, consisted of Quonset huts with cement floors, thin plywood walls, tin roofs, and screens on the doors and windows. There was little grass to be seen anywhere. Bryant cleared out a patch of earth, moved all the big rocks out of the way, and marked out a practice field. And then he went and figured out who was going to make his team.

After summer break, the A&M players reported to a team meeting. Bryant strode into the meeting and ordered the players to pack a couple changes of clothes and be ready to go on a little trip in 10 minutes. The team packed quickly and were standing in front of their dorm when the buses pulled up. Everyone boarded, and no one asked where they were going.

After a 10-hour drive, the team arrived in Junction and posted up at a camp just outside town. Bryant gave the team the rest of the day off, and most players spent the time cooling off in a nearby creek.

And then the coach unleashed hell.

At Junction, the players would rise before breakfast for an initial workout. They'd nap, get lunch, and then came the dreaded afternoon practice—a hot, dusty ordeal that induced vomiting every single day. They'd collapse into bed, exhausted, and wake up the next morning to find their pads still damp from the previous day's sweat. Players shed pounds, suffered heatstroke, and fainted in the Texas summer heat.

Many just packed up and left. They'd sneak out in the dead of night, thumbing a ride back to College Station. Or they'd pace around in front of the coach's door, sipping from the water fountain and trying to get up the courage to knock. When enough had quit in a day, one of the assistant coaches would pile them all into a van and drive them to the bus station.

Bryant shrugged off any criticism of his methods. "If a man is going to quit," he said, "I want him to quit in practice, not in a game."

As the players stepped up or dropped out, Bryant began shaping his philosophy of what makes a good team. Strategically, he started with the defense and worked outward from there. He preferred speed to size. Those two elements—defensive intensity and speed all over the field—would come to dominate his football philosophy throughout his career, and would serve as the foundation for the championship teams he would assemble in the coming years.

When Gene Stallings, one of the original Junction Boys and later a coach at A&M and Alabama, was asked if Junction was as tough as the legends held, he responded with a good line: "All I know is that we went out there in two buses, and we came back in one."

Just 29 players returned to College Station after the Junction ordeal, bonded as a team. They'd been through hell together, and it was time to test the strength of their loyalty and their love for one another.

They promptly lost their first game to Texas Tech, 41–9, and ended up losing nine of their 10 games that first season. So much for the Junction Boys becoming a fearsome fighting unit, right? Look a little closer, though. In every single game after the Texas Tech loss, A&M had a chance to win in the fourth quarter. The team wasn't there yet, but they were close.

A&M had tradition, loyalty, fidelity, and honor. What it didn't have was either a strong football tradition or coeds. Both factors made recruiting exceptionally difficult for Bryant. Perhaps because of these restrictions, or perhaps because of the influence of wealthy, overzealous A&M

alumni, the new coach found himself in almost immediate trouble with the NCAA.

Charges of recruiting violations landed A&M on probation for two years despite their abysmal 1–9 record in Bryant's debut season. He grumbled that rival schools were doing their best to sideline him before he could get A&M up to ramming speed.

"With his unquenchable thirst for victory in mind, [Bryant] grew overpersuasive in tempting promising college prospects to think of a future in Aggieland," Kern Tip wrote in the book *Football Texas Style*. Bryant denied illegally recruiting any players himself, but allowed that, yes, perhaps some illegal recruiting had been done by boosters of the program, and yes, perhaps he might have encouraged it. Maybe.

Either way, the pieces were falling into place in Aggieland. A&M had a spectacular rally against rival Rice in Bryant's second season, anchored by Stallings snaring an onside kick that led to the win.

"Most games are decided by five or six plays," Bryant would later say. "The secret to winning in football is having the right players on the field when those five or six plays happen."

Bryant had two rules for being a successful college football coach: a five-year contract and an understanding wife. At A&M, he had both, and all seemed right in his world.

But then Mama called.

Chapter 10

CHAMPION TIGERS

The *Birmingham News* included a portentous line in its 1956 season preview: "The Tigers look good in '56, [but] they might be great in '57." Elsewhere, the newspaper summed up Coach Jordan with a devastating, on-point characterization: "Perfectionist type, he can be quickly bitter toward a player putting out only 99.4 per cent [*sic*]."

The 1956 season wasn't much to remember. Perhaps the only highlight—or, rather, lowlight—was the "Battle of Chattahoochee," a fistfight that broke out between Georgia and Auburn after some debatable tackles. (The Chattahoochee is the river that runs along the border of Georgia and Alabama.) Georgia and Auburn were, and remain, the Deep South's oldest rivalry, and that familiarity has a different character than Auburn's blood rivalry with Alabama or its hated-neighbor rivalry with Florida.

Then came 1957, the year Jordan's preparation paid off like a savvy long-term investment. He had kept the majority of his coaching staff in place, and hired on a few new faces like former player Vince Dooley, back in Alabama after a two-year stint in the Marines. Early that year, Jordan sent his assistants to Oklahoma with the stated intention of learning about the Sooners' quarterback option scheme. But the truth was, he wanted his coaches to understand what was necessary to achieve a national championship–level program, from the ground up.

The year began on a rocky note, with Jordan facing some significant personnel challenges, to put it mildly. His starting quarterback and fullback had violated team rules, culminating with an incident in which they wandered into a girls' dormitory and drank beer. Not exactly a mortal sin, especially on a college campus, but rules were rules, and discipline needed to be administered. No player was above Jordan's law.

"Right after spring practice we had to make a move as a coaching staff that could make or break any season," Jordan wrote in a short piece, titled "By Reason of Spirit," in the book *National Champions*. "It had a tremendous psychological effect on the team. They knew that the coaching staff was serious about team discipline and morale." In other words, he lit a fire under that team and terrified them into staying on the straight and narrow.

That left Auburn without a quarterback, and Jordan tapped a 5-foot-11, 175-pound left-handed fullback by the name of Lloyd Nix. It would prove to be one of his finest personnel moves.

Before then, though, Nix and the rest of the Tigers needed to survive practices that would now be considered unconscionable cruelty. "We didn't get any water or ice at practice," right guard Tim Baker later told Jordan's biographer. "We'd go out in pads in that afternoon heat, then we'd run 100-yard sprints. But no water. I've seen other football players, plus myself, take sweaty towels and squeeze 'em to try and get moisture in our mouth and all we could spit out was cotton."

Expectations for the Tigers ran high. Auburn came into 1957 picked to finish second in the conference, behind Tennessee. (Alabama was picked to finish dead last.) The season started slowly, with a grim 7–0 win over Tennessee in Knoxville in which Nix completed just three passes. But a win is a win, and this one contained the seeds of what would be a theme for the entire season: no mistakes.

Auburn spent all of the 1957 season methodically crafting a beautiful record. The Tigers beat Georgia Tech in Atlanta 3–0, and then Auburn began climbing up the polls—No. 5, No. 3. They closed the season with a wicked trio of Georgia, Florida State, and Alabama. The Tigers took care of business by dispatching Georgia, and then absolutely boat-racing Florida State in Tallahassee.

"Playing Auburn is like entering battle without any guns," Florida State head coach Tom Nugent said afterward. Their victory over the Seminoles gave Auburn a national No. 1 ranking.

The probation handed down after the Beaube twins scandal meant Auburn wasn't eligible for a bowl, so that year's Iron Bowl was a de facto national championship game for the Tigers. Alabama wasn't expected to present much of a challenge; the team was 2–6–1 and more than ready to move on from Ears Whitworth.

The Tigers had plenty of motivation. Ohio State head coach Woody Hayes, who believed his team deserved to be at the top of the polls, thundered his disgust. "Whom have they played?" he said of Auburn. "We've beaten the best teams in the toughest league in America. It'll be a dirty shame if we aren't No. 1." In response, Auburn put a big blue *1* on the dressing room bulletin board.

So Auburn was fighting more than just the Tide, but the Tigers needed to take care of their in-state rival. "Don't nurse them," Jordan said prior to the game. "If you do, they'll stay with you and make it tough. Go get 'em from the start. Show 'em why you're No. 1. Show 'em why you deserve it."

Auburn annihilated the Tide, dropping 34 unanswered points in the first half and clearing the benches in the second. The Tigers were named national champions in early December, and the entire town turned out for a parade and a free day off school.

In retrospect, that Auburn team was simply magnificent. The defense gave up only 28 points all *season*, with none of those coming on the ground: one was a pick-six; the others came through the air. The defense was smothering, leading the nation in a range of categories, and shutting out six SEC teams: Tennessee, Kentucky, Georgia Tech, Florida, Georgia, and Alabama. Most notably, considering the alleged source of the information that led directly to Auburn's probation, the Tigers beat Alabama by a combined score of 74–7 in 1956 and 1957. That didn't get Auburn off probation any faster, but it took away a bit of the sting.

And then the hammer came down. In April 1958, Auburn got hit with an additional three-year probation—1958 through 1960—that was both widespread and severe. No bowl games, no sharing in postseason conference revenue, no participation by other sports teams in their postseason events until September 1, 1961. The impetus this time around: a Guntersville High School quarterback by the name of Don Fuell.

Fuell signed with Auburn on December 7, 1956, ending a furious 14-school battle for his services. But rumors swirled that Auburn had offered him a car—and Auburn believed Alabama was behind the rumormongering. Despite years' worth of Auburn testimony and protestations of innocence, the NCAA thundered down with its draconian punishment, at the time the third most severe in NCAA history.

Auburn officials howled their innocence, and skulduggery of the highest and silliest order ensued. Auburn contended that Alabama had been behind the push to get Fuell off the Auburn roster, and Alabama said there was no proof of that. Auburn officials claimed they were being convicted by evidence that was circumstantial at best, and didn't warrant the kind of overarching penalty the NCAA had doled out, regardless.

At yet another hearing, the NCAA declared that Fuell had come into possession of a $1,700 motorboat, an air conditioner, an apartment, and appliances that all just happened to be connected to Auburn alumni. They pointed out that the cost of these items was out of whack with the Fuell family's circumstances—the quarterback's father didn't even have a bank account. Fuell, for his part, was kicked out of school.

"The Southeastern Conference missed a great opportunity to grow up and become a real conference today," Jordan raged. "The commissioner missed a great opportunity to grow up and be a real commissioner."

Auburn's many probations had kept the team off television for the entirety of their 1957 national championship season. But the Tigers opened 1958 with a nationally televised game against Tennessee, and the NCAA permitted the broadcast to go on. The result was one of the greatest defensive showcases in SEC history, as Auburn held Tennessee to minus-30 yards of total offense and zero first downs, winning easily 13–0.

The team finished that season 9–0–1 and ranked fourth in the country. Had they been featured on more than just one national television broadcast and not been locked out of bowls, Jordan might have been among the most famous coaches in the country. As it was, he was by far the most famous in Alabama.

For the moment.

Chapter 11

FAITH REWARDED

The writers crowded into Bear Bryant's tiny office in College Station. The air was thick with sweat and cigarette smoke and nervous energy. The Aggies were steamrolling through the 1957 season without a defeat—hell, with hardly a point scored against them—but there were dark clouds on the horizon. Rumors swirled about the head coach's plans for next season and the future, and Bryant decided to address them head-on with the most memorable metaphor of his career.

"When you were out playing as a kid, say you heard your mother call you," Bryant rumbled. "If you thought she just wanted you to do some chores, or come in for supper, you might not answer her. But if you thought she *needed* you, you'd be there in a hurry."

Alabama needed Bear Bryant, and it was time for Paul to answer Mama's call.

After suffering through the run of horrendous coaching by Ears Whitworth, Alabama officials and boosters had seen quite enough. Losing was simply not an Alabama trait. Plus, over there in East Alabama, Shug Jordan was building himself a behemoth. It was time to hunt big game. Hundreds of elementary-school children in Tuscaloosa wrote letters begging

Bryant to come coach the Tide. Alumni reminded Bryant of what Alabama had already done for him, hauling him out of little Moro Bottom and giving him the foundation to become the man he now was.

Bryant was leery of offending his old recruiter, Hank Crisp, who was Alabama's athletic director at the time. Crisp allayed those concerns by flying to Houston, locating Bryant, and declaring, "Now come on. Get your ass back to Alabama so we can start winnin' some football games."

A&M's John David Crow won the Heisman that season, but Bryant was oddly muted, his mind clearly elsewhere. He did offer one comment that may well have tipped the scales: "If John David doesn't win the Heisman, they ought to stop giving it."

The Bear Bryant era ended at A&M with losses of one, two, and three points. It was an ignoble end to one of the most mythologized, if brief, eras in college football. "With his resignation," a prescient editorial writer in the campus newspaper wrote, "Texas A&M is no doubt losing the greatest coach in America today."

Bryant arrived in Alabama to find a football desert. In the previous three seasons, Alabama had won a total of four games under Whitworth. The Tide had scored just once against Auburn over that stretch, and not at all against Tennessee. This simply would not do; Alabama was no one's doormat. So when Bryant arrived, the expectation was that he wouldn't just turn the program around—he'd launch it into the sky.

"Coach," a writer from the *Birmingham News* said at his first press conference, "the alumni are expecting your team to go undefeated next season."

"The hell you say," Bryant grumbled. "I'm an alumni, and I don't expect us to go undefeated."

Bryant knew that this would be his most important rebuilding job, so he brought to Tuscaloosa everything he'd learned doing the exact same thing at Maryland, Kentucky, and Texas A&M. At his first meeting with the Alabama team, he laid down his law.

"Everything from here on out is going to be first class, which includes living quarters, food, equipment, modes of travel," he declared. "And my staff and I are going to see that you play first-class football." He spoke of pride and writing your momma and making your bed, and he spoke for 23 minutes, and he took no questions. "I don't know any of you and I don't want to know anybody," he growled. "I'll know who I want to know by the end of spring training."

Bryant officially started his tenure at Alabama at 5:30 a.m. on New Year's Day 1958, his white Cadillac—still bearing Texas plates—rolling into a silent, dark parking lot on the Alabama campus. Stripped of the ability to grind his charges into dust, he had to use more orthodox methods. He sized up his team in the spring of 1958 as a "fat, raggedy bunch." He summoned players to Tuscaloosa early that summer, and then gave them instructions on how to practice, since he couldn't oversee them himself before the season officially began.

Bryant took a special interest in the Alabama freshmen. He pledged that anyone who stuck with him would be a national champion. He stormed into the locker room of the freshman Tide team one game at halftime and chewed out players and coaches alike, scaring a dozen players into leaving the program right then and there.

After going 5–4–1 in Bryant's first year, the Tide didn't receive an invitation to a bowl—invites to the postseason contests were both more rare and more prized than today—but after that, he would take Alabama to a bowl every single year for the rest of his career. Bryant liked bowls not because of their money, or prestige, or their gifts to the players, or the exposure for his program. No, he liked bowls because they gave him a sanctioned extra month for practice. That allowed him to get a start on the next season that much faster.

Bowls also allowed Bryant to push the edges, and that included social customs as well as NCAA rules. He was never the white stalwart that his more segregation-minded fans would have liked, and from his first days at

Alabama, he began laying the groundwork—slowly, but unmistakably—for massive social change.

In 1959, Bryant, newly hired university president Frank Rose, and Alabama's segregationist governor John Patterson worked out a deal to suspend the state's "gentlemen's agreement" banning games against integrated teams, allowing the Tide to take on integrated Penn State in that year's Liberty Bowl in Philadelphia. Perhaps it was a chance to quietly advance Alabama society forward, perhaps it was the opportunity to play in the school's first bowl in six years, perhaps it was the $150,000 payment that enticed Alabama to Philadelphia.

Whatever the reason, Bryant and the Tide traveled north to play a Nittany Lions team that featured a young assistant coach by the name of Joe Paterno. This would be Bryant's first bowl game as Alabama's head coach, and Alabama's first nationally telecast game.

"This team has an excellent chance to regain much of the prestige that was lost in recent years by showing the East what kind of football is played in the South—and by this Alabama team in particular," the *Tuscaloosa News* wrote.

Bryant was deliberately defying the prevailing order, both of his university and his society, by facing an integrated team. A telegram from the Tuscaloosa Citizens' Council chairman declared, "We strongly oppose our boys playing an integrated team . . . The Tide belongs to all Alabama and Alabamians favor continued segregation."

The *Tuscaloosa News* advocated a more progressive position by appealing to the egos of Alabama fans: "It is a fact of life that the young men who play on Alabama's football team—or in any other sport—will meet players of other races if they enter a professional career. In sports centers of the East, Midwest, and Far West sports attractions and teams are not segregated. This year's Alabama team can help the cause of the Tide and the University if it goes to Philadelphia, plays a hard, clean game of which it is capable, and demonstrates sportsmanship at its highest level."

Alabama lost that particular game 7–0, but the point had been made. Bryant would play where he wanted, against whomever he wanted.

The Bryant aura drew in players with the same mindset. Pat Trammell was Bryant's first signed quarterback, a leader who claimed control of the team despite his relatively average statistics. According to local legend, as a freshman, Trammell once barged into a room of players who were also looking to play quarterback. He jammed a switchblade knife into a tabletop and asked which of them were quarterbacks. No one answered, and from then on, he had no competition for the job.

Trammell was the first in a long line of unconventional—to put it politely—quarterbacks who could draw Bryant's ire but managed to play their way out of trouble. Competing in the era where substitutions weren't permitted, Trammell was a de facto coach on both sides of the ball. Irate at his own offensive line, he once quick-kicked on third down, and told Bryant, "They're not blocking anyone, so I thought I'd see if they could play defense."

"He can't run, he can't pass, and he can't kick," Bryant said of Trammell. "All he can do is beat you."

In 1961, Trammell led the Tide to a monstrous season, a year in which Alabama went undefeated and outscored its opposition by a total margin of 297 to 25. The Tide finally ascended to No. 1 in November, and beat Arkansas 10–3 in the Sugar Bowl—on Trammell's touchdown—to claim Bryant's first national title at Alabama. Those 1958 freshmen who had stuck with him indeed got that national championship in their senior year.

Sadly, Trammell would live only a few more years. He was diagnosed with testicular cancer and died on December 10, 1968, at age 28. Wracked with grief and sadness, Bryant would call the day of Trammell's death the saddest of his entire life.

As 1960s-era football collisions go, it didn't look all that bad. But the effects would nearly topple the entire Alabama program, reshape the football future of a different university, and deeply stain the image of Bear Bryant.

The date: November 18, 1961. Alabama, in the midst of a season that would end with a national championship, was absolutely murderous. The defense in particular was brutal, having allowed only 22 points all season, and currently boasting a three-games-and-counting shutout streak. Early in the fourth quarter, Georgia Tech was once again punting, and one of the players assigned to cover the punt was Tech halfback Chick Graning.

Several days earlier, *Atlanta Journal* writer Furman Bisher stopped by the Tide's practice to size things up. He noticed Alabama's Darwin Holt wasn't in full gear. This would prove to be a portentous observation. "Coach Bryant tells us not to let him wear pads at practice," a team manager told Bisher. "He's afraid he'll hurt somebody."

As Graning raced downfield toward the Alabama punt return man, Holt cut into his path and slammed him with a forearm. An ugly play, but nothing apparently unusual in the rub-some-dirt-on-it era. There was no flag on the play, and Holt jogged back to the sidelines as if nothing was wrong.

Only . . . Graning didn't get up. He'd been knocked unconscious by Holt's blow. He was stretchered off, and in the hours after the game, the severity of the injury became clear: he had suffered a concussion and fractures all over his face, losing five teeth at once, with the rest of his upper teeth likely to follow.

Reporters from the *Atlanta Journal* were incensed, and called for Bryant to dismiss Holt immediately. For his part, Bryant said that Holt "came to me after the game and was all torn up and said that he had hit the Tech boy. He said he didn't know why he did it. He said he wanted to apologize to Graning."

Georgia Tech head coach Bobby Dodd implored both Bryant and Alabama president Frank Rose to take action. A few months later, Dodd announced he would end the long-running rivalry with Alabama after the 1964 game, and soon afterward, Georgia Tech would leave the SEC entirely.

Alabama went on the attack, sending out game film that demonstrated how, in Bryant's opinion, Tech was every bit as dirty, if not more so. But he had raised the ire of the *Journal*'s Bisher. Bryant may or may not have heard Mark Twain's line about picking a fight with a man who buys his ink by the barrel, but it likely wouldn't have mattered. He wasn't going to back down to some *reporter*, not when it came to defending his own team.

"There's no doubt Darwin fouled Chick Graning, and the officials should have penalized us, which they didn't," Bryant wrote in his autobiography. "But it could have been anybody in the secondary, not just him. I probably would have disciplined him my own way if those Atlanta sportswriters hadn't set out to crucify him. A penalty is one thing, a crucifixion is another."

Shortly before the 1962 season began, the NCAA released a memorandum to its members with the provocative title "Unwarranted Viciousness and Brutality in Our College Game." The memo condemned "a laxness of officials" and "the unwillingness of a few coaches to be worthy of their noble profession by properly instructing and disciplining their boys with regard to brutal play." The implication was clear, even if the NCAA couldn't quite muster up the courage to call out Bryant by name.

Bryant's rapid ascent to the top of the college football pyramid delighted Alabamians looking for a combination of victory and validation. Much like in 1926 with the Rose Bowl, a certain strain of Alabamian looked on the university's football triumph as proof of the innate superiority of the Southern man, on the battlefield or the gridiron.

"Football in the South was so enwrapped with state and regional pride that one could barely separate Saturday afternoon heroics from the politics of race," wrote E. Culpepper Clark. "It was our little skinny boys against theirs, and if theirs happened to be from outside the South, then it was their big, well-fed boys. It was as if the strong young men dressed in Alabama crimson and white transformed magically into butternut-clad Confederates, gaunt, ghastly, readied for battle."

"Your men stood like Stonewall Jackson," US Representative Frank Boykin of Alabama wrote Bryant after one triumph, adding that "they should now name you not just Bear Bryant, but General Bear Bryant." The reference to the famed Confederate general and the Tide's military bearing was in no way accidental; Bryant was now the epitome of Alabama's—and, by association, the entire South's—declaration that it was the equal of the North, regardless of how that Late Unpleasantness had turned out a century ago.

"Well, the Alabama football team showed the world, the whole wide world what our men could do," Boykin continued, echoing the thoughts of multitudes across the region. "There was so much joy, there was so much pleasure that you gave all of the home folks and people all over the South and people all over this Nation that want us to keep some part of our way of life."

That phrase—"our way of life"—was key to the arguments of Boykin and so many others, a not-particularly-subtle reference to a world of white supremacy and Black subservience. It was a "way of life" that, at that precise moment, was under assault from every direction—from federal government orders, from Black leaders, from Northern activists. What scanned as progress in the rest of the country felt like an invasion to many white citizens of Alabama.

Even as terrifying, heartbreaking, and devastating images filtered out of Alabama and onto the nation's nightly news, Bryant and the University of Alabama gave the white people of Alabama and the South a rallying cry as they pictured themselves as the embattled party. Bryant himself was a testament to the virtues of hard work and an up-from-poverty ascension, a stern leader who nonetheless praised the virtues of respecting church, home, and Mama. Not only that, but his teams were all white . . . even if he was working behind the scenes to change that.

But most people don't see behind the scenes. They only see the images in front of them, and those images were disturbing indeed. As professor Andrew Doyle noted in 1997, Bryant embodied to the rest of the nation a terrifying specter of what Southern historian W. J. Cash called the "savage ideal"—lawless, fearless young white men tearing apart society with abandon, wreaking havoc on Blacks and progressive whites alike. *They're defeating us on the football field today; will they come for us on the streets tomorrow?*

Even as Bryant was winning significant football games, police and segregationists were dealing out vicious beatings on Freedom Riders across the state, bombing buildings all over Birmingham, and generally cementing the image of the South as a sinister hellscape.

National media, with the civil rights atrocities as a backdrop, tore into Bryant. In 1961, just weeks before he would win his first national championship, *Time* magazine called Bryant "a relentless and brutal taskmaster" and "a shrewd recruiter, an admitted plagiarizer of football tactics, a chronic weeper, and a flagrant headline chaser" who "drinks Salty Dogs, runs up scores, browbeats sportswriters, cusses his players, and believes in corporal punishment—usually a size 12-D shoe applied to the seat of the pants." *Sports Illustrated* said he gave off the image of "a tyrant, a slave driver on the practice field, a recruiter without scruples, a ruthless opponent."

Bryant was a cultural Rorschach blot: you could see what you wanted in him, and you were never quite sure what the truth was. Which was exactly how he liked it. And his adoring fans loved him for it.

"When he came to Alabama in 1958, Alabama was a beleaguered place," says author Keith Dunnavant. "The state needed someone to look up to, to believe in, someone who helped us deal with our inferiority complex as a state. Bryant was the antidote to the scorn that Alabama people felt from the rest of the country. And not just that, but the way he ran his program was all about excellence. It was about doing the right thing, as cliché as that sounds, but that's the way we felt about it. He was our hero, in the literal sense of that word. We looked up to him because he let us feel better about ourselves, and our little place in the world."

Chapter 12

WHEN THE CHAIN HIT THE PIPE

When a chain hits a lead pipe, there's a distinctive ringing sound. It carries. And if you happen to be a player who suited up for Bear Bryant during his tenure at Alabama, the sound of a chain hitting a pipe will still have you jolting awake, as if from a nightmare.

Bryant wasn't the first head coach to use a tower to watch over his teams as they practiced; as far back as 1921, George Foster Sanford oversaw Rutgers football practices from a tower. But Bryant was the first to use a tower to grant himself godlike powers of observation and intimidation. Every day, as practice began, he would ascend 33 winding stairs, past a red-lettered sign that read "Do Not Stand Under Tower," climbing 20 feet up into his gleaming, white-painted citadel, then linking the chain behind him across the top of the staircase. He'd stand there, alone, a tin roof shielding him from the brutal Alabama sun. And he would watch, like a disapproving Old Testament God.

But Bryant wouldn't just watch. He would scan. He would observe. He would *see*. As the legend went, he would zero in on one player every day, and watch that player from the moment he stepped onto the practice field, through every drill and every contact, right up until the player limped off. He'd watch how that player engaged, how he fought, how he hit. And if that player loafed or slacked off, well, he could bid farewell to ever seeing game action.

Maybe it was true; maybe it wasn't. But Bryant was so far up in the tower, watching from above, that it was impossible to tell whom he was watching. So he could always be watching *you*.

Sometimes, he'd see something that angered him, and that was when the troubles began. When the chain hit the pipe—when Bryant unhooked the chain and it banged against an adjacent pole—it meant he was on his way down to rain hellfire on some poor bastard, dog-cussing him and threatening to call his momma and daddy and tell them what a sorry, misbegotten piece of trash they had for a boy. When the chain hit the pipe, it was enough to make the toughest men in Alabama afraid.

"Man, you could hear him coming," Lee Roy Jordan, Alabama's legendary linebacker and the second-most-fearsome man in the state, recalled to writer Tommy Hicks in 2006. "He wore those big ole military boots at that time, and you could hear him coming down those metal steps, his boots clanging on those steps. You just prayed it wasn't you he needed to correct."

No one accompanied Bryant into the tower, and few were ever permitted to climb its stairs. So it was no small shock in 1961 when Bryant invited a kid from Pennsylvania up to have a conversation.

A kid he dubbed "Joe Willie."

Beaver Falls, Pennsylvania, isn't the kind of place you'd expect to find a legendary SEC quarterback. Deep in the heart of mining country, it's remote and quaint, the kind of place where people can live full, happy, quiet lives without ever straying too far from town. Unless, that is, you're born with a wild streak.

Joseph William Namath grew up in Beaver Falls, the son of a millworker and the grandson of Hungarian immigrants. He grew up in a racially and ethnically integrated neighborhood, running and playing ball with Blacks and whites, Italians and Irish alike. His parents split up when he was in the seventh grade, and he lived with his mother above a tavern called Club 23.

Even as a boy, Namath had a sense of style. While playing outfield for his high school baseball team, he sported sunglasses called "cheaters." He pulled the black laces out of his cleats and replaced them with white ones that shone bright against the black leather.

Like most boys of his era, from Bart Starr to Nick Saban, Namath clashed with his father even as he craved the old man's approval. The two once nearly came to blows in the dugout after the senior Namath criticized one of Joe's teammates for making an error.

Joe had talent on the ballfield—enough to get himself a $50,000 contract offer from the Chicago Cubs his senior year. But after a meeting with his family, the decision was made: college, not baseball. He took visits to Arizona State, Miami, Michigan State, Notre Dame, Maryland... anywhere that was outside the boundaries of western Pennsylvania. He had his heart set on Maryland, but didn't get a high enough score on the SAT... which brought Alabama into play.

In August, Howard Schnellenberger, then the tight ends and wide receivers coach for Alabama, visited Namath and his mother. In less than an hour, Schnellenberger had charmed Namath's mother, and she packed Joe's suitcase, handed him a five-dollar bill, and said, "Honey, you're going with him."

When Namath arrived on campus as a freshman in 1961, fall practice had already started. Namath showed up wearing sunglasses, a checkered sport coat, and a powder-blue straw hat with a pearl in the band. This kid, in other words, wasn't there to blend in. He arrived at practice, and Bryant offered him the highest of honors—an invitation to join him atop that fabled tower. Until Namath, no player had ever been extended such a momentous invitation.

"We talked for fifteen minutes," Namath later recalled in his autobiography, "and I didn't understand a word he said." He recollected Bryant pointing out various players and saying "Stud," and he grasped that he was about to be joining an entire pack of studs.

As Namath tells it, he also got an instant introduction to the world that was the South in the early 1960s. At the bus station, he spotted separate water fountains for Blacks and whites. He rode in the back of the bus, only to be told he was in the "wrong" seat. And passing through the town of Holt, he observed a burning cross surrounded by Klansmen. "Welcome to Tuscaloosa," a billboard outside town proclaimed, "Home of the Ku Klux Klan." On the billboard, a Klansman atop a rearing horse held aloft a flaming cross.

"I had never experienced much by way of segregation until I went to Alabama," Namath said. "When I arrived, I wasn't even aware the school was segregated, and if I had known, I probably wouldn't have gone."

Still, there was something special about Alabama, something that made him temper his initial reactions. "Something about Coach Bryant, though, and that practice, made me want to be a part of it," he said. "The desire to be on his team overrode my differences with the South."

The 1962 season—and Namath's varsity Alabama career—began with a game against the Georgia Bulldogs. The youthful Dawgs would be relying on a sophomore-heavy lineup, which meant Bryant hadn't been able to effectively scout the Georgia team. He had no idea what to expect, and he was placing his hopes in the hands of his own sophomore quarterback.

Prior to the game, Bryant—as was his custom—took Namath for a little walk around Legion Field. As they walked, he took a deep draw on his Chesterfield and turned to Namath. "Joe, you got the plan?"

"Yes, sir," Namath replied. "I think so."

"You *think* so?" Bryant growled. "Damn, son, it's time you *know*. The hay is in the barn."

On his first play from scrimmage, Namath was so nervous, he called a quarterback sneak just to rattle his own cage and set himself straight. It worked: three snaps later, he threw a 52-yard touchdown pass. Georgia crossed midfield only twice, and didn't get any closer to Alabama's end zone than the Tide's 45-yard line . . . and that was on the last play of the game. The 35–0 victory was so overwhelming that, ironically enough, it would end up becoming one of Bryant's greatest losses.

Namath would lead the Crimson Tide to a 10–1 record, with only a missed extra point against Georgia Tech standing between Alabama and a perfect season. The Tide won an invitation to the 1963 Orange Bowl, where they would face Oklahoma. The game was memorable for two reasons: President John F. Kennedy and Lee Roy Jordan.

Kennedy, the popular young president, was well aware that his brother, the attorney general, and other members of his administration were actively working to break the segregation hammerlock in Alabama. Perhaps in solidarity, Kennedy only visited the integrated Oklahoma locker room before the game, not the all-white Alabama one. Bryant used the "snub" as still more fuel to fire up his team.

In the game itself, Jordan didn't single-handedly beat Oklahoma, but it sure seemed that way. As the Tide stomped to a 17–0 victory, he amassed an astounding 31 tackles on the day, leading to one of the great Bryant quotes. "If they stay inside the boundaries," Bryant rumbled, "Lee Roy will get 'em."

Off the field, Bryant's troubles were starting to mount. After the 35–0 Georgia beatdown, the blood was in the water for the Alabama coach, and Furman Bisher, the Atlanta sportswriter, was the lead shark. Bryant feared no man, but Bisher did a good job of enraging him with an article in the October 20, 1962, issue of the *Saturday Evening Post* headlined "College Football Is Going Berserk."

In the article, no less than Shug Jordan himself condemned the rise of "this new hell-for-leather, helmet-busting, gang-tackling brand of football." Jordan also had a handy rationale for why the state of affairs was so terrifying: "Since Bear Bryant came back to Alabama," he said, "it's the only kind of game which can win."

The article accused Bryant of effectively encouraging his players to commit assault and battery in the name of winning a football game. That's the kind of claim that can veer into the libelous, and Bryant filed a $500,000 defamation suit against Bisher and Curtis Publishing, the *Saturday Evening Post*'s parent company.

If Bryant expected a lawsuit to scare off his pursuers, though, he was wrong. Within just a few months, he'd find out just how wrong he was.

TIMEOUT: WAR EAGLE

When you've built up more than 150 years of tradition, mascots and icons and motivations tend to get a bit snarled up and crosswise. Such is the case with Auburn's War Eagle, which is at once a rallying cry and an inspirational icon.

Everyone at Auburn agrees that the origin of War Eagle is a well-constructed myth, but then again, myths carry meaning too. The War Eagle legend began in 1864 at the Battle of the Wilderness in Virginia, where an Auburn student fought alongside his fellow Confederates under the command of General Robert E. Lee. The student suffered grievous wounds during the battle, and was left for dead. But when he regained consciousness, he found, yes, a baby eagle by his side. (It's best not to ask too many questions. Let the War Eagle legend fly.)

The student returned home, nursing both himself and the baby eagle back to health. Flash forward to 1892, when Auburn's George Petrie organized that first game between Auburn and the University of Georgia. The Civil War veteran was in the stands with his eagle. As Auburn marched downfield for the final time, the now-aged eagle took flight and began to circle the field, inspiring cries of "War Eagle!" Auburn scored, won the game . . . and the eagle promptly dropped to the turf and died.

There is absolutely no evidence any of that ever happened, but that's not the point.

At least three other versions of the War Eagle creation myth exist:

- In 1913, during a pep rally prior to another game against the University of Georgia, an eagle emblem fell off a student's hat; a cheerleader declared it was a "war eagle."
- In 1914, Auburn played the Carlisle Indians, whose best player was known as Bald Eagle. Auburn players keyed on Bald Eagle, calling out his name; spectators mistook the calls for "War Eagle," and the chant stuck.
- Ancient Saxons apparently used "War Eagle" as a battle cry, referring to the vultures that would land on a battlefield after a skirmish to feast on the dead.

There is, of course, a real War Eagle, which has been housed at Auburn's Southeastern Raptor Center since 1930. An eagle first took flight around Jordan-Hare Stadium as part of pregame ceremonies in 2000, and ever since, the War Eagle's flight has thrilled the tens of thousands of fans in attendance.

"War Eagle," the fight song, has been around since 1955, and is played after every touchdown: "War Eagle, fly down the field," run the first lines, "Ever to conquer, never to yield." (The song wisely dodges any attempt to rhyme the un-rhyme-able word *orange*.)

There's also the joyfully incomprehensible "Bodda Getta" chant:

> *Bodda getta, bodda getta, bodda getta, bah*
> *Rah rah rah*
> *Sis boom bah*
> *Weagle weagle*
> *War damn Eagle*
> *Kick 'em in the butt Big Blue . . . hey!*

"War Eagle" remains the calling card of choice for Auburn grads and fans all over the planet, a two-word acknowledgment that they are part of the same family. Regardless of how the story began.

Chapter 13

THE TARNISHED CROWN

In late January 1963, the bottom dropped out on Bryant. Even with the 1962 libel suit from the college football brutality article hanging over its head, the *Saturday Evening Post* published a legitimate bombshell of a story: that Bryant and former Georgia head coach Wally Butts had conspired to fix the previous year's game between the two teams.

The article appeared in the March 23, 1963, edition with the provocative headline "THE STORY OF A COLLEGE FOOTBALL FIX." According to the story, Bryant received secret information from Butts in a telephone call nine days before the two teams would play at Legion Field.

The source of the allegations: an Atlanta businessman named George Burnett, who claimed he'd been plugged into the conversation via crossed wires on September 13, 1962. Burnett had been attempting to call Jackson 5-3536, the number to the public relations firm in Atlanta where Butts often made his phone calls, and to his shock, Burnett could hear an operator say, "Coach Bryant is out on the field, Coach Butts, but he is on his way to the phone. Do you want to hold, or do you want him to return the call?" Butts said he would hold, and Burnett silently listened in.

Bryant came on the line. "Hello, Bear," Butts said.

"Hi, Wally," Bryant replied. "Do you have anything for me?"

Burnett took notes on the conversation, and those notes—and the line "Do you have anything for me?"—became the basis of the article.

Burnett listened as Butts, who was Georgia's athletic director at the time, ran through his players, his coaches, his formations, and his plays for almost 15 minutes. Bryant offered nothing about Alabama, and only spoke to ask questions of Butts.

Burnett then showed his business partners the information, and they emphasized that he should forget he heard anything. And he did, until he saw a headline: "Tide Mauls Bulldogs." He read about how badly Alabama had beaten Georgia... and matters began to take shape in his mind.

Burnett kept his silence until January 1963, when he talked to a colleague who was close with Georgia's head coach, Johnny Griffith. When Griffith and Burnett met, Burnett showed the coach his notes, and Griffith was outraged.

"This looks like our game plan," he said. "I figured someone had given information to Alabama. This game was like a couple of others; we were just stymied—couldn't get anything going." (Furman Bisher would later allege that Butts, wounded at being relieved of his coaching duties at Georgia, would make several such calls around the Southeastern Conference.)

Once Georgia officials took possession of Burnett's notes, an investigation cranked up. At the same time, freelance writer Frank Graham Jr. was dispatched by the *Saturday Evening Post* to investigate the story. The *Post* paid Burnett $2,000 upon acquisition of the story and another $3,000 upon its publication.

In an editor's note, the *Saturday Evening Post* left no doubt about its perspective on the issue: "Not since the Chicago White Sox threw the 1919 World Series has there been a sports story as shocking as this one... The corrupt were two men—Butts and Bryant—employed to educate and to guide young men."

"This was the damning aspect of the situation," Bisher would later write, "not what Graham had written, but this lead-in that likened the action to the Black Sox baseball scandal of 1919, an out-and-out case of game-fixing."

The article closed with a thunderous declaration: "The chances are that Wally Butts will never help any football team again. Bear Bryant may well follow him into oblivion—a special hell for that grim extrovert—for in a very real sense he betrayed the boys he was pledged to lead."

Both Bryant and Butts held press conferences to denounce the charges, and both indicated that they had warned the *Post* against publishing the article. The magazine ran the story.

The reaction was immediate and immense. The attorneys general of both Georgia and Alabama opened investigations into the matter. Bryant went on statewide TV in Alabama to declare his innocence, and the Alabama establishment supported him. Butts, meanwhile, passed a lie detector test, but didn't enjoy the same level of institutional backing.

Time, *Newsweek*, and *Sports Illustrated* all pointed out the holes in the *Post* article. Red Smith of the *New York Herald Tribune*, quoted in the *Birmingham News*, summed the entire issue up: "If it were established that one embittered man had done the old school dirty, this would hardly constitute evidence of corruption in a conference," Smith said. "Nothing more has been charged than unseemly conduct between two men."

Sports Illustrated convened a panel of experts that agreed there was little information that Bryant could have used to his advantage. Butts's assessments as described in the article were some combination of opinion, meaninglessness, and self-evident obviousness.

Alabama Governor George Wallace gleefully torched the messenger, saying, "I don't know anything about it, but I'll tell you this—the *Saturday Evening Post* is the sorriest authority on the truth." The Alabama legislature introduced resolutions condemning the *Post*, while a US district attorney in Birmingham even called for a federal grand jury investigation of the magazine.

Georgia Governor Carl Sanders, a Georgia alum, directed the state's attorney general to investigate the matter to determine if criminal prosecution was warranted. The attorney general's report found no criminal violation, but nonetheless contended that the conversation "might well have vitally affected the outcome of the game in points and margin of victory."

The *Saturday Evening Post* was already fighting one battle against Bryant; a second article, documenting his underhandedness, would only help both the publication's bottom line and its court battle. Crucially, the *Post* never did get a look at Burnett's notes, which remained in the possession of Georgia officials who were investigating the story themselves. The *Post* relied only on Burnett's affidavit, as well as hearsay and secondhand information. Finally, the *Atlanta Journal*, which had intended to publish a concurrent article, backed away from the story—a story on which its own writer was a contributor—which by all reasonable means of investigation should have been a strong clue to the *Post*.

In its April 27, 1963, issue, the *Post* stood behind its charges, adding, "Our philosophy is radical. We believe that any coach who rigs a football game should be exposed. We will continue to cling to this radical belief despite what our detractors in and out of the publishing business may say about us." Bryant, in response, filed a second lawsuit for another $5 million.

This was a high-risk gambit for Bryant. Had Butts lost his case against the *Post*, there would be calls for Bryant to be fired. And if Alabama refused to do that, the SEC could boot Alabama from the conference, or the NCAA could sanction the Crimson Tide itself. Bryant was as close as could be to untouchable, but the charges, if proven true, would be tough for even the Bear to outrun.

Butts was an easy figure for mockery. His drinking, womanizing, and poor investments had left him nearly broke, and he was effectively forced out as coach of Georgia after the 1960 season. He had coached for 35 years, 20 of them at Georgia. But for some reason, he was still permitted to serve as athletic director.

Bryant pursued another avenue. Months earlier, he had flown to Washington, D.C., to meet with Robert Kennedy, attorney general of the

United States. Bryant and Kennedy discussed the allegations—which had not yet been made public. Kennedy indicated that his department had already investigated the rumors and found nothing to incriminate Bryant or Butts.

"I know that," Bryant said. "I just wanted to be damned sure you knew it." Bryant and Kennedy didn't speak again on the matter, although Bryant was apparently preparing to support—at least quietly—Kennedy's campaign for president in 1968.

Even so, Kennedy's assurances to Bryant didn't stop the rumor mill from churning throughout the summer. The US Senate's McClellan Committee, tasked with investigating racketeering and improper labor practices, began looking into the gambling aspects of the story.

Butts's $10 million libel action went to court in Atlanta in August 1963. Burnett testified that the *Post* paid him $5,000 for his information—more than $50,000 in 2025 dollars—without ever seeing the notes he made.

Griffith, the current Georgia coach, was a surprise witness, and his testimony was devastating to the *Post*. He indicated that the secrets the magazine described as "significant" were not particularly important, and that Georgia's "slot right" and "pro set" formations that year had been used in previous seasons. The implication was that Bryant probably already knew about those formations.

One of the article's most significant assertions was Georgia end Mickey Babb's claim that Alabama players taunted Georgia players in the midst of the 35–0 defeat, saying, "You can't run 88-pop [allegedly, a significant Georgia play] on us." There was just one problem: Griffith said Georgia had no "88-pop" play.

The trial's highlight came just after Curtis's attorneys rested their case. Bryant himself strode into the courtroom to testify, at once regal, commanding, and slightly terrifying. Dressed in a gray seersucker sport coat, white slacks, and brown alligator shoes, Bryant was forceful, definitive, and clear. He wasn't aw-shucksing his way around the situation; this was no press conference. He was there to clear his name and to strike fear in the hearts of his accusers. He even went to a blackboard to diagram a few plays, a move that clearly thrilled the all-middle-aged-male jury.

Bryant dismissed the idea that he learned anything of value from Butts, saying, "If I didn't know that, I oughta be bored for a hollow head."

When Butts's attorney read the indictment out loud to Bryant, charging him and Butts with being "corrupt," Bryant could barely contain his seething anger. Asked if the charges were in any way true, he didn't hesitate.

"Absolutely not," he replied. "If we did it, we ought to go to jail. And if we didn't, anybody who had anything to do with this [article] ought to go to jail. Taking their money is not good enough."

Butts, on the stand, held firm for a time but eventually broke down in sobs at the accusations. He refuted the allegations in the article, point by point. (For instance, Butts had allegedly told Bryant that one cornerback overcommitted on running plays and was vulnerable to deep passes. In the game film, it was clear that Alabama didn't throw in his direction one time.)

In the end, there was no smoke and no fire. The *Post* was at a loss to explain why Alabama would need to fix a game it was favored to win by two touchdowns. The jury found in favor of Butts, awarding him general damages of $60,000 and punitive damages of $3 million, later reduced to $300,000.

When Butts called Bryant, the Bear's immediate response was, "That's fine, but what happened to the rest of it?"

Alabama president Frank Rose, at that exact moment, was—as he put it during testimony in the Butts trial—"going through two crises at that time as far as the University was concerned." At the same time he was dealing with the Butts-Bryant call, he was in the midst of an ongoing standoff with Wallace that made national news. The governor had put Rose in an untenable position, and for once, college football was not an easy refuge.

Rose and Bryant's own lawyers went to visit Bryant at his home. Harry Pritchett, one of Bryant's attorneys, cut straight to the point: "Paul, what would you settle for?"

Bryant didn't want to "settle for" a damn thing. He wanted to rip the entire $10 million out of the heart of Curtis Publishing. But he also knew which way the wind was blowing. He understood the toll a long trial would take on him, his family, and the University of Alabama. He also may have known that private investigators hired by Curtis were digging into his past at the University of Kentucky, asking questions and looking for anything they could bring to bear.

Bryant agreed to split $25,000 with Darwin Holt over Bisher's "brutality" story, and for the "fix" story, he settled for $275,000 in damages and $20,000 in expenses. In the end, he netted $196,000 for the entire affair, and no evidence linked him to gambling on the game.

The *Saturday Evening Post* lawsuit forced Bryant to look in the mirror. He was a fierce leader, perhaps even a cruel one. But he had always perceived himself as a sportsman; now, with the story about fixing the Georgia game and how quickly so many people had believed it, he had to reckon with the fact that perhaps his own self-image and the way he was viewed were starkly different. He didn't want to be thought of as a coach who was dirty, but there it was.

Chapter 14

BIGGER THAN BALL

In the summer of 1963, the challenge to Bear Bryant's reign was the second-most-pressing problem facing the University of Alabama. It had taken nine years, but progress—in the form of the federal government—had finally come to Tuscaloosa. In 1954, *Brown v. Board of Education* had struck down segregation in public schools, but Alabama politicians regarded the Supreme Court's ruling as something between a nuisance and a campaign opportunity. Universities across the state denied admission to hundreds of Black students—only Autherine Lucy had managed to enroll at Alabama, and then only briefly—and Governor George Wallace thundered his declaration: "I draw the line in the dust and toss the gauntlet before the feet of tyranny, and I say, segregation now, segregation tomorrow, segregation forever!"

Finally, in 1963, several Black students applied to Alabama, and a federal district judge ordered that they be admitted to the school. The judge blocked Wallace from interfering in their enrollment, but did not block him from appearing on campus... a loophole the governor happily exploited.

Wallace was an instigator, a race-baiter, and a demagogue, but he was also a politician, and he understood that his state couldn't afford a repeat of the deadly riots that had broken out over at Ole Miss the previous September. So he privately worked out a deal with the Kennedy administration that allowed him to thunder his opposition to the move—and then step aside and let the students enroll. Local law enforcement warned nearby white supremacist groups like the Ku Klux Klan to stay out of town.

On the morning of June 11, 1963, Vivian Malone and James Hood preregistered for their classes in Birmingham, and then traveled to Tuscaloosa and Foster Auditorium, just a few blocks away from the football stadium, with the intention of paying their fees and confirming their schedules. The Kennedy administration had initially considered taking Malone and Hood straight to their dorms, but realized Wallace wanted to put on his performance for the cameras.

"I would not take the students up to the schoolhouse door," Nicholas Katzenbach, the Kennedy administration's deputy attorney general, later said. "I would not have *them* refused. He could refuse me, but he couldn't refuse them. It was just a question of dignity, and I didn't want that picture on national television, his turning down two Black students. It seemed to me the better confrontation was federal and state authority, not the racial one."

As 150 law enforcement officers looked on and temperatures soared above 100 degrees, President Kennedy allowed Wallace to unleash a brief stemwinder on states' rights, but then the Alabama National Guard calmly put an end to the governor's speechifying. The two students registered without further incident, Wallace got to make his speech for his base, and the University of Alabama took baby steps into the future.

University president Frank Rose and many members of the university's board of trustees watched the entire affair unfold from Bryant's nearby office. Bryant was not on campus, and the university's leaders likely chose his office as a place where they could observe the goings-on in privacy. They understood the gravity of the moment, even as they were powerless to change or redirect it.

Joe Namath, meanwhile, stood near the auditorium as Malone and Hood prepared to register. "She seemed scared," Namath recalled of Malone, who would later become a friend, "and all I could think about was how brave she was. It was a heavy position to be in. She had poise."

Tensions ran high the next few days, as the National Guard remained on campus, prepared for a potential repeat of the riots in the wake of Lucy's enrollment. But this time, the campus remained calm, and life went on. The federal government had achieved integration, and Wallace could frame himself as a victim of an oppressive federal government and a defender of states' rights. He also tarred the image of his entire state for decades to come.

"Racism is a worldwide problem, and it's been [like that] since the beginning of recorded history," musician Patterson Hood, Alabama native and Drive-By Truckers founder, says in the song "The Three Great Alabama Icons." "It ain't just white and Black, but thanks to George Wallace, it's always a little more convenient to play it with a Southern accent."

A postscript: Katzenbach later revealed that after Malone registered, she went down to her dining room to eat lunch. Rose feared a riot, but Malone sat down at a table by herself, and according to Katzenbach, six to eight students soon joined her at the table.

There was no lower moment in Alabama's civil rights history than September 15, 1963, when four members of the Ku Klux Klan planted 19 sticks of dynamite beneath the steps of the 16th Street Baptist Church in Birmingham. Shortly before 10:30 a.m., the bomb exploded, killing four girls—Addie Mae Collins, Carol Denise McNair, Carole Rosamond Robertson, and Cynthia Dionne Wesley—who were in the basement changing into choir robes. The act of terrorism outraged and horrified the nation, but most of white Alabama—including Bryant—remained largely silent on the civil rights trauma wracking the state.

"We are as out of contact with the trouble in our state as you are in Los Angeles," Bryant once said in response to an out-of-town journalist's inquiry. "I learn about it mostly by watching television out of New York." Had the bombing happened in a later era, Bryant would have been called to speak out on the matter, but the sportswriters of the day kept politics and sports separate. There was football to be played, after all.

Namath's junior season was an unspectacular one from a record standpoint, with losses to both Florida and Jordan's Auburn, and ended abruptly. The weekend of December 7, 1963, Alabama had a free week—a game against Miami still loomed, postponed in the wake of President Kennedy's assassination. But a free week in a college town is a troublesome thing for players, and on this night, Namath and a teammate allegedly had a few too many drinks and ended up "directing" traffic downtown. No one did anything in Tuscaloosa without the Bear's knowledge, and Bryant soon found out and confronted his quarterback.

Namath had actually been helping push a teammate's car out of the intersection. The problem was that he had also gone to a fraternity party and had a Seven and Seven. Sipping alcohol was forbidden, and the word of the Bear was law.

Bryant knew he had to take action, so he suspended Namath, forcing him to move out of the football dorm and even floating the idea of transferring. Over a single drink? Yes, but more than that, it was about Bryant's reputation. If he bent the rules for Namath, what good were the rules at all?

Most of Alabama's coaches wanted to suspend Namath. Gene Stallings, the former Junction Boy, wanted to go even further, kicking him off the team entirely, since that's what Bryant would have done to anyone else. Bryant opted for an indefinite suspension . . . but while Namath was between dorms, he spent a few nights in the basement of Bryant's home. So, yes, there were exceptions.

The 1964 season is a case study in Alabama's fraught history of claiming national championships. In Namath's senior season, Alabama stormed through their schedule, posting wins over every program they faced, including rivals Auburn, Georgia, LSU, Tennessee, and Florida. That was enough to give the Tide their second national championship ranking... before playing the bowl game.

In those days, the polls didn't take bowl finishes into account, which was good news for Alabama. No. 5 Texas held off the Tide in the Orange Bowl, 21–17, a game that featured a controversial did-he-get-in-or-not goal line dive by Namath.

Namath insisted to Bryant that he'd crossed the plane, but Bryant didn't want to hear any excuses. "If you can't jam it in from there without leaving any doubt," he snarled, "you don't deserve to win."

In all the years since, Namath has trotted out a reliable explanation every time: "I was over the line, but I didn't score."

"We've gotta live with it," Namath would later write in his autobiography. "There weren't instant replays back then and there aren't replays in life, so deal with it."

The national championship was a pretty good consolation prize, even though retroactive analyses have awarded the 1964 title to other schools. Alabama, while claiming titles it wasn't awarded at the time, has no intention of relinquishing one that was bestowed on it, regardless of how the season actually turned out.

Alabama's second national championship under Bryant—and under the segregation and strife that wracked the state—incensed national commentators. "So Alabama is the 'National Champion,' is it? Hah!" wrote Jim Murray in the *Los Angeles Times*. "'National' Champion of what? The Confederacy? This team hasn't poked its head above the Mason-Dixon Line since Appomattox."

"It is unfashionable to say anything nice about Alabama and Coach Bear Bryant because they are segregationists," Bud Collins—who would later become famous for his tennis commentary—wrote in the *Boston Globe*. He then took aim at the dire condition of the entire state of Alabama, from the Selma marches, to Wallace's absurd propping up of his wife Lurleen as governor, to Birmingham Commissioner of Public Safety Eugene "Bull" Connor, the law enforcement official responsible for setting dogs and fire hoses on protesters . . . and, incidentally, a friend of Bryant's.

"Poor Alabama. It has Selma to live down, as well as Lureen [sic] and George, and Sheriff Bull O'Connor's [sic] police dogs," Collins wrote. "Surely there's something worthwhile down there. Yes—it has the best football team."

In the years to come, Bryant found himself caught between his own state's hard-line segregation and the rapid advancement of the rest of the country away from the Deep South. Wallace could happily rail against the federal government and take loss after court loss, each one entrenching him in the minds of his base as the last bastion of righteousness against overreaching federal authorities. Bryant couldn't do that; he understood that he needed to change with the times or be left behind. And he had a long-term—some would say *too* long-term—plan for how to keep up with the rest of America.

In December 1966, Bryant appealed to the country to help Alabama keep pace with the rest of the college football nation: "A few years ago, we had segregation problems. But now, we'd like to ask the help of you fellows up above us in the North, who have been our critics, to help us get games with the Big Ten, the Big Eight, the Pacific Coast."

Murray, of the *L.A. Times*, happily skewered Bryant for his plea. "Dust off the courthouse at Appomattox! Get ready for a new era of Reconstruction! Bear Bryant and the sovereign state of Alabama have handed over their swords!"

But at the same time, Bryant's teams were gracious in victory over an integrated Nebraska team in 1966. The fact that Alabama could play integrated teams without incident was no shock to anyone who knew the team—Bryant was far too disciplined to allow any kind of racist absurdity to derail his men—but it still surprised some of his Northern critics, and pleased the more progressive residents of the state.

"The sportsmanship that everybody exhibited was so marked," Montgomery businessman Winton Blount wrote Bryant in 1967, "and with 40 million people watching I don't know how we could have done anything more effective in this area which so badly needs help."

Namath, for his part, went on to sign with the Jets, and happily sparred with national reporters who didn't think much of the Alabama program.

"Tell me, Joe," one said, "is it true you majored in basket-weaving at Alabama?"

"No," Namath replied, "basket-weaving was too tough, so they put me in journalism."

Namath was one of the few players to come out from under the Alabama banner and become more famous after he left than he was when he was there. His Super Bowl III declaration—"We'll win. I guarantee it"—is still the most famous guarantee in sports history, all the more so because, in true Bryant style, he carried through on it.

Chapter 15

FALLING OFF THE PACE

Shug Jordan seethed. The NCAA probations in the late 1950s had cost him not just exposure, but recruiting muscle as well. Bryant was building a colossus across the state, and Auburn simply couldn't compete. Bryant had the good fortune of being able to recruit his initial classes while Auburn was on probation, and the Bear took full advantage of his rival's woes.

Counter-recruiting is an important tool; part of the job of getting a recruit to come to your school is to convince him why he shouldn't go to the other guy's. Bryant had a handy justification right there—*Why go to Auburn, where you won't play in a bowl for years, when you could come to Alabama and start playing for titles right away?*

Bryant also had power that Jordan envied: as athletic director, he could make decisions that Jordan couldn't. And at the same time, Alabama shut out Auburn four straight years. Four years! An entire class of Tigers didn't score a single point against Alabama! That would not do.

But not even Bryant could control the changing cultural tides sweeping over Alabama. At the same time Bryant was dealing with the Butts lawsuit, and Jordan was trying to put together some kind of functional team amid probation, the Civil Rights Movement was swarming down on Alabama.

Auburn struggled to handle the changes sweeping across the South. Shortly after James Meredith's disastrous enrollment at Ole Miss in fall 1962, Auburn's president, Ralph Draughon, brought up the issue of Black enrollment to the school's board of trustees. While Auburn could fight applications from Black applicants on a piecemeal basis through the courts, Draughon said, it might be a better idea to admit a qualified Black student.

Shortly after Governor Wallace stood in the schoolhouse door over in Tuscaloosa, Draughon again met with trustees to suggest admitting a Black student. While the school had received only 13 serious initial applications—and none completed—from Black students in the past few months, Draughon noted that the applications would only grow in number. The board decided to avoid voluntary desegregation, opting instead for a just-try-it approach and waiting for the courts to make the call.

Soon enough, the courts came calling, in the form of *Franklin v. Parker*. Harold A. Franklin had graduated from Alabama State College, a historically black institution that was unaccredited by the state. Franklin wanted to pursue a master's degree in history and political science at Auburn, but the graduate school dean, William V. Parker, denied him admission without an accredited bachelor's degree.

The problem for Franklin was that no historically black colleges were accredited by the state, one of the wicked little legal paradoxes that served to trip up aspiring Black students. But Franklin decided to step right over the barrier and take his case to court under the Equal Protection Clause of the Fourteenth Amendment. A federal district court judge ruled that the state of Alabama had failed to provide him with an opportunity to continue his education solely based on his race.

Franklin arrived on campus on January 4, 1964, to register for classes at the library, facing a battalion of more than 100 state police officers. The director of the Alabama Department of Public Safety, Albert J. Lingo, was also present on campus; Lingo would soon become infamous for his role in the bloody protests at the Edmund Pettus Bridge in Selma, 100 miles to the west. Despite some tense confrontations—Franklin was asked to produce his student identification, which he didn't have since he wasn't yet registered—the registration proceeded without violence.

"I don't think we ever had a protest march at Auburn during the turbulent 1960s," Jordan once said. "Maybe it's because of the pastoral setting around Auburn, the small-town atmosphere of Auburn. I think things like that have been handled beautifully at Auburn to avoid situations like that."

And in a classic probably-shouldn't-have-said-that line characteristic of a bygone era in Alabama, Jordan added, "Now we have had some panty raids at Auburn, but I think the women encouraged it just about as much as the people that did the raiding."

SEC football had begun integrating in 1966 in Kentucky, but it would be three more years before integration would truly come to Alabama's top universities. James Owens, a running back from Fairfield, became Auburn's first Black scholarship football player in 1969, and suffered through both physical and spiritual trauma.

"The first three years that I was [at Auburn], there were days I got up and said this is the day," Owens said in 2012. "I'm going home. It's not worth it. And I would call my mom and say 'I'm coming home.' And she'd say, 'No. Stay.'"

In 1970, receiver Thom Gossom walked on to the team and made the squad; he would later become the first Black athlete to graduate from Auburn, even though he was briefly kicked off the team in a battle with Jordan over hair length.

"We knew where not to go," Gossom would later write in his autobiography, "and which professors not to take."

Although Alabama would receive far more national attention for its integration following its famous "game that changed the South" against USC in 1970, the truth was that Auburn got there first—and that was due, in part, to Jordan's efforts.

"I don't think there was a racial bone in Coach Jordan's body as far as football was concerned," quarterback Phil Gargis told Jordan's biographer. "Everybody was treated as athletes, not Black, not white. You work hard, you get a chance to play."

"I don't give a damn whether competitors are red, white and blue, green or even turquoise," Jordan said.

Regardless of Jordan's personal beliefs, de facto segregation remained entrenched at Auburn. In 1985, as part of a Justice Department investigation into the racial makeup of Alabama's higher education system, a federal judge issued a 103-page opinion that declared Auburn was the most racially segregated of all of Alabama's universities. At the time, 3.3% of the 17,200 students enrolled at Auburn were Black, compared to 12.5% at Alabama.

"The evidence tends to support the widespread perception of Blacks in Alabama that, except for the presence of Black athletes and the changes mandated by federal laws and regulations," Judge U. W. Clemon wrote, "Auburn's racial attitudes have changed little since the '50s."

Starting in the mid-1960s, Auburn football began a slide. Every staff loses coaches, but Jordan saw some significant departures, including Auburn freshman coach Vince Dooley, who left The Plains to take a job as head football coach of the Georgia Bulldogs. (He would perform admirably in the role.)

Still, Auburn had juice. *Sports Illustrated* picked the Tigers to win the national title in 1964, running a painting of Jimmy Sidle on the cover and proclaiming 1964 "The Year of the Running Back," with an inside headline that continued "... and Auburn runs the most." (Sidle played quarterback, but he ran the ball too.) The article astutely compared Auburn, the town, to Green Bay, Wisconsin, in its single-minded devotion to the local football team.

But Sidle didn't even make it unscathed out of the first game; on an ugly tackle, he tore his rotator cuff and later moved to tailback. The season implications of that injury are one of the what-ifs that haunted Jordan for the rest of his days.

Hal Herring, Jordan's defensive alchemist, moved on to the Atlanta Falcons coaching staff. And Jordan began to face recruiting battles on two fronts—against Bryant in Alabama and, now, against Dooley in Georgia. So he attempted to step up his recruiting of elite players, but he also began a low-level program to identify walk-ons and unrecruited high school players. The chances of finding a gem in the dirt were slim, but better than if Auburn wasn't even looking at all.

The strategy paid dividends—All-American defensive back Buddy McClinton and All-SEC lineman Gusty Yearout were products of the look-under-every-rock strategy. Plus, because Auburn's depth charts were so slim, every recruit and walk-on got an honest, legitimate chance at a starting job.

On the plus side, this was the point at which the Iron Bowl got its name. The 1964 season was in ruins, yes. Auburn had lost three times that year and would not be going to a bowl. Asked how he would deal with the disappointment, Jordan simply responded, "We've got our bowl game. We have it every year. It's the Iron Bowl in Birmingham."

Birmingham's geography made it an ideal location for steel mills, as it's one of the few locations in the world where all three elements necessary to create steel—coal, iron ore, and lime—are right there in the ground waiting to be mined. Birmingham's first blast furnace, Sloss Furnaces, was built about four miles away from Legion Field. The industry drew in both Black and white workers from all over the state, and those workers found community and tribal attachment in college football teams, whether or not they'd actually attended school there.

"Football has kind of been historically a poor person's game, and football was a way out for a lot of poor people in Alabama," sportswriter and historian Kirk McNair says. "Alabama was a poor state, and it's still not a rich one."

College football gave a highly divided Birmingham a reason to unify, building familial bonds and connections that would last long after "The Magic City" transitioned out of the steel industry. The city is now a hub for financial services and health care, and the Alabama–Auburn game left Legion Field decades ago, but the Iron Bowl moniker remains, a testament to the city where it began, and the first fans who cheered it on.

Football "transcended even the segregation that was a chief defining factor of the state," says college football journalist Spencer Hall. "If you want to know why football is so important, I think it's because people need a place where they can be happy or proud. They can set most [problems] down, even if it's an illusion."

By the end of the 1966 season, the grumblings about Jordan's suitability for the job were starting to reach the surface. An alumni gathering in Birmingham for the express purpose of questioning Jordan's job security ended quickly when new president Harry Philpott, who had arrived at Auburn the year before, declared that the coach would not be fired. Instead, the alumni began a push for Jordan to get a younger, more connected staff.

Jordan, naturally, knew what was going on. He had spies in the meeting, and they fed him reports prior to the game with Alabama, varying between "fired" and "retained." Ultimately, he stayed on; one losing season since 1952 wasn't enough to cost him a job. Yet.

Chapter 16

THE BEAR VS. THE SNAKE

By the 1960s, Bryant's coaching tree had begun to spread its branches outward across the country. Washington, Virginia Tech, Kentucky, Oklahoma, and many others—including, eventually, Auburn itself—hired Bryant alumni as their coaches. Then, as now, the assumption of proximity to coaching greatness was the same—anybody who'd shared a sideline with Bear, anybody who'd learned at the feet of the Bear, anybody who'd breathed the same air as the Bear ought to be able to bring a little of that Bear mojo to our campus, right? Sometimes it worked. More often, it didn't.

But one hiring in particular stuck in Bryant's mind, and in his heart. Texas A&M, Bryant's old stomping grounds, hired away Gene Stallings, one of the original Junction Boys, as their head coach in 1965, and the move brought out an unexpected emotion in the old coach.

"It's the first time I've cried in 20 or 30 years," Bryant told the *Houston Post*, "and believe me, I really did. I cried because I'm so proud that one of my little Junction boys is going back there to take over. And, secondly, I cried because I'm so upset over losing him. Shoot, with Stallings gone I may have to go back to work."

Every year, there was another challenger coming for the houndstooth hat. Bryant kept holding them off, but the challenges came from all sides. Sometimes, even from inside the program.

Ken Stabler was born on Christmas Day 1945, and to many of his future coaches, wives, girlfriends, and opponents, that was as close as he ever came to being holy. The son of a World War II machine gunner–turned–auto mechanic who went by the name "Slim," Stabler grew up in Foley, Alabama, and played every sport he could. Whip-thin—his old man once said Stabler could "drink a strawberry soda and look like a thermometer"—the boy who would become Snake threw himself into both athletics and partying like a man on a ticking clock.

"I like to get out and get after it," he would say years later, as a pro with the Oakland Raiders. "So what if I go out and drink, shoot some pool, chase women, stay out late, don't come home. All the time I'm doin' that I'm bein' nice to people. I go into bars and sign autographs and shake hands and shoot the bull. What's wrong with that?"

A 6-foot-2, 175-pound lefty, Stabler earned his nickname in high school as a kick returner. When he returned a punt 60 yards for a touchdown, slithering between defenders all the way, his coach remarked, "Damn, that boy runs like a snake!" The name stuck.

Stabler led Foley High to back-to-back undefeated seasons his junior and senior years, and that put him squarely in the recruiting sights of both Auburn and Alabama. He also had a mean fastball—his chief rival was a kid from a nearby high school named Don Sutton, a future Hall of Famer—and turned down a $20,000 signing bonus from the Yankees to play baseball.

Stabler—in a move that would be repeated over decades, much to the frustration of Auburn—opted for Alabama, which at the time was a far more winning program. Not only that, Slim Stabler bore such a resemblance to Bear Bryant that when he was in the stands, fans would mistake him for Bryant . . . right up until the point where, fueled by a bit too much whiskey, he'd retort, "Wouldn't you think if I was Coach Bryant that I'd be with my team before a game, and not up here in the goddamn stands?"

Stabler arrived on campus in 1964 carrying little more than underwear, socks, his Foley High letter jacket, and $5. The university hooked him up with a job, and that suited Stabler just fine. "The job gave me spending money," he later wrote, "and I made friends with some guys who also liked to play basketball, throw around a football, drink beer, and get close to girls. Girls were everywhere: blondes, brunettes, redheads. I had never seen so many great-looking women in one place." And then the words that should have set off alarm bells:

"The University of Alabama. It was definitely my kind of place."

Namath was a senior by then, but he and Stabler introduced themselves to one another over a supposedly friendly game of one-on-one. The two future Super Bowl–winning alphas locked horns, and in years to come, each would insist the other had gotten the better end of the battle.

Stabler's college exploits have taken on the tone of Alabama legend. He once survived a car crash in which he'd been driving 110 miles an hour. His stories of A-Club hazing echoed those of Starr years before. According to Stabler, he had to survive everything from being left out in the country to hitchhike home, to a phenomenally painful procedure where he tied a string around his manhood, ran the string up through his shirt, tied a pencil to the other end of the string, and had to carry a notepad and get 25 girls to sign their autographs with the pencil. Some obliged, and some knew the game and purposely misspelled their name a few times just to keep the pain going.

He also found a way to entertain the ladies, wherever they might be. He fell in love with an unnamed paramour in Mobile, and he would leave Tuscaloosa at nine o'clock at night, drive to Mobile, spend a few hours with his lady friend, and drive back in time to—maybe—make it to class.

Not that he had to work particularly hard in his classes. "It was not easy for football players at Alabama to fail courses, particularly education majors," Stabler wrote. "All you had to do was show up. I took such classes as audio-visual aids, where I learned how to plug in and turn on a movie projector."

Stabler's true introduction to the Bryant wrath came during his sophomore year against Tennessee, when the score was tied 7–7. He drove the team 50 yards, down to the Vols' 10-yard line, and then on third down threw the ball out of bounds to stop the clock. There was just one problem: he'd misread the scoreboard. It wasn't third down—it was fourth. Game over, tied.

"Stabler," Bryant bellowed, "have you lost your fucking mind?"

Bryant stormed through the bowels of Neyland Stadium to find the visitors' locker room locked. He smashed that door off its hinges, and when the team had gathered, he sent all the assistant coaches and non-players out of the room. He pulled the broken door closed and turned to his team.

"I want to apologize for me and my staff for not preparing you people well enough to win the game today," he said. "It was us, not you, who lost that game. I'm sorry."

Another time, Stabler attempted a jump pass, the move his predecessor Harry Gilmer was known for. He threw five straight completions, but the sixth was intercepted. "Keep your feet," Bryant growled, "on the fucking ground."

Stabler keyed the mighty 1966 Alabama offense, running option pitchouts and pitchbacks to perfection. Bryant's system at the time was an I-formation, rollout offense—the quarterback chose a side, and then either pitched to a running back or kept the ball himself. Once the defense began closing in to stop the run, Stabler would loft the ball over their heads. Harkening back to his old mule-calling days, Bryant ran the offense with two commands: "Gee" to go right, "Haw" to go left.

But Stabler wasn't content to be a cog in a machine. He'd Gee and Haw with the best of them, but he was also always looking for bigger gains. When he realized that the defense was reading his eyes, he began no-look pitches, which mystified opponents and enraged Bryant.

"Stabler," he grumbled, "you're luckier than a shithouse rat."

Lucky, yes, but also very, very good . . . right up until the moment the entire program's luck ran out. Alabama had won three national titles in five years in the early 1960s, even though by modern standards at least one of those wouldn't have counted. The Tide won the 1964-season title despite losing to Texas in their bowl game. As a result, the NCAA waited until after bowl games to award a champion in 1965. In 1968, the NCAA declared once and for all that polls would include bowl games in the national championship calculus. It was a move that seems commonsense now but, as always in college football, common sense is only visible in retrospect.

If Alabama got away with a title in 1964, it was robbed of one in 1966. That team won 11 straight games, six by shutout, outscoring its opponents 301–44. The Tide played Nebraska in the Sugar Bowl, whomping the Huskers 34–7. But Notre Dame had opted to play for a tie with Michigan State, and both of those teams, which finished 9–0–1, were ranked ahead of Alabama in the final polls.

Bryant seethed that a team that had played for a tie would get the national championship nod. Once again, Notre Dame had frustrated him. At that year's Iron Bowl, Alabama fans, seeing the writing on the wall, displayed a sign that read "Alabama plays football, Notre Dame plays politics: In your heart you know we're No. 1."

Why didn't Alabama win that 1966 title? The Tide had gone undefeated, allowing only 44 points all season. Mealymouthed excuses like "strength of schedule" didn't really hold up. The truth was, sportswriters—like much of the rest of the country—had simply grown fed up with the entire state of Alabama, and decided to take out their rage at the state's continued racial turmoil on its flagship university.

Even as other schools—and other leagues—across the country integrated their rosters, Alabama continued to schedule only all-white teams. As time wore on, that became tougher and tougher to do, leading to weaker opponents, tepid strength of schedule, and an overall disgust with how the program was handling itself.

Bryant would later claim that he had tried as far back as his Kentucky days to bring Black players onto the field. "I told the [Kentucky] president, Dr. Herman Donovan, that we should be the first in the Southeastern Conference to have Black players. I told him he could be the Branch Rickey of the league. But I didn't get anywhere," Bryant said. "You don't change people's thinking overnight. Not in Kentucky, not anywhere."

But the question of how hard Bryant really tried to upset the entrenched racial order in Alabama persists. The state's governor, George Wallace, spent much of the '60s blustering on about segregation, but Bryant had the gravitas to match Wallace's bloviating.

"He was the only public figure in the state who could have taken on George Wallace with credibility," civil rights journalist Howell Raines said years later. "They both knew they were the biggest cats in the forest. I don't think Coach Bryant would have been personally afraid of Wallace, so much as it would be a distraction, and if you wrestle with a pig, you're going to get muddy. So there was no upside to it. But the fact is, he never stepped out the way he should have."

In some perverse way, Alabama boosters enjoyed the fact that Bryant was winning with segregated rosters, contending that his success validated Alabama's all-white mandates. "At that point, that was the only claim to fame that white Alabamans had," Alabama federal judge U. W. Clemon told writer Don Yaeger. "I mean, we were at the bottom in terms of just about every other measuring stick. And there were avowed racists roaming this land, and they could all point to the all-white team of Alabama as vindication for their theory that you don't have to have integration, integration won't work, and we can do it without getting Blacks involved."

But as "early" as 1967, Bryant began recruiting Black players to Alabama. In April of that year, he invited five Black players to attempt to make the team as walk-ons. This was a nearly impossible task, but he was warming up the waters. Stabler recalled Bryant telling the white players before the Black players arrived that "we were to treat them exactly as we wanted to be treated ourselves."

Stabler, like everyone in the state, lived through Alabama's racial strife, albeit on the well-insulated sidelines. From the Freedom Riders in 1961 to the bombings in Birmingham, the entire state of Alabama spent the 1960s on edge, and Stabler would later profess his disgust with the entire system, if only for competitive reasons. "There were a lot of us that hated segregation," he said. "I despised it. Most of us wanted to play the Black players. We wanted to test ourselves. But more than anything, most of us hated segregation."

According to Stabler's daughter Kendra, none of the white players would talk to the Black walk-ons... that is, until Stabler went up to one of them and spoke to him as an equal. That changed the entire tenor of the locker room. Two of the five players, Andrew Pernell and Dock Rone, would dress out for the spring A-Day game, although they didn't make the final team.

Stabler gave all the credit to the Bear. "Coach Bryant had a knack for treating everyone fairly, and in a way that everyone thought was the same," he wrote. "You believed that he was as polite to the janitors cleaning up the stadium as he was to the president of the university, that he treated the fourth-team guard the same way he treated the All-American."

But Stabler knew he didn't do enough at the time. Years later, he and Raiders teammate Gene Upshaw, an outspoken advocate for Black causes, would talk about the Civil Rights Movement, and Upshaw would give Stabler a break.

"I always felt like he almost wanted to apologize for what happened in Alabama," Upshaw later told writer Mike Freeman. "I told him once, 'You didn't become like those others. That's a victory in itself.'"

Stabler did know how to look after his own interests, though. After the everything-but-a-ring 1966 season, he decided to leverage his fame. He went to a local car dealership, picked out a fine black-and-white Corvette, and damned if the salesman wasn't sporting a bright red Bama button on his lapel.

"I told him I was going to be a bit short on the down payment, and that I couldn't do a whole lot about the monthly payments either," Stabler later recalled. "When he didn't frown at that, I was encouraged."

Early in 1967, a spring practice knee injury sidelined Stabler for months, and he spent the time skipping class, getting into trouble, and generally finding a way to make a nuisance of himself. That was enough to get Bryant on his ass, and to get him suspended from the team for failing to maintain a sufficient GPA.

The telegram arrived with brutal brevity:

YOU HAVE BEEN INDEFINITELY SUSPENDED.
Signed, Coach Paul W. Bryant

A few days later another one came from Namath, who was once suspended for the sin of taking a sip of alcohol:

HE MEANS IT.

But Slim somehow managed to come through for his boy. He had a lawyer friend fake a letter from a draft board that threatened Stabler with induction into the Army if he didn't go back to school. Given that the Vietnam War was raging in early 1967, Stabler understood what was at risk. He got his act together and tried to plead his case to Bryant.

The stern old coach just puffed on his unfiltered Chesterfield and spit tobacco into the paper cup he held.

"Coach," Stabler said, "I've made myself eligible to play again and I want to come out and get back on the team."

"Stabler," Bryant growled, "you don't deserve to be on my team." Another spit.

"Well, Coach," Stabler said with forced bravado, "I'm coming out anyway."

In those days, Bryant had six different colors of jerseys representing the level of team each player achieved. Red was first team; white, second; blue, third; green, fourth; orange, fifth. The sixth and final team was brown, appropriate given that one of Bryant's favorite insults was "Turd."

Stabler got a brown jersey.

He fought his way up through the rainbow of jerseys, reclaiming the starting role . . . just in time for both the offense and the defense to begin sputtering. Things fell apart right out of the gate, when Alabama tied Florida State 37–37, the first time the Tide hadn't won a game in more than a year. A later loss to Tennessee—the first since 1960—ended Alabama's national title hopes.

But there was still the matter of the Auburn game. Stabler had one more Iron Bowl in him before he left Tuscaloosa.

IRON BOWL 1967: THE RUN IN THE MUD

There are days when college football in the South is everything that is right and glorious about the world, days when the warm sunshine and the smell of fresh-cut grass and the sounds of college bands playing fight songs can make even the stoniest heart feel a swell of pride.

And then there are days like December 2, 1967, in Birmingham, which was the opposite of all that sentimental hogwash.

The temperature at the 1:30 p.m. kickoff of 1967's Iron Bowl was 52 degrees and falling. The wind whipped out of the south, gusting up to 27 miles an hour, and the rain was falling hard. The field had been painted green by city workers, and within minutes, all that paint was on the uniforms of the Tigers and Tide players. Minutes after that, the paint had washed right off them and back onto the muddy ground.

Overhead, the Alabama and Confederate battle flags waved in the blustery wind. Umbrellas dotted the stands, where most of the 71,000 in attendance shivered, while a lucky few huddled under decks. They were all about to witness a classic, but they would pay dearly for the privilege.

Without a doubt, the 1967 Iron Bowl was one of the messiest, ugliest installments of the century-plus rivalry. The game started slow and never got any faster. Wind gusts hit 42 miles an hour. Umbrellas were turned inside out. The mud was up to the players' ankles, and no one could move with anything approaching game speed.

Upon seeing the carnage in front of him, Bryant decided to play conservatively and wait for Auburn to make a mistake on special teams. Alabama punted on third down with the wind at its back, and on fourth down going into the wind.

"I don't think anybody was going to put a long drive together under those circumstances," Bryant said after the game. "So we kept kicking on third down over and over and over. I thought for awhile there I might have played it too close to the vest, but I guess the percentages haven't changed."

In the first half, Auburn was stopped on fourth down twice inside the Alabama 10-yard line, and missed a 35-yard field goal attempt. Still, the Tigers frustrated Bryant's master plan by taking the lead on a 38-yard field goal early in the third quarter.

Then came the moment that would define the game forevermore. Stabler, facing third and three on the Auburn 47, ran to the right on an option, faked a pitch, cut back inside, spotted daylight . . . and stomped an ugly 47 yards through the mud for a touchdown. At the end of the play, he outran three Auburn defenders, and then eluded a fourth who had an angle on him. It was a masterpiece of situational running, and Stabler would go down in history for it.

After the clock expired, Bryant found Stabler in the muck and mire, thanking him not just for the win but for a magnificent career. "Son, I am as proud of you as I am of anybody who's ever been here," he said. "You've done a great job for me on and off the field."

Stabler's play irked Jordan, who groused for weeks about what he believed were illegal blocks that sprung the Alabama quarterback free. "I wonder if [Alabama's] number 84 thought he was on defense, because he made one of the finest tackles of [Auburn's Gusty] Yearout I have ever seen."

The numbers weren't pretty. Auburn totaled 13 first downs to Alabama's four, and 216 yards of offense to Alabama's 176, but it didn't matter; Alabama had the higher number in the only place on the stat sheet where it mattered: the 7–3 final score.

"I expect these were the worst conditions I've ever seen a football game played in," Bryant said. "This late into the season, Legion Field is the worst field in America because of all the traffic it has on it."

The game was Auburn's eighth loss in nine games to Alabama, the kind of streak that gets angry alumni even angrier. Shug was going to need something to turn around quickly. Fortunately for him, something did.

Alabama would go on to play Texas A&M in the Cotton Bowl—the same Texas A&M coached by Gene Stallings, Bryant's former Junction Boy. At the pregame press conference, the two coaches and old friends did their best to praise each other while downplaying their own chances.

"We recruited a bunch of kids who couldn't play for Alabama," Stallings said.

"Well, hell," Bryant replied, "we still have some you recruited, and they can't play for Alabama either."

The Aggies upset Alabama 20–16, and the postgame scrum produced one of the most memorable photos in Alabama history when Bryant hoisted Stallings up onto his shoulders, beaming in pride at his young protégé's success.

A few months after the Iron Bowl, the Houston Astros picked Stabler in the second round of that year's draft, even though he hadn't played baseball in two years. He kept the Astros at arm's length while he waited for the NFL to call . . . and in the second round of the 1968 draft, it did. Stabler would be an Oakland Raider, and the team would never be the same. And Alabama would never again have a quarterback quite like him.

Stabler would storm through the NFL, winning a Super Bowl with the Raiders, but he always remained connected to Alabama, and his days with Bryant were a major reason why.

"Without Coach Bryant saving me," he said, "I guess I'd be a bartender somewhere."

1967 IRON BOWL

Final Score: Alabama 7, Auburn 3

Chapter 17

THE PAT SULLIVAN EXPERIENCE

If you were to create an Auburn football messiah, you'd start with a quarterback with swooping brown hair and a soft accent. You'd give him a gentle personality and an arm that could throw a football into orbit. You'd make him an inspiration and a hero, the kind of man that young fans want to be, the kind of player that older fans would want as their son. You'd create the Anti-Stabler, as far from Tuscaloosa's pride as possible.

You would create Pat Sullivan, who came along at exactly the moment Auburn needed him most, and along with his go-to receiver, Terry Beasley, delivered The Plains some hope at the end of a dark and ugly decade.

Shug Jordan loved buttermilk. He loved coming home from a long day of practice, pouring himself a tall glass of buttermilk, and sitting down beside the telephone. He'd return calls from sportswriters late into the evening. "These people are as much responsible for building your program as anything you can do on the field," he said, knowing full well that sportswriters—so often accustomed to being abused, humiliated, disregarded, or flat-out ignored—would respond like gleeful puppies to some affection.

Jordan knew how to flatter his fan base too. He had his own television show, the *Auburn Football Review*, which aired on Sunday afternoons at five o'clock, right after Bear Bryant's show. Jordan started appearing on TV in 1955, and his audience grew to encompass the entire state. His one-liner delivered to host Carl Stephens—"You're so right, Carl"—became a catchphrase for decades around Auburn.

By the late 1960s, the stress of the job was starting to catch up with him. His health was deteriorating too. He was diagnosed with cancer in June 1968. Doctors advised him to leave the sideline behind, but he disregarded their orders and planned for major surgery in the offseason. Rolling into that surgery, he allegedly delivered one heck of a line: "Hell, I can't die now, not with Pat Sullivan and Terry Beasley coming up."

Sullivan, a 6-foot-tall 180-pounder out of John Carroll High School in Birmingham, was one of the most coveted recruits of 1967. And he was Auburn's to lose.

Children in Alabama grow up rooting for either the Tigers or the Tide. It was Auburn's good fortune that Sullivan grew up an Auburn fan; that gave Jordan an edge in recruiting him. For years afterward, Jordan would tell the story of how he visited Sullivan during the high schooler's senior year and drove him to an NFL exhibition game in Birmingham. En route to the game, Jordan's car overheated. He and Sullivan had to walk, and as they did, here came Bear Bryant, arriving with a police escort.

"Well, Pat, you can either go in the limelight with him," Jordan said, "or walk with me."

Sullivan opted to walk with Jordan, and Auburn was never the same.

Beasley, a wide receiver who also ran 180 pounds and a tetch under 6 feet, was a tougher sell. He had torched the competition at Robert E. Lee High School in Montgomery. He won the state track championship for Lee running—for the first time in his career—the third leg of the mile relay. He took the baton in fourth place, and handed it off in second.

Bryant invited him to Alabama, even taking him up into the old tower to watch practice. He grilled Beasley, saying, "You're going to be an All-American, and we want you to be an All-American at Alabama."

But Beasley remained unconvinced. Ultimately, he decided on Auburn for the same reason as so many others: he liked the idea of being an underdog. Since recruiting visits were unlimited in those days, Auburn staff wanted Beasley to stay out of sight and out of reach of Alabama recruiters, and they sweated out some nervous nights until he finally signed with the Tigers once and for all.

Sullivan arrived at Auburn in the fall of 1968 and, starting with the freshman game against Alabama—freshmen couldn't play on the varsity team in those days—immediately set about changing the entire culture of the school, even if few saw it at first. Auburn's Tiger Cubs were trailing Alabama 27–0 when Sullivan found Terry Beasley with a crucial pass that unlocked the Auburn offense. The Tiger Cubs would go on to win 36–27, and Auburn had itself a new passing duo.

Auburn by this time was hungry for any kind of high-powered offense. Tiger fans had ground their teeth watching Archie Manning at Ole Miss, Steve Spurrier at Florida, and—most brutally—Joe Namath and Ken Stabler at Alabama. Sullivan gave them exactly what they wanted and needed, a star of their very own.

After spending the 1968 season on the freshman team, Sullivan and Beasley rocketed into the SEC. Sullivan debuted under center in 1969 with three touchdowns—two on the ground, one in the air—in a 57–0 rout of Wake Forest. In his first game as a member of the varsity team, he was so pumped up that he lofted his first pass, in his estimation, 20 yards over Beasley's head. Tigers fans, so thankful for something approaching quarterback competence, cheered anyway.

He crashed back hard to the ground in his SEC debut against Tennessee, throwing five interceptions. But he got better, and fast. He ended up starting all 30 regular-season games during his three varsity seasons. He set an SEC career record of 7.03 yards averaged per play, as well as the seasonal mark of 2,856 yards of total offense in 1970.

On the other end of the tandem, Beasley caught everything in his area code. He set SEC career records with an average of 83.9 receiving yards per game and 29 touchdowns. Their specialty was a go-long bomb, where Sullivan would throw a pass high in the air, and Beasley would look backward and upward, like Willie Mays chasing that famous Vic Wertz fly ball in the 1954 World Series, and reel it in. The duo would practice the move until the sun went down.

The Tigers would go on to finish 8–3 in 1969, a season that included wins over both Florida (ending a Gator unbeaten streak) and Alabama, marking Auburn's first Iron Bowl win since 1963, back when Sullivan was a wee lad selling soft drinks in Legion Field's east stands. (That 1963 Iron Bowl featured one of Jordan's all-time great pregame speeches: "There is a time for everything. A time to live and a time to die, a time to love and a time to hate, a time for peace and . . . a time for war. And gentlemen, there's a time to beat Alabama. Now is the time.")

But it wasn't all joy for Sullivan that first year. Against Houston in the Bluebonnet Bowl on New Year's Eve, he got a little big for his britches. On a fourth and one, Jordan sent in the punter. Sullivan sent him back out, and then failed to convert the first down.

"I thought we should go for it," Sullivan said, attempting to explain himself.

"You sit your rear on the bench and don't get up until the game is over," Jordan shot back.

Sullivan entered his junior year of 1970 as the consensus second-best quarterback in the SEC after Manning. But when Manning broke his arm halfway through the season, Sullivan took the reins and led Auburn to a 9–2 record that included a whomping of Tennessee, the Vols' only loss of the season.

Player safety rules were somewhat different in those days. Against Alabama in 1970, Beasley was knocked unconscious after a catch on Auburn's first series. He hit the turf so hard, his teeth jutted through his lip. Doctors had to pull the lip off the teeth. They didn't stitch him up then and there, because he was going back in the game, of course, and another hit would wreck his lip even worse.

"They put some Juicy Fruit and cotton in there," Beasley later quipped.

He would eventually need 19 stitches to close his lip, and it would be years before he remembered the rest of the game. He was knocked out in daylight and woke up in twilight, with Auburn already trailing 17–0. He tried to get back into the game, but the coaches wouldn't let him—not to protect him, but because they weren't certain he was ready to catch passes. He finally went back onto the field shortly before halftime.

"I was out of breath quicker," he would later say of the effects of what was almost surely a severe concussion. "I was real nervous. It was a wonder I wasn't offside on every play. My body was literally trembling the whole time. I remember on the end-around play, I really should have scored, but my balance was so off once my brain was jarred that the gravity pulled me out of bounds." Auburn managed to win 33–28, but it was an ugly scene for Beasley. (In the years to come, he would suffer many more concussions, both in college and in the NFL, and his health sharply declined as a result.)

The paths of Manning and Sullivan would cross later that year, when Manning returned for the Gator Bowl, which set the two schools against one another. Auburn won 35–28, and Sullivan finished sixth in Heisman voting, even though he ended up leading the nation in total offense. Jordan wasn't present at that Gator Bowl; days before, he needed an emergency appendectomy, and complications from the surgery would affect him for the rest of his days.

As the 1971 season approached, with both Beasley and Sullivan in their senior years, Jordan felt an uncomfortable and unexpected sensation: anticipation, and fear. He spent countless hours looking over the practice field, patting down the grass, making sure no random hole or rock cropped up to twist the ankles of his beloved and indispensable duo.

Meanwhile, Sullivan navigated the pressure of being both a Heisman favorite and leader of a potential national champion. Jordan wanted his quarterback to win the award, in no small part because he knew that Alabama hadn't yet had a Heisman winner on any of its national championship rosters.

"Blindfolded, hands tied behind his back," Jack Doane wrote in the *Montgomery Advertiser*, "Pat Sullivan would be a one-point favorite at his own execution."

Against Tennessee, Beasley again got knocked out of the game, hitting his head so hard on a tackle that he briefly wandered over toward the Vols' huddle. He didn't remember anything between going up for the pass and resurfacing in the locker room. With Auburn down 6–0 at the half, he heard Sullivan's halftime declaration—"I just want to tell the defense that if they continue to hold them, we'll get the points we need"—and checked himself back into the game.

Beasley had a broken tooth and an injured toe, but that didn't stop him from serving as an especially attractive distraction; Sullivan simply spread the ball around the field, and Auburn came from behind for a 10–9 victory.

As pleasant as the victory over Tennessee was—and nobody at Auburn ever took a win over the Vols for granted—the bigger challenge came later in the 1971 season, when 8–0 Auburn faced 9–0 Georgia in Athens.

Pressure was building on all sides. Auburn was ranked 6th in the country; Georgia, 7th. Sullivan's Heisman candidacy, once seen as a sure thing, had started to spring leaks. *Sports Illustrated* even put Cornell running back Ed Marinaro—later a star on *Hill Street Blues*—on its November 1 cover just days before the Georgia game. Plus, Alabama's Johnny Musso was starting to siphon Southern votes from Sullivan.

So the Georgia game was widely viewed as Sullivan's last chance to secure that Heisman. But before he could even get to the field at Sanford Stadium, he and his teammates had to suffer the wrath and torment of Georgia fans in Athens.

Auburn's hotel wasn't far from Georgia's fraternities, and the Bulldog brothers decided to take a proactive approach to fandom—blasting music from the tops of the fraternity houses, leaping onto the roof of the hotel, banging on players' doors. Coaches even resorted to giving some players sleeping pills so they could sleep through the night. During the game, Georgia fans vandalized a state trooper's car and several of Auburn's buses.

The Dawgs were ready. Georgia offensive guard Royce Smith had a poster on his wall on which a teammate had written, "If the world was ending tomorrow, your one wish should be that we are playing Auburn today."

None of it mattered. The Tigers, seething with rage at the Georgia fans, rallied in the most effective way possible: by beating the hell out of Georgia on its own turf. Sullivan effectively clinched the Heisman on the very first play from scrimmage, hitting Beasley in stride for what would become a 70-yard touchdown. Final score: Tigers 35, Dawgs 20, Sullivan vindicated.

"If someone else does get it," Jordan said after the game, speaking of the Heisman, "I'll bet he's Christ reincarnated." Then he stopped. "Hold it. I'm a religious man, and now I'll be up all night saying Hail Marys." He amended his statement to say that anyone else who won the Heisman would have to be "ah, *magnificent*."

Jordan would look back on that win with love. "It was Southern football in all of its glory, in an Indian summer in all of its glory." He paused for a moment. "I feel a little poetic."

Bowl organizers announced even before the Iron Bowl that Auburn would be playing undefeated Oklahoma in the Sugar Bowl. Alabama and Nebraska would meet over in the Orange Bowl. Two of the four teams were destined to go into the game with a loss, since No. 1 Nebraska and No. 2 Oklahoma were playing on Thanksgiving, and No. 5 Auburn and No. 3 Alabama would battle two days later.

Nebraska knocked off Oklahoma, 35–31, in one of the great games in college football history. Now it was down to Auburn and Alabama to carve out their share of a shot at the title. But first, there was the small matter of the Heisman.

Sullivan was named the Heisman winner at halftime of the Georgia–Georgia Tech game on Thanksgiving Day 1971, and Auburn as a school and a town lost its collective mind. The joy hit a hard wall two days later. The Tigers hadn't been thinking of the Tide, and Alabama made them pay. Alabama torched Auburn 31–7, using the still-new wishbone offense to pick apart the Tigers' vaunted defense. There was grumbling on The Plains that the Heisman celebrations had cost Auburn necessary prep time.

"I'm not saying that's why we lost to Alabama," Sullivan later said, "but I think it affected us."

Then came Oklahoma, also using the wishbone, to debone what was left of Auburn in the Sugar Bowl. A despondent Jordan attempted a halftime speech: "I want you to go out there in the second half and remember who you are." But either Auburn forgot, or couldn't muster up the energy, because Oklahoma walked away with the game and the Sugar Bowl title, 40–22. Auburn finished the season ranked an ugly 12th.

Sullivan would continue to get grief from unexpected quarters—Howard Cosell called him "a nice kid who is not a great quarterback by college standards"—but conducted himself with almost supernatural grace. "As Dandy Don Meredith would say," Sullivan responded, "I'd rather not talk about old Howard." (Auburn fans were less forgiving; one booster wrote "Harry Cosell" at ABC suggesting that Cosell was fortunate to have Meredith and Frank Gifford "to 'carry' you on your sports program [a.k.a. *Monday Night Football*]; otherwise you would be a flop and a dud.")

If you were going to select the most important figures in Auburn history, you might get an argument between Shug Jordan and Pat Dye, or between Bo Jackson and Cam Newton. But you would get no argument—none whatsoever—about the sweet, soft-spoken kid from Birmingham.

"When he was playing ball, he was the best player on the field, no question," recalls Stan White, who quarterbacked Auburn in the 1990s. "But you know what? He made other players feel like they were the best player. And he took that off the field with him as well. And that's just a phenomenal trait to have."

TIMEOUT: ROLL TIDE

You hear it everywhere in Alabama—it's greeting and farewell, benediction and declaration, blessing and curse, comfort and call to arms. It rolls easily off the tongue, gliding smoothly from vowel to consonant to vowel again, and once spoken, it summons others from miles around:

Roll Tide.

But where exactly did the phrase come from? According to the Paul W. Bryant Museum, Auburn, of all places, gets credit for providing the inspiration, while sportswriters get credit for coining the term.

In 1907, Auburn was a heavy favorite to wallop Alabama. But the game ended in a muddy 6–6 tie, in what would be the last Auburn–Alabama matchup for more than 40 years. Hugh Roberts from the *Birmingham Age-Herald* wrote that Alabama's mud-soaked team looked like a "crimson tide." The *Birmingham News*'s Zipp Newman, who chronicled Alabama for decades, firmly secured the phrase in the popular imagination.

Where exactly the "Roll" came from is a bit of a mystery. It could be a simple declaration of what the Tide does to its opponents. It could have come from Alabama's fight song "Yea Alabama," which in its original version included the phrase "Go! Roll to victory!"

However "Roll Tide" evolved, it's now an indelible part of the sports lexicon, and as much a cheer as a threat for the rest of the sports universe.

Chapter 18

THE GAME THAT CHANGED THE SOUTH

There's a tendency, when one decade ends and another begins, to view history as changing chapters in a book. But the real world doesn't sort itself out that neatly. Eras don't end just because the calendar does. The decades bleed into one another, and from 1969 into 1970, there was blood everywhere in America, particularly in Alabama. The war in Vietnam raged on, growing even less understandable and more asymmetrical as it became clear that there was no strategy other than simply pummeling the enemy into submission. The worst battles of the civil rights era were over, but the scars of one side and the seething resentment of the other persisted, making this a "peace" in name only. Violence pierced the heart of another American college campus—Kent State—and the students there, including one young man named Nick Saban, would carry the tragic images of that day with them for the rest of their lives.

Alabama—the state and the university—clung stubbornly to the old ways as the 1970s dawned, even as it was clear the old ways were almost over. The day of the lantern-jawed, yes-ma'am, no-sir football player with close-cropped hair was ending; hair was longer, attitudes were looser, and crusty old football coaches weren't intimidating the new generation the way they had the earlier ones. In 1969, a student-initiated lawsuit targeting Coach Bryant demanded he resign for failing to sign Black players, and other students petitioned for his resignation. He wasn't going anywhere, but the fact that he was even being challenged by students was indicative of how much society had changed outside the lines of the football field.

Bear Bryant was the most popular man in Alabama—far more popular than George Wallace, although he detested the petty nature of politics—but even Bryant couldn't break through the unspoken ban on Black players at the University of Alabama. Entrenched racism and deep-rooted tradition were too much for him to upend with a few well-chosen words on his Sunday TV show, and he knew that Wallace could be vindictive when threatened. If he crossed the governor too openly, he put the university itself at risk.

"He could have pushed harder given his stature in the state, but that wasn't his job," Andrew Doyle says. "His job was to win football games." And as the championship-less seasons started to pile up, Doyle adds, "people were turning on Bear Bryant by the late '60s."

A football coach to his core, Bryant knew that there were assets out there just waiting for his acquisition. He recognized the level of talent in Alabama's Black high schools, and he understood just how those players could vault his program to untouchable heights. He also saw other schools across the country tapping into this wellspring of talent, and he understood that before long, Alabama's dominance would be over . . . and it would be from a self-inflicted wound.

Behind the scenes, Bryant continued to work angles throughout the state. He'd spent his entire coaching career planning for what could happen next, and he'd observed enough societal change to understand that what had been the law and custom of the land for so long wasn't going to last forever. He had begun quietly laying the groundwork for the inevitable, years before integration happened—too quietly for some, but definitively all the same.

Prior to the 1970 season, the NAACP called on Bryant. He surprised them by not only agreeing that sports teams needed to be integrated, but by pulling out a sheet of paper with the 15 best Black players in Alabama. He said he'd have a scholarship waiting if any of them enrolled at Alabama. None did.

"Any time you got good players, you come see ol' Bear," one high school coach later recalled him telling Tuscaloosa-area Black high school coaches. "I want 'em, and one day, I'm going to get 'em." Bryant understood that if he could position himself as a man with his eyes on the future, he'd have the assistance of the people he needed the most.

The season schedule had always hemmed Bryant in, with its 10 games and mandatory conference matchups, but in 1970, the NCAA unwittingly gave him an opportunity to make a bold move. That year, the NCAA permitted teams to schedule an 11th game, and while most coaches simply added a cupcake to pad their stats—Nebraska, for instance, welcomed and then whomped Wake Forest—Bryant saw a more meaningful big-picture opportunity.

He and John McKay, the legendary head coach at the University of Southern California, were longtime friends, in the way that men who have ascended the mountaintop share a common bond of knowledge. Together, they'd won five of the previous nine national championships, and they were two of the most famous men in the country. (Bryant and McKay once showed up at Chasen's in West Hollywood on a night when Frank Sinatra was dining there. Sinatra sent word that the men should come by his table. Bryant sent back word that Sinatra could come visit *their* table. Thirty seconds later, there was Ol' Blue Eyes.)

In January 1970, Bryant met McKay in a Los Angeles airport lounge with a proposal: bring the Trojans to Alabama for a season opener, for a cool $150,000. McKay heard the offer and raised Bryant one: a home-and-home series for 1970 and 1971, for $250,000. The deal was struck, and two of the most famous programs in America would clash in the fall at Legion Field, just a few blocks from where the worst battles of the civil rights era had been fought.

Legion Field was less than two miles from Birmingham's 16th Street Baptist Church. The fires of the 1960s were out, but the embers still smoldered, and the smoke was in the air. "We'd heard the stories," USC's star running back Sam "Bam" Cunningham would tell Yahoo Sports decades later. "We'd seen the news. We knew enough to be thankful we didn't live there."

Cunningham was big. He was fast. And he was Black. For a state accustomed to having all the advantages on its own side of the field, the game was a humbling experience. Cunningham and USC didn't just upend Alabama's worldview; they demolished it.

The game took place on September 12, 1970, amid avalanches of hype. Alabama's national championship–winning tradition against USC's glamor and muscle? These were the kinds of matchups that college football created, demanded, needed.

From the start, Cunningham pummeled the Tide, and USC rode in his wake. By midway through the third quarter, USC held a 32–7 lead, and many of the Alabama fans had begun heading for the Legion Field exits. They'd seen enough, and they'd seen exactly what Bryant wanted them to see. By the end of the game, the only sound audible among the seats where the dejected Alabama fans slumped was the "Co-Cola!" call of vendors walking up and down the aisles.

Final score: USC 42, Alabama 21, and it wasn't even that close.

The game's stat line was monstrous: USC ran for 485 yards; Alabama for just 32. Six different USC players rushed for more than 50 yards. Cunningham himself scored two touchdowns and averaged better than 10 yards every time he touched the ball, totaling 135 yards on 12 carries.

After the game, Bryant shook hands with McKay, and a photograph of the two—which hung in McKay's den for years afterward—showed Bryant smiling. *Smiling.* Later, he made his customary visit to the winning locker room, congratulating first McKay and then Clarence Davis, who had lived in Birmingham but had been unable to play football at his home state's flagship university.

One myth that made the rounds after the game held that Bryant brought Cunningham, still bare-chested and sweating, into the Alabama locker room and declared that he "and his Trojan brothers just ran your slow-motion asses right out of your own house. Raise your heads and open your eyes, this is what a football player looks like." But that entire story appears created from thin air; no member of the Alabama team nor any reporter nearby recalled anything like that happening, as thrilling as it might have been for the ardent Alabama-haters of the day. Cunningham himself later said he met with Bryant, but outside the Alabama locker room, not inside it.

Bryant instead used a more muted tactic to get his point across. "There is nothing we can do about this one," he told the media after the game. "I hope we will suck our guts up and use it as a stepping stone to try and improve, to try to keep building for the future. Whether the future will be the distant future or how long, I just don't know."

He was speaking about the football team's on-field prospects, but you didn't have to listen very hard to hear that he was talking about the university, the state, and the entire region too.

Jim Murray of the *L.A. Times* cheerfully acknowledged the changing times, declaring that Alabama had at last "joined the Union" after they "took the field against a mixed bag of hostile black and white American citizens without police dogs, tear gas, rubber hoses or fire hoses. They struggled fairly without the aid of their formidable ally, Jim Crow. Bigotry wasn't suited up for a change. Prejudice got cut from the squad."

It's worth noting that when Alabama and USC met in 1970, the NFL—via its professional pigskin predecessors—had been integrated for 50 years. The NBA had integrated two decades before, and Jackie Robinson had suited up as the first Black man to play professional baseball in 1947. Universities around the country had integrated their teams everywhere but in the South.

"Sam Cunningham did more to integrate Alabama in 60 minutes than Martin Luther King did in 20 years," gushed Jerry Claiborne, a Bryant assistant. While that line is ridiculously dismissive of King's life's work, it did hit on an important element of integration: white Alabamians weren't going to be persuaded by protests, or violence, or calls to higher moral character. The easiest route to convincing them to join the rest of the country was the realization that the rest of the country was going to stomp them every fall Saturday afternoon hereafter unless Alabama picked up the pace and joined America's forward progress.

"Some Black civil rights leaders thought sport was problematic and identifying Black achievement as only physical was going to create problems," says Mark Dyreson, a professor of history at Penn State. "But even they recognized, given the popularity of sport in the United States, that maybe [sport] can alter the long conflicts over race relations that exist in the United States."

Cunningham dismissed any comparisons between him and King. "There might be a drop of truth in it," he said, "but there's no possible way in my mind [that] what I did should be compared to Dr. King."

Also notable: the contributions of Davis, the USC halfback, who, like Cunningham, ran all over the Tide and scored a touchdown of his own. But while Cunningham was from California, Davis had been *born in Birmingham*. The implication was clear—he could have been wearing crimson instead of stomping on it.

As the years have passed and the game has taken on a mythical importance, it's worth reexamining some of the key elements of that significant afternoon. Was Bryant simply challenging a friend? Or was he trying to make a larger point, showing the people of Alabama that they wouldn't be winning any more national championships if they didn't make their peace with integration? Did he know Alabama was going to lose, or was he testing himself against the inevitable? It was a high-risk gamble—if all-white Alabama had blown out an integrated USC team, it could have set back integration efforts even further—but did Bryant see it as a gamble, or was it just another football game?

"If I'd known this game would be this important, I would have paid more attention," Cunningham joked years later. "I was just focused on playing well enough to play next Saturday against Nebraska."

Bryant had already been preparing for the inevitable, making his moves on several fronts. He'd scheduled the game against an integrated Penn State team more than a decade before, and he'd brought those five Black players to spring practice in 1967. He'd signed a Black player to a scholarship in 1969. And he'd been keeping that list of Black high school players, as he noted in a 1970 deposition in the lawsuit filed against him by his own school's students.

"Three or four years ago, we began looking in the State and this was prior to the time when they started Blacks and whites playing each other," Bryant said. "And our thing was that [if] any good ones came along, we certainly didn't want them to get away, and if we wanted to start, we wanted to start with Alabama boys." (He later said he "hoped like hell" Auburn never got a look at his list.)

Two Black players were already in the Tide pipeline. A young Alabama assistant by the name of Pat Dye recruited running back Wilbur Jackson out of tiny Ozark, Alabama, and on December 13, 1969, Jackson became the first Black player to sign a scholarship at Alabama.

"That 1970 Southern Cal game has been so misunderstood through the years," author Keith Dunnavant says. "It did not cause Alabama to integrate. However, it was very powerful symbolism, in terms of contrast between the future and the past, and so it was certainly helpful for Bryant's cause at that point."

Soon after their fateful Birmingham matchup, McKay ran into Bryant at the Bob Hope Desert Classic in Palm Springs, and mentioned that he had an interest in a young defensive end out of Mobile, Alabama, named John Mitchell. Bryant excused himself, called Tuscaloosa, and had his assistants track down—and sign—Mitchell. If McKay was interested in him, that was good enough for Bryant, and in 1971, Mitchell became the first Black player to play in a game for Alabama.

"We did a lot," Cunningham said after the USC game, "but the lion's share of the credit goes to the Black athletes who decided to become a part of those programs . . . I can only imagine the guarantees Coach Bryant had to make to the parents of the young [Black] men who came to play for him. A lot of stuff was still happening even at that time."

"If you have a problem," Bryant told Jackson and Mitchell, "come and see me. Don't see anybody else. Just come and see me, and it'll be taken care of." But neither Jackson nor Mitchell ever had to go see Bryant. Jackson would go on to win both a national championship and a Super Bowl, while Mitchell would later become a coach under Bryant.

"We have black players, and we play against them, and that's progress," Bryant said in his 1974 autobiography. "I don't say I agree with everything Martin Luther King said, but I saw the wisdom in most of it."

"[Integration in the SEC] had been going on for four years before he got involved," says Michael Oriard, an emeritus professor of English at Oregon State University. "He was just unwilling to put himself at political risk. He's got a racist governor and a civil rights–resistant population in the state of Alabama. Maybe he could have talked them into it sooner by just saying, 'Look, folks, if we want to be able to beat the best football teams, we need to have the best football players, and some of those best football players are going to be Black.' I absolutely have no idea if he could have done it sooner than he did, I just know he didn't."

"Could Bryant have been earlier? Of course he could have," Dunnavant says. "In reality, he got it just about right, because you have to remember his primary job with the young men that he brought in was to keep them safe. He had seen what had happened, for instance, at Ole Miss [where riots over James Meredith's enrollment led to the deaths of two people]. He didn't want to bring a young man into Alabama and not be able to keep him safe from the yahoos out there who didn't get it."

Neither Bryant nor McKay mentioned their motivation for the game in their autobiographies. But then again, the silence might well be the point.

"If he had a plan to use this game to change the minds of Alabama fans, and I believe he did, then the worst thing he could do was talk about it," Florida State University head coach Bobby Bowden would say years later. "All he needed to do was praise USC and never mention the race of the players who beat him. That's what he did."

On the field, Bryant got his revenge on USC. The next season, after sending USC spring game film of their offense, a customary practice between rivals, Bryant launched into a fire drill, ordering his team to learn the wishbone offense in just three weeks, with no observers permitted.

Bryant tapped Texas head coach Darrell Royal to help him develop the wishbone offense for Alabama, visiting his old friend in Austin and later calling him as many as five or six times a day. Alabama rolled out the wishbone just three weeks before the USC rematch, a stunning change in offensive philosophy. Coaches usually install new offensive schemes in the spring to give teams a chance to work out the kinks and think on it all summer.

But Bryant decided to pull a fast one. When the SEC press tour rolled into Tuscaloosa, he ran the old pro set offense during practice, making it appear for all the world like Bama was going with the same old, same old.

The sneak attack worked. The move caught the Trojans flat-footed in the first game of the 1971 season, and before USC could adjust, Alabama scooted out of LA Coliseum with a 17-10 victory. Two years later, Bryant—with a fully integrated team—would win his fourth national title. Two more would follow, in 1978 and 1979, and as Black players became stars, captains, and NFL draftees, Bryant's belief in integration was proven correct. That, combined with his willingness to alter his offensive philosophy, unlocked an entire new decade's worth of success.

During the 1970s, Alabama won eight SEC titles and three national titles. The Tide was the team of the '70s, even if Notre Dame had frustrated Alabama throughout the decade. It was Bear's era, Bear's time, Bear's reign.

But there's often a burr under the saddle that can take the joy out of the victory ride. A blue-and-orange one.

IRON BOWL 1972: PUNT BAMA PUNT

Losing an Iron Bowl is bad enough, but losing it in a way that generates bumper-sticker taunts for years to come . . . oh, that's absolutely the worst. It's not enough to marinate in your loss for a year; if it's bad enough, you'll be reminded of it in traffic, on T-shirts, in one-liners that can last long after the particulars of the game are forgotten. Long before there was Kick Six, there was Punt Bama Punt.

The outcome of the Iron Bowl "determines your identity for 364 days," ESPN's Ryan McGee says. "The final score of that game gives you the ability, until Thanksgiving weekend a year later, to walk into the breakfast diner, the break room at work, the golf course on a Saturday morning in the spring with the high ground." Nowhere was that more clear than on December 2, 1972, a day that will live in Iron Bowl glory . . . or infamy.

Paul Bryant had spent the 1960s winning championships and effectively wiping Auburn off the map. The Tigers couldn't get out of their own way, and not even Pat Sullivan and Terry Beasley could slow the Tide's momentum. Alabama possessed both a powerful offense and a quietly superior defense. By 1972, the new wishbone was in full effect, and everything was clicking for the Tide.

But Auburn was quietly putting together an impressive run of their own, rolling through the season at 8–1, ranked ninth in the nation when they faced the 10–0, No. 2–ranked Crimson Tide. Alabama was mighty in all phases of the game except one . . . the kicking game.

"I have never seen an Alabama football team as sloppy as they are in the whole kicking game," Auburn defensive coordinator Paul Davis told Jordan prior to the game. They'd spent extensive time watching film, and they'd seen players from other teams break through the Alabama line and get to the kicker but miss the ball. Davis and Jordan decided to stick with Auburn's eight-man rush but throw in some wrinkles . . . wrinkles that wouldn't be apparent until later.

Early in the game, Alabama leaped out to a commanding 16–0 lead, and everything seemed just fine for the Tide. Everything was not fine. Late in the game, an Auburn drive stalled at fourth and eight on the Alabama 24. Jordan opted to kick the field goal, and the boos rained down. Shug turned and looked at trainer Kenny Howard, smiled, and said, "They don't think we're gonna win, do they?"

And then the Tide's woes began.

The next Alabama drive stalled, and the Tide prepared to punt. But the Auburn line realigned itself, confusing the Alabama line. The Auburn players zipped through the B gap—the space between the guards and tackles—and swarmed Alabama punter Greg Gantt. Bill Newton blocked the kick, and David Langner recovered the ball at the 25 and ran it in for Auburn's first touchdown. One extra point later, and Alabama's lead had shrunk to 16–10. There was 5:30 left in the game.

Alabama took the kickoff and gained two first downs to reach its own 42. With 2:10 remaining and facing a crucial third and four, Alabama rolled right—and Auburn was there to throw the Tide for a 5-yard loss.

It was time to punt again. Bryant grumbled, and told Gantt to move up 2 yards and just boot the ball into the open field. No need to worry about precision—just get the damn thing out of the backfield.

The problem was, the Auburn rush had come from the middle. Moving Gantt up toward the line of scrimmage only put him in the teeth of the snarling Tiger defense. Newton was on top of Gantt in an instant, once *again* blocking the kick, this time on the 35. The ball *again* bounced into Langner's hands, and he *again* took it to the house. Auburn now led 17–16 with 1:34 left.

And then, Langner, as if he hadn't already done enough, intercepted Alabama's Terry Davis to seal the win and end Alabama's dreams of a perfect season and a national title.

The 17–16 victory was Shug's *Mona Lisa*, his *David*, his Ninth Symphony. A work of art. Brilliance unforgettable to anyone who saw it live, memorable to all who heard about it through the years. And for another four decades, it would be the decisive Auburn-over-Alabama win.

"I like to think we outsmarted Bear on that one," Jordan said.

"I have a hard time looking at people in the eye," Bryant groused a few days later.

"Everybody can remember where they were when Kennedy was shot, when the man walked on the moon, and if you're from the state of Alabama, when Auburn blocked the punts," Auburn linebacker Mike Neel later recalled to Jordan's biographer.

An Alabama fan once asked Auburn's Terry Henley why Auburn fans kept chirping about the blocked punts. "I'll make you a deal, pal," Henley replied. "Y'all quit singing about the Rose Bowl, and we'll quit talking about the kicks."

Punt Bama Punt was the pièce de résistance of an Auburn team that would come to be known as "The Amazins," a crew that went 9–1 during the regular season and then stomped Colorado in the Gator Bowl, 24–3. The Tigers finished the season ranked fifth in the country. Jordan was named SEC Coach of the Year, nearly 20 years after he'd won the award the first time, back in 1953. And best of all, they had a new slogan that still burns Alabama to this day, half a century later—a slogan that would carry them through the 10 long years of losses to Alabama that were about to come.

"Maybe Auburn was lucky. Maybe Auburn couldn't do it again in 10 years, a hundred years, maybe even a thousand years, but that doesn't matter," Auburn's David Housel wrote in 1973. "It's all academic. What matters is that they did do it, and as the sun sank slowly in the West, Auburn, [Alabama,] was the football capital of the whole universe. It would be that way for days, weeks and months to come."

1972 IRON BOWL

Final Score: Auburn 17, Alabama 16

Chapter 19

THE LAST DAYS OF SHUG JORDAN

College football is a cruel and pitiless sport. It comes for your body and it comes for your dreams. The players see their days on the field end in their early 20s. The coaches can stave off the darkness for longer—sometimes decades longer—but eventually time comes for everyone.

By the 1970s, Shug Jordan had restored some of the glory to an Auburn program that had suffered mightily in the mid-1960s. Having Pat Sullivan as your quarterback will do that. The Tigers were coming off three straight third-place finishes in the SEC and four top-20 finishes in the country. But around the margins, the cracks were starting to show.

One day, halfway through the 1971 season, Auburn's offensive coaches were scheming up plans to challenge Georgia Tech in Atlanta. Tech had fallen far from the heights of its glory days, and was 2–3 coming into the game. But you never underestimate a rival, and Jordan walked into the room to see how the preparations were coming and offer up a few "suggestions."

He walked up to the blackboard and drew up a standard scheme—two tight ends, three running backs. Exactly the kind of offense he'd used to win a national championship... in 1957.

"What do you think about this?" he asked his assistants. "What would Tech do if we came out in this?"

The assistants looked at one another silently, no one wanting to voice the obvious truth. Finally, offensive coordinator Gene Lorendo, who'd been with Jordan from the very start, said what they were all thinking: "They'd just beat the hell out of us."

Disgusted, Jordan threw down his chalk and stormed out of the room. Auburn would go on to win the game, 31–14.

Jordan wasn't much for grand gestures; he was a man who preferred action to words, deeds to monuments. But even he had to admit, getting an entire stadium named after him was quite the honor.

Auburn renamed Cliff Hare Stadium in 1973, dubbing it Jordan-Hare Stadium. It was the only stadium named after an active head coach in the country, and the honor was a testament to the way Jordan had vaulted the Tigers to national prominence. Over the course of his tenure since 1951, the stadium had grown in capacity from 21,500 to 61,261, and had changed shape twice—from parallel grandstands to a horseshoe in 1960, and then to an enclosed bowl in 1970. When Alabama added Bryant's name to Denny Stadium in 1975, Jordan happily gloated that the Bear had copied him.

The growth of Jordan-Hare Stadium had an immediate impact on Auburn's standing. Even though the Tigers still trekked to Birmingham each year to play Alabama in the Iron Bowl, the increased size of Auburn's home field made it a viable destination for other teams. In 1974, for instance, the Tennessee Volunteers came to Auburn for the first time. Previously, Tennessee had only deigned to come play the Tigers in Birmingham. And Auburn fans got to let loose on their long-standing grudge against the Vols for not making the journey to The Plains: at least one Tennessee coach was pelted with an orange thrown from the stands in the course of the 21–0 Tigers victory. Auburn was tired of playing the little brother role, and embraced its newfound strength.

Even as his on-field impact declined, Jordan's influence reverberated with players he'd coached, and he never stopped recruiting. He once had a famous exchange with star linebacker Mike Kolen, who'd suited up for

Auburn in the 1960s and went on to play for the Miami Dolphins during their back-to-back Super Bowl seasons of 1972 and 1973. Jordan wanted Kolen—nickname: Captain Crunch—to serve as an advance scout, checking on high school prospects in the Miami area.

"There are mainly three types of high school players," Jordan said. "The first type will get knocked down on the field and he'll crawl off to the sidelines and quit."

"I know we don't want that type," Kolen said.

"The second type, when he goes down, he jumps right back up. But when he goes down again, he'll crawl off and quit."

"We don't want him either," Kolen replied.

"The third type is raw bone tough. He'll get knocked down again and again but he'll get up every time and continue to give 110 percent."

"That's the type we want, right, coach?" Kolen said.

"No," Jordan said. "You find the guy that's been knocking him down."

In mid-December 1974, shortly before Auburn was scheduled to play Texas in the Gator Bowl, Jordan sat back and looked at his accomplishments: a national championship, a Heisman Trophy winner, an Outland Trophy winner, SEC Coach of the Year, countless All-Americans. Twenty-five years at Auburn, 65 years old—not a bad way to go out. It was time to walk away, and Jordan told athletic director Lee Hayley that it was time to choose a successor.

"I'm not tired of coaching," Jordan said. "I just wanted to get out when I was ahead. I don't feel like I'm a legend."

The choices for Jordan's replacement came down to offensive coordinator Doug Barfield and assistant coach Paul Davis. Jordan favored Davis, but the administration had an eye on Barfield, and in this case, Jordan did not get his way.

The plan was to offer the job to Barfield and introduce him as the head coach at the same time Jordan announced his retirement. But the news leaked early, leaving Davis out in the cold. Jordan was deeply disappointed at how the story broke, getting out to friends and players before he could tell them himself.

Rivals like Bryant and Georgia Tech's Bobby Dodd praised ol' Shug, but sadly, Jordan didn't get his grand farewell. Auburn went 3-6-2 in his last year, only his third losing season as head coach. The fractured coaching staff—with Barfield's promotion and Davis chafing at the disrespect he endured—didn't help.

Even as the sun was going down, Jordan took issue with the NCAA telling him that visiting teams could dress out only 48 players, while the home team dressed 60—a rule he deemed "asinine" and "silly."

"I have enough states' rights in me to resent being told how many people you can dress out," Jordan said, a subtle indication that the old times in the South weren't forgotten . . . or even all that old.

Jordan's final home game came on November 8, 1975, against Mississippi State. The sellout crowd of 64,796 stood and applauded Shug as he ran onto the field in his traditional attire of light windbreaker and khaki pants. He raised his right hand to acknowledge the crowd, and wiped tears from the corners of his eyes.

Jordan next met Vince Dooley, his old player and longtime rival, in Athens. During Dooley's tenure, he and Jordan had each won six games, and Dooley got the last win. They met at midfield, and Dooley broke down. "This was my coach," he said. "This was the one who gave me a start."

Then came the Bear.

Jordan and Bryant had done battle 17 times in the Iron Bowl. Jordan had won only five, but that was still more than any other coach had ever managed against Bryant. Alabama rolled into the game 9-1; Auburn was a mere 3-5-2, with only four players who had started in the previous year's game still in uniform.

Jordan wore a suit and tie for what was to be his final game. Bryant walked over to his rival, removed his houndstooth hat, and shook Jordan's hand. There would be no emotional displays from the Bear, but none would be needed.

In his final speech to his team, Jordan struck a gentle tone. "If you can walk off the field after the game and feel like you did your best, then I'm satisfied," he said. "If you win, you win; if you lose, you lose. But you will always feel good about yourself knowing you did everything you could to win."

Alabama respected Jordan, but this was the Iron Bowl. Richard Todd and Ozzie Newsome helped the Tide bludgeon the Tigers, 28–0. Asked whether he wished he had another chance to coach, Jordan didn't hesitate. "I'm sitting right now wishing," he replied. "But that's impossible. There comes a time you must get out."

He tried to rally the spirits of his despondent locker room after the game. "This season will stay with me as long as I'm alive," he told his players. "I'd like to have another time at bat. But it just can't happen."

The next day, the *Auburn Football Review* on WSFA in Montgomery held its final Jordan show. Former players, including Pat Sullivan, Lloyd Nix, and Bill Newton and David Langner of Punt Bama Punt fame, visited the studio, and Jordan's wife, Evelyn, paid her first visit to the set.

"I think I can teach him how to act like a fan," said Evelyn in an immaculate coach's-wife blonde bouffant hairdo and pantsuit. "He can learn how to stand up on kickoffs and cheer on the team and holler at the coaches like we do in the stands." Jordan was presented with a set of stadium seat cushions, since he and Evelyn had never watched an Auburn game together.

In the course of the show, Jordan offered up one final "You're so right, Carl," to his longtime cohost, Carl Stephens. And then it was time to go. As the Auburn fight song played, Jordan's players came in for one last handshake, and the credits rolled.

"There comes a time to quit," Jordan said, "and this is it."

Jordan joined the Auburn board of trustees, where he proceeded to become a thorn in the side of university president Harry Philpott, the same man who had refused him the opportunity to be both head coach and athletic director. He played golf, badly. He mowed the lawn. He and Evelyn traveled once—to Istanbul—and Jordan vowed never to leave the United States again. After that, he journeyed about as far as Montgomery. He spent days in his office on the phone, but tried to stay out of Barfield's way.

Jordan helped spearhead a massive expansion of Jordan-Hare, adding an upper deck on the stadium's west side, increasing VIP seating, and boosting capacity to 72,169. Opponents of the idea said the millions spent on expanding the football stadium should go into academic disciplines rather than athletic ones, particularly when the program was under yet another NCAA investigation. But the stadium expanded, and then expanded again in 1987, adding a second deck to the east side to bring capacity to 85,214. That would make it the largest stadium in Alabama for nearly two decades.

By early 1980, Jordan's health began to decline. In April, he was diagnosed with acute leukemia. On April 29, he had a pacemaker implanted following a heart attack. A few weeks later, he moved to a bed in his home to live out his final days.

A stream of well-wishers visited Jordan, but in his last days, he turned away many, wanting them to remember him as he was—younger and vibrant, not withered by disease. One of the final people to see him was his longtime friend and Auburn supporter Billy Thames.

"Billy," Jordan said at last, "say goodbye."

Jordan passed on July 17, 1980, at the age of 69, with his family around him. Funeral services were held at Holy Trinity Episcopal Church at Auburn, just a block from Jordan's home. Several of his players, including Sullivan, Beasley, and Phil Gargis, served as his pallbearers.

Governor Fob James and other dignitaries, including Vince Dooley, came to Auburn. A coterie of Alabama coaches made the trip, and Bryant stayed at the back of the tiny 250-seat church, preferring not to call attention to himself.

The service lasted just 15 minutes. Reporters from around the country asked Reverend Bill McLemore for a copy of his planned sermon. "The people gathered here," Reverend McLemore replied, "are the sermon for Coach Jordan."

It's impossible to overstate the influence Jordan had on the Auburn family, the way he lifted the entire spirit of the university community for more than a quarter-century. He was folksy, cranky, charming, irascible, witty, temperamental—if Bryant was a stone icon, Jordan was a man of the people, reflecting their best nature and expecting them to live up to what they could be.

"He taught the Auburn people to feel good about themselves, and he became their main point of pride," recalled Dooley in the foreword to Jordan's 1993 biography. "The people shouted 'War Eagle!' with a conviction and a devotion unheard of in the past. He challenged them to stand tall and believe in themselves and reminded them that being an Auburn person was something that was very special indeed."

On one of his final trips outside the house in the summer of 1980, Jordan and his son, Ralph Jr., traveled to Jordan-Hare Stadium to get a look at the nearly completed grandstands rising on the west side of the stadium. Hayley let them in through the South Gate—a gate where, a few decades in the future, a statue of Jordan himself would stand—and father and son drove slowly around the field, marveling at what Jordan had inspired in this tiny town. This stadium had been such a place of joy for him, as a young man and as an adult. Memories of this place had inspired him on a faraway beach in Normandy. Belief in this grass, these stands, these people kept him going, and the belief that he put back into this field would inspire countless members of the Auburn family for decades to come.

Chapter 20

THE SIGN OF THE WOLF

The young coach sweated inside his new suit, and not because of the weather. He was about to meet the legendary Bear. The young coach knew that the Bear could make or break his fledgling career, and so he had handwritten a letter to Bryant asking for a job. He got the interview, and he kept his voice and face steady under the Bear's gaze.

It was only after he left the Bear's office that the young coach realized he'd never taken the tags off his new suit.

The young coach's name was Pat Dye, and better days in the Bear's presence lay ahead.

Pat Dye was born on November 6, 1939, at a farm on the banks of the Ogeechee River in South Georgia. When he was just three months old, his family moved to Blythe, Georgia, about 20 miles southwest of Augusta. The Dye family lived right next door to the Baptist church in Blythe, and as a young lad, Pat fell asleep listening to the choir practice.

Southern men become who they are in an effort to please their fathers, and young Pat had one hell of a challenge in getting the approval of his daddy, Big Wayne. A former semipro baseball player, Big Wayne looked like the ideal father to a boy, regularly going hunting and fishing when he wasn't farming cotton, peanuts, corn, peas, wheat... whatever was in season. The family tended hogs too; one of them even bit off a piece of Pat's big toe when he was a youngster.

But Big Wayne didn't own the land he farmed; he leased it. And he had a thirst for drink and a love for cigarettes, smoking as many as five packs of Camels in a day. Those vices would eventually come to claim Big Wayne... and they'd loom over young Pat's life too.

Dye grew up picking cotton alongside Black families, and he would later claim that gave him a special perspective on race relations that others who grew up in more segregated worlds may have lacked. "I've got the advantage of having worked, black and white, goin' down the cotton rows together," he wrote in his autobiography. "That's the way I grew up. The blacks were just as important as we were."

When Pat wasn't working, he and his friends would hitchhike into Augusta to watch movies starring former Alabama standout Johnny Mack Brown. Pat attended Richmond Academy in Augusta, playing football there and even winning a state championship as a 185-pound senior guard in 1956. Every night after football practice, he'd have to find his way back home, 20 miles, and he'd walk, hitchhike—whatever it took.

Big Wayne knew Shug Jordan, and young Pat's football prowess was enough to put him on Auburn's recruiting radar. But his heart as a high schooler lay with the University of Georgia, his mother's alma mater, and so off to Athens he went.

Dye had the misfortune to join Georgia in the late 1950s, a time when the perpetually dysfunctional staff was particularly chaotic. He was teammates with Fran Tarkenton, and played well enough to get an invitation to join other college All-Stars on *The Perry Como Show*, but other than that, his college career was largely undistinguished. After he graduated from Georgia in 1960, he played a couple seasons for the Edmonton Eskimos of the Canadian Football League, but with the expiration date on his playing time fast approaching, he realized he needed to make a career change. He served in the Army for a short period of time to satisfy an outstanding ROTC obligation, and then, in 1964, he started looking for work.

Right around this time, Gene Stallings left Alabama to coach at A&M, and that presented an opportunity for the ambitious young Dye. He wrote a letter to Bryant pitching himself as a coach, and despite the price-tag fiasco, Bryant hired him at the princely sum of $500 a month.

At Alabama, Dye worked out of a windowless office. His task was to figure out how to maximize the Tide's linebackers—and *only* the linebackers. Especially with young coaches, Bryant maintained a level of need-to-know secrecy that would have done the Pentagon proud; young coaches didn't get a look at the entire playbook on the likely chance that they would pick up and leave for Tennessee, Georgia, or some other rival.

Dye excelled at recruiting. Tasked with covering the entire state of Georgia and the southeast corner of Alabama, he crisscrossed his territory, glad-handing high school coaches and offering up honest talk for the recruits. With no limits on recruiting visits in those days, the only constraints on Dye's efforts were how far he could go before needing to refill his gas tank... or collapsing.

Bryant was a celebrity, and this often presented problems on the recruiting trail. Many high school seniors just wanted the cachet of saying the Bear had come to *them*, regardless of how interested they were in playing for Alabama. It thus became Dye's job to weed out the dilettantes and the casuals, putting only the finest possible recruits under Bryant's eye.

"I'm gonna recruit you. Coach Bryant ain't coming to visit you. If you want to talk to Coach Bryant about coming to Alabama, you'll go to his office on his time," Dye would tell recruits. On the other hand, "If you know you want to come to Alabama, and you're ready to sign, then Coach Bryant will come sign you." The technique worked; Dye began delivering recruits by the truckload.

On the field, however, matters didn't exactly begin well for Dye at

Alabama. In his first game on the coaching staff, Alabama lost to his alma mater, Georgia, 18–17. To make matters worse, he locked his car keys in the trunk.

Bryant didn't take to losing well. "Men," he said in the locker room after the game, "it's kinda obvious that we don't have a very good football team. But if you are the kinda people I think you are, we'll have a good football team before the year's over." And then he proceeded to rain hell down on them at practice the next Monday. Bryant was such a fearsome presence after losses that players were known to bed down in the practice facility rather than oversleep and miss practice.

The lessons took hold with Dye. It wasn't just about the talent; it was what he could do with the talent. Bryant was an absolute master at taking what others had done, adopting and adapting their strategies, and then—more often than not—beating the exact people he'd swiped the ideas from.

"He could get more out of his people than you could get out of yours," Dye wrote in his autobiography, speaking of Bryant. "He grew up hard in the country in Arkansas, and he was naturally a hungry person. He did not want to go back to plowing mules at 50 cents a day. And that's the way he coached."

Like so many other coaches, Dye blossomed under Bryant's intense gaze. Once he got the go-ahead to start recruiting Black players, he began visiting still-segregated Black high schools. He traveled to Carroll High School in Ozark, Alabama, to meet with Wilbur Jackson, and made him a pitch that would resonate.

"Wilbur," Dye recalled telling Jackson, "there's no way for me to tell you what it's going to be like, because I don't know. I don't know how the other students on the campus will treat you. I do know our football players will respect you as a man." Jackson would be the first Black player offered a scholarship at the University of Alabama, and would go on to win both a national championship and, later, a Super Bowl.

"We live in an age, and it will probably last forever, where the Black kids in this region make the difference in football," Dye wrote in 1991. "If there are 10 college prospects in Alabama, seven are gonna be Black."

Dye would spend much of his 1991 autobiography attempting to defend himself from charges of racism, but through a 21st-century lens, he comes off as either patronizing or defensive—"The Black athlete has speed and size and hunger. And all the intangibles. And the kids are good kids." Race relations lurked just below the surface for every white Southern football coach, and for Dye, they would erupt in the coming years.

Eventually, every one of Bryant's coaches left the nest, and in Dye's case, that meant a job at East Carolina to start the 1974 season and, later, a year at Wyoming. In 1980, he heard about an opening at Auburn. Doug Barfield had struggled in Jordan's wake, losing at least three games in each of his five years, and Tigers leadership was ready to make a change.

Vince Dooley was Auburn's primary choice, but Dooley, who had begun building a powerhouse at the University of Georgia, opted to stay in Athens. That meant the job was open, and Dye, never shy about asking for what he wanted, lobbied for the job all the way up to Alabama Governor Fob James.

One day, when he was deep in the interview process at Auburn, Dye's phone rang. An unmistakable growl rolled from the receiver.

"You're aren't going to take that job," Bryant declared.

"I am if they offer it," Dye replied.

"You're going to get *this* one," Bryant said, meaning the Alabama gig.

"If I come to Alabama," Dye countered, "I'd be trying to maintain what you've already done. At Auburn, I can build a program."

"Well," Bryant replied, "you're not going to beat me."

"Maybe not," Dye retorted, "but the one that follows you, I'm gonna beat him like a stepson."

So Dye continued interviewing, and one of the first questions was the most important: "How long will it take you to beat Alabama?"

"Sixty minutes," he replied. He wasn't being glib; he knew that he would need 60 minutes of effort to beat Bryant. He had coached at Alabama, played at Georgia, and pitched himself as the only man who knew both programs well enough to make Auburn competitive with both. He got the job, and even though he called his new employer "The University of Auburn" at his introductory press conference, hopes were appropriately high.

Dye's first practices in the spring of 1981 were what he called "wolf-sign" practices—"damn blood and hair and tore-up ground all around." They'd entertain high school coaches for clinics, then usher the coaches out, lock the gates, and start getting down to real business. Bodies would fly; coaches would pounce on fumbles and knock heads with their padded players. This was serious business, right from the jump, and Dye had a strategy behind his meanness.

"I can tell you this," he later wrote, "when we came out of that spring, they weren't afraid. Of anybody. I think they had a different feeling about themselves. They knew there weren't any faint-hearted people playing for us."

Dye's men also began hitting the recruiting trail hard, outhustling the Bear at every stop. They knew the old man's style, and that meant they knew how to beat him. In particular, Dye listened with interest as his assistant Bobby Wallace, the Birmingham-area recruiter, talked about a new kid out of Bessemer they had their eye on but Bryant hadn't yet seemed to notice.

Still, those opening games were rough ones. After beating Texas Christian, Auburn lost three straight, to Wake Forest, Tennessee, and Nebraska. Against LSU, Auburn played four quarterbacks—including Joe Sullivan, little brother of Pat—rotating them in one play at a time. Losses to Mississippi State and Georgia followed, and by the time the Tigers reached the last Saturday in November, Auburn stood at a wobbly 5–5. A date with history awaited.

IRON BOWL 1981: THE RECORD

He was almost at the mountaintop. Bear Bryant owned the imagination of an entire nation, but he didn't quite have that magic number: 315. That was the number of wins he needed to put himself one ahead of Amos Alonzo Stagg for most NCAA wins in a career.

By now, the lines in Bryant's face were deep. The cigarettes, whiskey, steaks, and late nights were taking their toll. The rumble in his voice had cooled to a low hiss. He was showing his years, and even though he was younger than President Ronald Reagan, who was 70, Bryant had the world-weary look of a man who had seen it all, many times, and was determined to press onward.

He'd won three more national championships throughout the 1970s, and he'd etched another indelible moment into Alabama history: the 1979 Sugar Bowl, where the Tide challenged Penn State and Joe Paterno with the national title on the line. In the game's waning moments, leading 14-7, the Tide prepared for a literal goal-line stand—Penn State ball, fourth and inches to the end zone. Penn State's Mike Guman took the handoff and barreled toward the line, where he met an array of Tide defensive linemen. Alabama linebacker Barry Krauss met Guman head-to-head in an impact so fierce and severe, it broke Krauss's helmet. The Tide held on for the victory and a national championship (split with USC), and the goal-line stand became the subject of a Daniel Moore painting that still hangs in homes and bars all over Alabama.

As the 1981 season began, Bryant knew his ultimate victory was within sight, and that turned him contemplative. "I'm just a plowhand from Arkansas," he once said. "But I have learned over the years how to hold a team together. How to lift some men up, how to calm down others, until finally they've got one heartbeat, together, as a team."

Even as he neared the career wins mark, the state of Alabama had to pass a special law exempting Bryant from then-current rules, since mandatory retirement age for state employees was 70. When Alabama Governor Fob James—the old Auburn grad—signed the law, there was outrage from teachers, but not a single politician would dare vote against the Bear.

In 1981, the Tide was coming off a 1980 season that would have been a tremendous success had it not been for Herschel Walker tearing up the SEC and leading Georgia to a national championship. Most of the Alabama team that had gone 10–2 and reached the Cotton Bowl was returning, and they had a singular mission: to get that record for their coach.

One look at the Tide's schedule was all it took for the national media to begin preparing travel plans for October 31, 1981, the day Alabama would welcome Mississippi State to Tuscaloosa. Surely the Tide would be undefeated at that point, and a ninth win on the season would mean the record would fall in T-Town.

Alas, it wasn't to be. Alabama lost the second game of the season and then, somehow—how the hell could this happen?—*tied* Southern Miss, both matchups at Legion Field. On November 14, Bryant tied Stagg's record with a win over Penn State and Paterno, who would go on to break Bryant's record a few years later. And that pushed Bryant's date with destiny to the last week in November . . . against little ol' Auburn and its brand-new—but in no way unfamiliar—head coach.

Dye was working his way through his first year at Auburn, and a locker room speech after a brutal loss to Tennessee set the tone for his entire tenure. "There's gonna be a lot of days when you lay your guts on the line, and you come away empty-handed," he said. "If you'll keep fightin' like you did today, if you keep playin' like that, you can build a foundation that we can live a long, long time on at Auburn."

Not that Bryant ever needed any more motivation to beat Auburn, but the record—plus the prospect of a New Year's Day bowl game, plus the outside shot at another national title—made that Iron Bowl one of the legendary ones. Auburn, meanwhile, was appearing on national TV for the first time in two years, the result of yet more sanctions levied against the program.

On that day in 1981, *315* signs dotted yards all over Birmingham. Fans painted *315* on their faces and wore "I was there when Bear won 315" buttons.

Shortly before the game, Bear walked onto Legion Field—partisan Legion Field, a stadium so Bama-focused, even the ushers were pulling for the Tide—and strode around his territory, projecting his traditional menacing alpha-wolf confidence. Dye knew the move, and he caught the Bear at midfield. There are several variants of the conversation, but all run roughly like this:

"Coach, I just want you to know," Dye said, "we're fixing to get after your ass."

"What are you trying to do, boy?" Bryant smiled. "Scare me?"

"I ain't trying to scare you, Coach," Dye replied. "I just want you to know we ain't scared of you any more."

Bryant just laughed. Former Bryant assistants had lost 28 straight games to the Bear.

That Saturday in Birmingham was cool, but the sky was a brilliant blue, all the better to give the Almighty a good look at the game of the week. The Tide was a 12-point favorite, but still, Bryant conceded to ABC's Keith Jackson before the game, he was "scared to death."

Early on, Auburn had opportunities to get after Bryant's ass but kept squandering them. The Tigers could have been up as much as 23-7 at the half, but thanks to three missed field goals and an interception in the end zone, they went into the half tied, despite leading Alabama significantly in all statistical categories except the one that counted.

At the half, Bryant told ABC's Verne Lundquist that the Tide was playing like it was "afraid of hurtin' somebody's feelin's."

Dye exhorted his team to victory, saying there would never be a better chance, with the Tide on the ropes. In Legion Field's other locker room, Bryant seethed. "You're acting like you're playin' your little brothers, or something," he growled. "Like you're afraid you're going to get hurt, or hurt them."

Matters didn't sort themselves out early in the second half. Through three quarters, Alabama had committed an unthinkable five turnovers. But Auburn was penalizing itself into oblivion, and the score was still knotted at 14. Auburn briefly took the lead early in the fourth quarter, but Alabama roared back immediately with two touchdowns to clinch the game and the record for their coach. Ballgame, 28–17.

Bryant strode off the field, ensconced in a phalanx of security guards. One officer held the Bear's houndstooth hat under his arm.

"It looked like the good Lord wasn't gonna let us win for awhile," Bryant told Lundquist underneath the Legion Field stands. He later received congratulations from both President Ronald Reagan and former president Jimmy Carter.

In the postgame press conference, Dye praised Bryant, who walked in just as he was wrapping up.

"What the hell are you doing up here speaking?" Bryant growled, and Dye ceded the stage.

Bryant was clearly in a surly mood. When one reporter asked him to move closer to the microphone so he could be heard, Bryant rumbled, "I'm old. I'm going to sit where it's comfortable for me."

Still, he proceeded to offer kindnesses to Dye and the Auburn team. "It's a good start," Bryant said of Dye's performance, "but I don't want him to get biggety."

After the celebrations of Bryant's 315th victory began to subside, reality crept in. Alabama lost to Texas, 14–12, in the Cotton Bowl. This was not the same Bear, not the same Alabama. They were losing recruits, unable to close the deal with players they would have nabbed a generation, or even a few years, before. And it finally cost them the biggest prize in college football history.

1981 IRON BOWL

Final Score: Alabama 28, Auburn 17

Chapter 21

BO

Paul W. Bryant didn't make mistakes. But he did make miscalculations. In 1981, he made one of his worst, miscalculating exactly how far he could push a young running back out of Bessemer. Bryant invited the young man up into his tower—one of the few recruits ever accorded that honor—and told the high schooler that he could be a star for the Tide, "offense or defense."

Bo Jackson was *not* going to play defense. And so Bryant learned early on what defenders all over the country would soon realize: you don't push Bo anywhere he doesn't want to go.

Vincent Edward Jackson was raised in Bessemer, Alabama, a suburb of Birmingham that was a thriving mining town until the mines closed. Birmingham moved on from the mining industry—it's become a hub of tech, finance, and health care since then—but towns like Bessemer didn't. In a way, it's not unlike Monongah, West Virginia, or Selma, Alabama, or Fordyce, Arkansas, where other legends of the Iron Bowl were raised. Times were good then, and they're not so great now.

Born a fighter, Bo was the eighth of 10 children born to Florence Jackson. His father, a steelworker by the name of A. D. Adams, was married to another woman when Bo was born on November 30, 1962. Jackson tells the story of how he got the nickname "Bo"—that growing up, he was "tough like a wild boar," which got shortened to Bo. Jeff Pearlman, in *The Last Folk Hero*, suggests there's a more sinister origin story—that the name comes from the time Jackson led a crew that slaughtered a local farmer's boar hogs. In his autobiography, Jackson confessed to slaughtering the hogs—and to ratting out his friends who did the deed with him.

Jackson grew up roaming the streets, becoming an athlete without even trying. He honed his arm by whipping rocks at passing cars. He honed his speed by running away from those cars' drivers. "Kids wanted to be my friend just so I wouldn't beat them up," he would later write. "I was hard on everybody who wasn't my friend."

He learned to run and weave and throw on those streets, in those woods. And when he signed up for Little League at age 10, he was too much for the other kids his age to handle. He had been held back a year because of his stutter, and that was enough to put him well ahead of his classmates physically.

Jackson wasn't permitted to play football, on the orders of his mother. But he tried out in the ninth grade anyway, and made the junior varsity team. He competed in track and field—he was a natural high jumper—and the first hints of the legend he would become started to show themselves there. In his second game as a member of the McAdory Yellow Jackets football team, Jackson, in a blowout, returned a punt an astounding 89 yards for a touchdown. He wasn't yet *Bo*, but he was getting noticed.

Jackson formally hit the big time on April 16, 1980, in an article in the *Birmingham News* titled "McAdory High's Vincent Jackson Is All-Around Athlete, but in Track No One Believes He's Just a Soph." By his junior year, he was a legitimate phenom, and soon began getting recruiting notices. The first came after the 1980 football season from Indiana University and its coach, Lee Corso.

Meanwhile, in the spring, Jackson kept on dominating, in both baseball and track. He was still a national unknown, with most of the attention on high schoolers focused on a basketball player named Patrick

Ewing. Things changed again on July 20, 1981, when Jackson appeared in *Sports Illustrated*'s "Faces in the Crowd" feature. The snippet noted that he "won four events at the state AAA track meet," set a state record, and helped McAdory win the state title while hitting .432 for the baseball team. No mention was made of football.

Auburn's defensive backs coach, Bobby Wallace, was the first one to target Jackson in person, at the state decathlon. When Dye saw his film, he was astounded. "This kid Jackson is out front, leading a play, and blocks three people at one time," Dye would later recall. "He just runs through 'em, stacks 'em up like cordwood. I'm not sure he ever hits the ground, just runs through the three of 'em."

But Jackson still wasn't the most famous running back in the South. He had to live in the shadow of Marcus Dupree, who played in the town of Philadelphia, Mississippi. Dupree was the biggest target in all of college football up to that point and the subject of one of the great sports books of the day, Willie Morris's *The Courting of Marcus Dupree*.

Where Dupree got plenty of touches, Jackson was part of an offense-by-committee. Where Dupree could be genial, Bo was standoffish, hiding his insecurity behind a mask of dismissive arrogance. He didn't have much of a family life, didn't take well to structure, and was on the right side of the law only by the grace of God, given how many times he nearly got himself arrested.

Despite all the tempting recruiting offers, the potential what-ifs—*Bo Jackson at USC! Bo Jackson at Colorado! Bo Jackson at Nebraska or Tennessee!*—there was never really any chance Bo was going to leave the state of Alabama. He wanted to be close to his mother, and so he would be. The only real question, then, was the one that vexed many high school stars in the Yellowhammer State: Auburn or Alabama?

At Auburn, Dye had instituted a recruiting tactic that blanketed the entire state of Alabama. After every Thursday afternoon practice during the season, he'd send Auburn's 12 assistant coaches out on one of the school's two airplanes, to be dropped off throughout the state. They'd watch Thursday night games, hit the Friday night games, and then jet off to wherever the Tigers were scheduled to play that week.

Bo was largely unknown to recruiters, a sharp contrast to Herschel Walker, who had a Georgia assistant coach living in an apartment in his hometown during his entire senior season. Bo wasn't even listed among the 100 best high school players in America, which suited Auburn's recruiters just fine.

When he recruited Jackson, Dye characterized his two challengers for the running back position as "a 6-5 split end with a lot of heart" and—in a now-regrettable description—"a midget. A talented midget."

"Bo looked at our people and knew he could come over and play," Dye wrote.

On the other hand, Alabama assistant coach Ken Donahue gave Jackson the standard Alabama pitch: work hard, and you might be able to play by your junior year. Donahue knew how fiercely Auburn was recruiting Jackson, and he scoffed at the little ol' village on The Plains having anything to offer that mighty Alabama couldn't match. That thinking was as big a blunder as the old tale of the record executive who dismissed the Beatles in 1962, declaring that guitar groups were a passing fad.

It wasn't entirely Donahue's fault, of course. Appealing to players' competitive nature and playing the Alabama card had worked countless times before. Donahue and Alabama's recruiters had met talented players, and they'd met stubborn players. They'd just never met one quite so talented, or so stubborn, as Bo.

Bryant, meanwhile, didn't much care about Jackson one way or another . . . until Auburn took an interest in him. The Bear wasn't about to let his in-state rival grab a prospect—or, at least, he wouldn't have had he been the old Bear. By this time, he was weathered, nearly broken. The years of smoking and drinking had carved deep trenches in the old man's face, and deeper scars on his heart and liver.

Bryant had the opportunity to take a run at Jackson, but never really bothered to do it. He didn't get around to visiting Bessemer, even though it was less than an hour away. He made a phone call to Jackson, but no in-person visit. When Jackson visited Alabama, that cinched it. He met with Bryant atop the coach's fabled tower . . . and that's where Bryant made his miscalculation.

"Bo," Bryant said, "we'd love to have you down here. We think you could help us in a lot of ways. Offense or defense." That possibility—that he might be stuck on *defense*, away from the ball—soured Jackson. That, and the fact that he would've been stuck behind Alabama's legion of running backs already on the roster.

"Auburn was my second choice," Jackson said. "I was going to Alabama before that day."

"You don't push Bo," Dye wrote. "You just don't push him. That's not the way you deal with him. You sit down and reason with him."

Auburn, meanwhile, rolled out the blue-and-orange carpet for Jackson.

"If you come to Auburn," Dye told him, "I'm not gonna give you anything. You got to earn it. Don't expect to be put up on a pedestal. You've got to work your ass off. But if you do, the accolades will come, the pros will look at you and you will be compensated."

Dye made sure to visit Florence Jackson in her home, and then asked Bo point-blank if he was interested in coming to Auburn.

"Yes," Jackson replied, "I am."

"All right," Dye said, "that's what I wanted to know."

The Jackson family took an official visit to Auburn in September 1981, flying via private jet—Jackson's first time ever on an airplane—and enjoying the high life of a prospective star recruit.

"We need you in our program," Dye said. "You can be our Herschel Walker." Dye signed off on Jackson's desire to also play baseball and run track, and that was pretty much that. The deal was sealed, even though signing day was months away.

Before Auburn, though, there was the matter of baseball. Jackson was a simply incredible ballplayer—he had a combination of speed, talent, and power that had rarely, if ever, been seen before. But he ended up getting picked in the second round of the MLB draft, 50th overall, by the New York Yankees, falling so far primarily because it was clear he wasn't giving up football. The Yankees couldn't even reach him for several days after the draft; he dodged all their calls. New York was prepared to offer him a six-figure contract, but he refused.

Auburn, it turned out, had been waging a war against the Yankees, making sure Jackson knew that the organization was backstabbing, corrupt, and likely to screw him over, rotting from the head—George Steinbrenner—on down. The psychological warfare worked, and when the Yankees complained that they'd been hornswoggled—and that Jackson had received all manner of impermissible benefits from Auburn—nobody much felt sorry for them. Despite the rumors that Florence Jackson got herself a brand-new Cadillac or a chain of 7-Eleven stores, Bo has always insisted that he didn't get any money to play for the Tigers.

Jackson entered Auburn in the summer of 1982, and was put to work painting yellow parking lot stripes at the nearby Auburn Mall. It was a nefarious task designed by Dye to test the mettle of his incoming freshmen. Those who bitched or complained their way through the job would be starting the season a step behind in their coach's eyes.

Jackson was part of a planned running resurgence at Auburn. Coming off a 5–6 season, the team was anemic at most positions, but primarily in the backfield. When it came time to pick jerseys, Jackson wanted No. 40, got No. 41, and traded it for No. 34—the number worn by Walker over in Athens, and Walter Payton and Earl Campbell in the NFL. If you were a running back and you dared to wear 34, you'd better back that up with some game.

Once practice began, Dye transformed from the affable, friendly fellow who sweet-talked mommas and pledged that recruits would have themselves a fine ol' time down on The Plains into a vicious, relentless taskmaster. A player who showed up late to practices or team meetings would be kicked out of the coach's sight and ordered to run before dawn the next morning.

While other coaches would hold two-a-day practices, Dye would have three-a-days. Starting the workouts at 5:30 a.m., and running his players until 6 p.m., he withheld water, which was a lawsuit waiting to happen. His choice of punishment: stadium steps, where players would hold a cinder block in each hand and walk to the top of the stadium, and then turn around and walk back down. That was one "stadium," and players got nailed with one stadium for every minute they were late to practice.

The team wasn't particularly good on the scoreboard, but the players were mean as hell and tough, and that set the Tigers up for success, provided they had the right horses. And in Jackson, they had a thoroughbred capable of winning the Kentucky Derby by 10 lengths.

Early on in his Auburn career, Bo began showing off his prowess to his teammates. He leveled defensive tackle Donnie Humphrey, a 275-pound future NFL player, on one of his first carries. He leaped over a Volkswagen. The legend was approaching liftoff speed.

In the run-up to his first game, against Wake Forest, Jackson was sleeping in the locker room. *Sleeping.* "Other guys would get all pumped up in the locker room," he later recalled. "I'd be yawning. The closer we got to the game, the sleepier I got."

It didn't matter. Jackson thundered right over the Deacons, running for 123 yards and two touchdowns on just 10 carries. And the legend of Bo Jackson was born at Auburn.

Auburn struggled later in the 1982 season, losing a game to Florida that effectively ended their chance at a bowl game. But there were signs that better days were ahead. The Tigers nearly beat Georgia and Herschel Walker, leading 14-13 before eventually losing 19-14, driving toward the end zone when time ran out. In the locker room after the game, the players wept, knocked sideways by the enormity of the upset they'd nearly pulled off. Dye struggled to find the words for the moment. "I really don't have a talk ready for losing," he said.

Then, from outside the locker room, they could hear it—60,000 fans chanting, "It's great to be an Auburn Tiger! It's great to be an Auburn Tiger!" That was as good a postgame speech as any, and it gave the Tigers new hope and new life. For the first time in forever, Auburn had hope, and soon, they would have the talent to make that hope a reality.

Over in Tuscaloosa, matters had turned dark. Sportswriters picked Alabama to win yet another title. But behind the scenes, all was not well. Bryant wasn't anywhere near his best, not anymore. Alabama fell to Tennessee in October, and then, three weeks later, lost to LSU. After that game, Bear offered up one of the most drastic commentaries in his entire tenure at Alabama: "We need to make some changes, need to start at the top." Many took it as a sign that Bryant was hinting at his own impending retirement.

One week later, the worst game of the year—maybe the worst game of Bryant's life—came in a 38-29 loss to Southern Miss at Bryant-Denny. That was the moment it dawned on the Tide faithful that maybe, just maybe, something was very, very wrong with this year's edition of the Tide. Alabama had won 57 straight at home, and then to lose to... Southern Miss? What the hell?

At the same time, Dye projected confidence in a way Auburn hadn't seen in forever. The Tigers were always optimistic—it's part of the curse of the Auburn family, that belief that better days are always ahead—but now they had good reason to be hopeful. By November, the Iron Bowl had rolled around again, and this time, the Auburn Tigers had Bo in the backfield.

Or did they?

IRON BOWL 1982: BO OVER THE TOP

Bo Jackson sat in the Auburn bus station, staring at each bus that arrived, watching each one that left. He knew he could get on one and be back in Bessemer in just a few hours, out from under all the pressure and the drama and the fear. Just a few steps, and he'd be up those stairs and into that seat, and away from Auburn once and for all.

But each time a bus would come by, he would imagine what his family and friends would say if he quit, joining the ranks of so many who had come back to Bessemer and stagnated. "I don't want to be *nothing*," he thought. "I want to be *something*."

He sat there for seven hours, watching the buses come and go. Finally, he talked to assistant coach Bobby Wallace, who patiently explained—at 1:30 in the morning—that there were many options available for him if he stayed, but none at all if he left.

It was days before the Iron Bowl, and Bo wasn't sure exactly how he fit into this rivalry. But he was about to find out.

The shadows were growing long, and the old man knew it. Bryant was nearing the end of the line, one way or another. And on a gray November

Saturday in 1982, Alabama got a look at just how much the balance of power had shifted in the Yellowhammer State.

Coming into the game, tensions ran high on both sides of the state. Bryant kicked three players off the team for not having a "winning attitude." Dye nearly booted three players of his own who were caught smoking marijuana the night before the game. He relented and suspended them for just the first half.

The general belief around the state, and around the country, was that even a wounded Bear was more than a match for Dye. But this was a new day, a new era. And Dye was pulling some old tricks that Bear had once employed, faking out prying eyes and installing a new offense—the I formation, with two backs lined up behind the quarterback—rather than the traditional wishbone. The Tigers practiced the new formation inside their "Bubble"—a covered field well protected from public view. Would it work? Well, Auburn had Bo Jackson, and he had a way of making every play a little easier.

And then it was game time. As the cameras caught Dye jogging to the sideline, ABC's Keith Jackson remarked, "I get the feeling today that Paul Bryant is more worried about Pat Dye than Pat Dye is worried about Paul Bryant."

At halftime, Auburn led 14–13, but Bo Jackson had largely been kept in check. Alabama had been the superior team according to the box score, but had nothing much on the scoreboard to show for it.

In the fourth quarter, Jackson woke up. By then, Alabama was ahead 22–14. But Jackson was ready. He was back in the wishbone, and took the ball at the Auburn 34. He found a hole and shot off downfield like a missile. He was finally run out of bounds at the Alabama 13, and a field goal cut the Alabama lead to 22–17. A fortunate (and debatable) pass interference call on Alabama's Jeremiah Castille that overturned a Tide interception gave Auburn the ball on the Alabama 9, with 3:19 remaining. After three plays, including a Jackson rumble down inside the 1-yard line,

Auburn stood 18 inches away from the end zone, just 2:30 remaining on the clock.

What happened next was the stuff of legend.

Jackson had been a high jump champion in high school. So the theory was, if he couldn't go through the Alabama defensive line, well, he could simply go over it. Auburn had been working on just such a play to exploit Jackson's skills. The play—Bo Over The Top—was elegantly simple: Jackson would gather momentum 4 yards behind the line of scrimmage, and then, well... go over the top.

The problem was, Alabama knew it was coming.

The Tide knew quarterback Randy Campbell wouldn't throw the ball, so they brought all 11 men to the line. Auburn countered by putting seven men on the line, with the quarterback and the three players who formed the wishbone in the backfield.

Campbell took the snap, pivoted, and handed the ball to Jackson at the 2-yard line. Jackson took the ball, leaped into the air, and hit his apex just as he was crossing the goal line. He reached forward, and scored perhaps the unlikeliest touchdown in Iron Bowl history... to that point, anyway.

But the game wasn't over yet. The two-point conversion failed, leaving Auburn ahead by just a single point, 23–22. On the next possession, Auburn's Bob Harris intercepted the pass, and it certainly seemed like he'd just ended the game. All Auburn had to do was run around the field for a couple minutes, and the game would be over.

First down, a 5-yard gain. Second down, a 4-yard gain. Third and one, and Auburn called a timeout with 1:13 remaining. And then the Tigers did the worst thing possible—went back to Bo Over The Top. From the sideline, Dye bellowed, "Tell Bo to squeeze the ball!"

Jackson stepped, leaped, flew—and *fumbled*. He didn't squeeze tightly enough, and an Alabama defender planted his helmet right on the ball. The ball popped loose and ended up in Tide hands.

Jackson lay on the ground, stunned, thinking he might have just lost the game for the Tigers. But the Auburn defense bailed him out, shutting down the Alabama offense once and for all.

The game technically never ended. After Auburn's final play from scrimmage, Alabama called a timeout with six seconds left on the clock. Auburn fans surged over the fences and onto the field. An official made his way to Bryant and asked if he wanted to clear the field for one final play. Bryant looked out over the chaos and shook his head no. The inevitable was here. The clock wound down to one second and stopped there.

"I looked over at the sidelines and I saw Bear Bryant and he looked like someone had walked along and stepped on his sandcastle," Jackson later wrote. "Then I looked at Ken Donahue"—the assistant coach who had told Bo he would have to wait his turn and that Auburn would never win—"he looked like he had just swallowed a wad of shit."

The Auburn fans—so often outnumbered at Legion Field—stormed the field, tore down one goalpost, and ripped up chunks of the sod for souvenirs.

Dye, his eyes wet with tears, exuberant over the victory, was lifted onto the shoulders of his team. Bryant looked haunted, lost, in what would be his final Iron Bowl. Jackson was relieved, able to breathe again after winning the Iron Bowl and then almost losing it in the space of about a minute of game clock. Behind them, the goalpost fell beneath the weight of the Auburn fans.

In the locker room, the Auburn players whooped, embraced, wept with joy. Finally, Dye stood and pointed at the door back to the field. "What I'd like for you to do, I'd like for you, the ones that want to, I'm gonna go back out there, and thank our people." The jubilant team followed him, and the celebration on Legion Field lasted for nearly an hour more.

Two weeks after the Iron Bowl loss, Bryant announced his retirement.

"There comes a time in every profession when you need to hang it up, and that time has come for me as head football coach at the University of Alabama," he said. "This is my school, my alma mater, and I love it. And I love the players, but in my opinion they deserve better coaching than they've been getting from me this year, and my stepping down is an effort to see that they get better coaching from someone else."

Auburn fans gloated—and not without justification—that they had forced Bryant into the sunset. For the moment, they had a victory they could cherish. For the moment.

1982 IRON BOWL

Final Score: Auburn 23, Alabama 22

Chapter 22

THE LORD GETS
HIS FOOTBALL COACH

The procession stretched from Tuscaloosa to Birmingham. By some estimates, more than a quarter million people lined Interstate 65, watching the solemn parade make its way from T-Town, home of the Tide, to the Iron City one final time. The Lord would be welcoming His football coach home.

By the 1980s, Paul Bryant had become an indelible symbol of a vanishing America, a place where children loved their mommas and still said "yes, ma'am" and "no, sir." As the hedonistic '70s gave way to the neon '80s, Bryant was willfully, determinedly out of step, a relic of a bygone era who could adjust his play calling, but wouldn't adjust his mindset. You played on the Bear's terms, or you didn't play at all.

As his fame grew, so did the demands on his time, and as a result, Bryant had to endure all kinds of frivolity. One example: Senator Jeremiah Denton of Alabama organized a banquet on March 8, 1982, for Bryant in Washington, D.C., humbly titled "America's Tribute to Paul (Bear)

Bryant." It was the kind of affair where Bob Hope made bland jokes like "He's so tough that the inside of his hats are lined with real hound's teeth."

The five-hour-long affair ground on Bryant, and by the end, he was done. "I've always said I wanted the biggest funeral in Alabama," he said, and then looked at Mary Harmon. "Mother, if I croak now, all you have to do is just lay me out."

Meanwhile, Alabama's disastrous 1982 season was about to collapse, culminating in that backbreaking "Bo Over The Top" Iron Bowl. After Alabama lost its final three regular-season games, the Tide received what amounted to a charity invitation to the Liberty Bowl.

Bryant had loved those bowl invitations, lobbying for them every year because they gave him extra time to prepare for next season, but this time, there would be no next season. This would be the end of the line for the Bear. On December 15, he announced that he would be staying on as Alabama's athletic director, but not as its head coach. Bryant had effectively fired himself.

"There comes a time in every profession when you have to hang it up," he said, "and that time has come for me as head football coach at the University of Alabama."

Bryant kept the succession drama to a minimum. Although Gene Stallings and Howard Schnellenberger came under consideration, in the end, Alabama opted for another Tide alumnus—Ray Perkins, one of Bear's players and, most recently, the head coach of the NFL's New York Giants. Perkins would take the crimson reins in 1983, but first, there was one more game to be played.

The Liberty Bowl is a uniquely uninspiring place for a farewell to a legend, a saddle-shaped, aluminum-bleachered concrete bowl in the middle of some fairgrounds in central Memphis. But it was there that Bryant made his final farewell, coaching his team to one last victory, a 21–15 win over Illinois. As he left the field, lights on the scoreboard blinked out GOOD-BYE, BEAR, WE'LL MISS YOU.

In the locker room before the game, Jeremiah Castille, overcome with the moment, rose to his feet and thanked Bryant for the chance to play at Alabama. "Not knowing that Coach Bryant would not live a month after I shared that with him," Castille said years later, "it humbles me now that I got a chance to thank my coach."

Shortly before Bryant would coach his final game, *Sports Illustrated* writer John Underwood called him up to ask why he was calling it a career.

"Because four damn losses is too damn many," Bryant said. "I'm up to my ass in alligators, John. These new young coaches just have too much energy for me. We need someone younger."

"So you really are tired?" Underwood asked.

"Naw," Bryant replied. "To tell you the truth, I feel great. I got so many things I've been wantin' to do for so long, and now I'm gonna get to 'em."

He wouldn't. Bryant had long suffered from coronary artery disease. He had a major heart attack in 1980, but after taking some medication, he was back on the practice field in a week. In 1981, he suffered a light stroke that caused some paralysis on one side of his body. But once again, he treated the symptom, not the underlying disease, and returned to the sideline.

Less than a month after the Liberty Bowl, early in the evening of Tuesday, January 25, Bryant was at the home of a friend when he began suffering massive chest pains. He was rushed to Druid City Hospital, and woke up in the morning feeling better. He sat upright with a yellow notepad in his hands, writing down a list of things to do and things to say to the most important people in his life. Perkins stopped by to say hello, and Bryant chided him for being at the hospital and not out recruiting.

But at 12:24 p.m., as he ate lunch, Bryant's breathing became labored. Within 15 seconds, his heart stopped beating, and a Code Blue alarm sounded through the unit. A brief heartbeat fluttered, but it wouldn't last.

At 1:30 p.m. on Wednesday, January 26, 1983, Paul W. Bryant was pronounced dead. When he died, he was wearing the ring the Junction Boys had given him at their 25th anniversary reunion.

Bryant's death led all major news broadcasts. President Reagan called Mary Harmon to offer his condolences. "The Bear is dead," NBC's Tom Brokaw reported. Alabama schools interrupted classes to break the news to their students.

The day after Bryant died, a service was held at Alabama's Memorial Coliseum. His closed coffin, covered with red and white carnations, lay in state, and more than 6,000 mourners passed by it, weeping and paying their final respects. Steadman Shealy, a quarterback on Bryant's 1979 team, delivered the eulogy. Bryant, Shealy said, "was a winner here on earth, and I am convinced now that he is a winner with God."

A Friday morning service was held in Tuscaloosa at the First United Methodist Church, barely a mile down the road from the football stadium, but the 400-seat chapel was far too small to contain everyone who wanted to be there. Every SEC head coach was present, as were Nebraska's Bob Devaney, Ohio State's Woody Hayes, Penn State's Joe Paterno, and Grambling's Eddie Robinson. The ceremony was broadcast by closed-circuit television to nearby churches. Outside a crowd estimated at 10,000 gathered and listened to the eulogy over loudspeakers. The organist played "Amazing Grace" and "A Mighty Fortress Is Our God," and tears flowed all over Alabama.

Eight players from the 1982 team, Bryant's final squad, served as pallbearers, carrying his casket from the church into a waiting white hearse. More than 200 photographers were on the scene to document the solemn, heartbreaking moment.

Then a 3-mile-long motorcade traveled to Birmingham for the burial in Elmwood Cemetery. Somewhere between 300 and 400 cars would make the 60-mile drive. The entire 1982 team followed their coach one last time in three buses. The motorcade rolled down streets lined with people five and six deep, and slowed beside Bryant-Denny Stadium, as if to give Bryant one last look at the palace from which he'd ruled college football.

On the way, an estimated 250,000 mourners—about one in every 12 people in the state—lined the route. They held up signs and banners: WE LOVE YOU, BEAR, and WE'LL MISS YOU, BEAR, and THANKS FOR THE MEMORIES, BEAR. Trucks and cars pulled to the side of the road in honor of Bryant.

"It is generally agreed," wrote Winston Groom, an Alabama graduate and creator of the famed Crimson Tide player Forrest Gump, "that the largest funerals held in the South were those of Jefferson Davis, Martin Luther King Jr., Elvis Presley, and Paul William Bryant."

The graveside service lasted just five minutes, at the request of Mrs. Bryant. And then the Bear was gone, and Alabama—the university and the state—would have to figure out the rest of their lives for themselves.

Chapter 23

BO DOES ANYTHING, NOT EVERYTHING

If, in 1983, Alabama fans were looking for a sign that the Bear Bryant era was over once and for all, they could go down to Cain Steel on 20th Street in west Tuscaloosa. There, lying on its side on a flatbed trailer, surrounded by weeds, lay Bear Bryant's tower, the perch from which he'd watched generations of champions. The days of Bryant were done. The era of Alabama head coach Ray Perkins, for better or worse, had begun.

In the months after Bryant's death, the city of Tuscaloosa renamed 10th Street Paul W. Bryant Drive. A nice gesture—except, of course, for the fact that devoted Tide fans kept stealing the street signs—it was an ever-present reminder of the legacy that Perkins was assuming. Not that he expressed any worry about the challenge of walking in the footsteps of the greatest coach in college football.

"When I took the job they asked me if I was intimidated by Coach Bryant. I said he wouldn't have wanted me if I was," Perkins told *Sports Illustrated* days before his first game. "I'm not replacing him; I'm following him. People say it's better not to follow a legend, but not everybody who follows a legend has to fail. The guy who says he'd rather follow the guy who follows the legend is too scared to be there in the first place. He doesn't deserve this job. It's the best coaching job in America."

Nearly 30 years younger than Bryant, with a stylish-at-the-time bob of brown hair, Perkins—who had been one of Bryant's fiercest athletes in the early 1960s—brought the same piercing intensity and my-way-or-else ethos to the Alabama sideline. He junked the tower, calling it a "distraction." He cleaned house in the athletic department, sending everyone from assistants all the way down to the radio color commentator out the door. He shut alumni and boosters out of practices. He increased his fees for the postgame show, running off longtime sponsor Golden Flake. He abandoned Bryant's wishbone and installed a pro-style offense. He removed players' names from their jerseys, declaring, "We've never won a national championship with names on the jerseys."

These were not the actions of a timid man. These were also not the actions that garnered a coach a lot of goodwill to get through the rough patches.

Alabama fans tried, in their own way, to get behind Perkins. Bumper stickers began showing up in town—IT TAKES A GIANT COACH TO FILL BEAR'S SHOES and THE TIDE JUST KEEPS PERKIN' ALONG—but the truest test of Perkins's ability would not come until kickoff.

While Tuscaloosa was adjusting to a new emperor, Auburn was trying to figure out what to do with the icon it had in-house . . . and how to deal with tragedy.

On August 20, 1983, fullback Greg Pratt, from Albany, Georgia, died after running—or attempting to run—the four 440s that Coach Dye required every player to complete in under 80 seconds, with only a 90-second break between each 440. Coming off the field, Pratt was sick and glassy-eyed, and his teammates attempted to cool him off by running water over him. In the shower, he recited the 23rd Psalm, and his teammates called 911 and hailed an ambulance. He didn't survive, and was pronounced dead at 2:35 p.m. of what a coroner deemed heatstroke. Dye later visited his body and sobbed, alone.

Players, particularly in the South, often died of heatstroke before mandatory requirements for their safety and protection. It was a sad, grim reality of playing August football in a region where the summer sun is unrelenting. Lee County coroner Jon Williams ruled Pratt's death "accidental," adding, "In my personal and professional opinion, this kind of accident could have occurred at any time strenuous activity was involved, even cutting grass. What happened on the Auburn practice field Saturday morning could have happened anywhere."

At the funeral, Auburn's players filled the tiny church in Albany. Perkins was there, and the Atlanta Falcons sent flowers. The pain was raw and real in the tiny church. Dye pledged that Pratt's mother would receive a $100,000 insurance payout from the university.

"[His] death affected me more than any one incident that has happened in my life," Dye wrote in his autobiography. "In some ways, it was more difficult than my daddy's death." But he did not apologize for running his 440 drills on a 96-degree day in Alabama. It may never even have occurred to him to do so.

Auburn was ranked No. 5 in the 1983 preseason poll and slated to face six top 25 teams. But the Tigers knew just how good they were, and—unfamiliar with the feeling—began gloating. That's where the troubles began.

The University of Texas stomped into the state of Alabama and caused the first bit of trouble, walloping Auburn 20–7 in a game that wasn't even that close. After the game, Jackson, still in uniform pants and a gray T-shirt, strode into the Texas locker room. He walked from locker to locker, congratulating every single player. It was a move, unconsciously or not, that echoed Bryant, acknowledging man-to-man when a foe had gotten the best of you.

After that loss, the Tigers turned up the heat and began throttling teams. They beat Tennessee soundly, knocked off Florida State with a touchdown inside the final two minutes, and annihilated Kentucky, Georgia Tech, and Mississippi State. Then came Florida.

Relations were always ugly as hell between the Gators and the Tigers. The rivalry had a long history of chop blocks and viciousness, its low point coming that year when a Florida student printed T-shirts with a line through the number 36—Pratt's number—and the message "At least we don't kill our players."

That day, Jackson ran wild—gaining 196 yards on 16 carries, including a couple of monster touchdowns—and helped haul the Tigers to a third-place national ranking. Auburn carved through the rest of the schedule, knocking off a good Georgia team. And then came the Iron Bowl. This time around, the Tigers fans were the confident ones; in the first year of the Perkins era, Alabama wasn't anywhere near as good as Auburn.

Auburn and Jackson were all but unbeatable by any mortal team. But a divine power had some influence on the game. At halftime, Perkins took a call from Tuscaloosa. Storms were battering T-Town, and they would soon be in Birmingham. If Alabama was going to win, they had to do it immediately or risk getting washed out entirely. A tornado was spotted in the area, but few fans left. Legion Field's steel girders were already swaying slightly in the breeze.

Then the bottom dropped out, the tornado warnings sounded, and Auburn held on for a 23-20 victory. Jackson—who had run for 256 yards on 20 carries—lay down in a puddle of water and waved his arms and legs in sheer delight. He'd beaten Alabama twice now, and he would be around for two more.

"I don't relish that thought," Perkins admitted.

"Bo's not a good practice player," Dye conceded after the game. "In fact, he barely gets by. I just tell the coaches the best thing to do is not worry, just be sure and get him to the game."

Meanwhile, Alabama was frustrated. "This is something that I will have to live with for the rest of my life," defensive tackle Randy Edwards said. "Today was my last chance to hit somebody from Auburn and not go to jail for it."

No. 3-ranked Auburn was scheduled to meet No. 8 Michigan in the Sugar Bowl. No. 1-ranked Nebraska, who would play No. 5 Miami in the Orange Bowl, and No. 2 Texas, facing Georgia in the Cotton Bowl, remained ahead of the Tigers in the rankings. If Auburn won and both teams ahead of them lost, the Tigers would be the national champions. Easy, right?

The Tigers held up their end of the deal, beating Michigan 9–7 in an ugly game. Georgia beat Texas 10–9, and in Miami, Tom Osborne made one of the most hotly debated calls in college football history when, with his Huskers down by one, he opted to go for two and failed, giving the Hurricanes a 31–30 victory.

So that meant both Nebraska and Texas had lost, while Auburn had won. That should have moved Auburn into the No. 1 spot. But this is college football, where nothing quite goes the way it ought to. Miami leapfrogged Auburn to take the national championship. It was a heartbreaker, one that devastated Auburn's players and coaches. It wasn't fair, it wasn't right, but it was the way college football always seemed to work.

By the start of the 1984 season, Bo Jackson was an unquestioned superstar. And the Tigers were in great shape, ranked No. 1 in the country in preseason polls. This was supposed to be the year Jackson ascended to total dominance, and the Tigers right along with him.

It didn't take long for Auburn to remember that nothing is a given, and everything must be earned in college football. Miami, led by new head coach Jimmy Johnson, beat Auburn 20–18 in Giants Stadium in the season's very first game, bloodying the Tigers' noses before they even set foot on Jordan-Hare's grass.

"I believe," Dye said after the game, "those folks who ranked us Number 1 made a mistake." To make matters worse, in the season's second game, Bo separated his shoulder after a punishing tackle by a Texas defender. Season over, for both Jackson and Auburn. Or so it seemed.

Jackson returned in November against Florida, but he posed a challenge to the then-existing order of things for Auburn. The team had won six straight in his absence, and now he was being awkwardly shoehorned back into the lineup. It wasn't an optimal fit, either for him or for the team. And it showed—the Gators won, 24–3.

Then, of course, came Alabama. The Tide was 4–6 entering the game, the first time they'd carried a losing record into the Iron Bowl in 27 years. Perkins wasn't handling the burden of leadership well, and Alabama was doomed to its first losing season since 1957 . . . not coincidentally, the year before Bryant arrived in Tuscaloosa.

So 1984's Iron Bowl lacked the luster of previous versions, and the game was pushed to a late-morning kickoff. Florida–Florida State got the marquee afternoon slot instead. Perkins also breached decorum by not participating in the usual pregame glad-handing and banter. Dye noticed and made note of it, and it would be years before the temperature between the two would warm.

Still, Alabama had pride. Throughout its athletic facilities, staffers hung signs that read "STOP BO." The rationale was simple: keep Jackson contained, and make everyone else on Auburn beat you . . . if they could.

Through three quarters, Auburn couldn't. Alabama led 17–7 at the start of the fourth, and Auburn seemed lost and discombobulated. The Tigers cut the lead to 17–15 with 9:11 remaining, and when Alabama's Mike Shula threw an interception that put Auburn on the Tide 17, victory seemed attainable, if not inevitable. Jackson rumbled right over Alabama's Cornelius Bennett and stormed all the way down to the Alabama 4-yard line. Auburn had momentum, and Auburn had Bo. The ending seemed foregone.

But this was the Iron Bowl.

Auburn drew a holding penalty and couldn't move the ball, leaving the Tigers looking at third and goal from the 9. A quarterback sneak got the ball down to the 1-yard line. Fourth and goal. Did Dye go for the go-ahead field goal, or the hammer strike?

Dye knew that Alabama's kicker, Van Tiffin, had a leg on him that could flip the game even if Auburn took the lead. So he opted to go for the touchdown. His plan would be a sweep, either right or left, the same play had won the game against Florida State six weeks earlier.

Just like before, Alabama piled all 11 men at the line of scrimmage. Just like before, Auburn pulled its formation in tight, seven men on the line, a quarterback and three rushers behind him. The assumption was that Jackson would be going over the top. But it wasn't to be.

Jackson heard the wrong play. He should have gone with 56 Combo—a sweep right. But he heard "57 Combo"—and so he ran the wrong way. Jackson should have gone right and helped block for Brent Fullwood. But he went to his left, where he bumped into Fullwood—who was instantly met by a horde of Tide defenders.

"I waxed the dude," gloated Alabama's Rory Turner.

This game went down in the history books as Wrong Way Bo, even though it wasn't over yet. Auburn held Alabama and got the ball back, and had an opportunity to win the game again—but kicker Robert McGinty missed a 42-yard field goal that would have given the Tigers a one-point win. The ball hooked deep into a crowd of Alabama fans, sailing at least 25 feet wide left of the goalpost.

In the locker room, Dye put the loss on himself. "When you win, you win as a team; when you lose, you lose as a team," he said. "This is certainly a team effort here today. Offense, defense, kicking and coaches. We all contributed, every one of us. And it starts with me. It starts with me."

Publicly, Dye hung the loss on Jackson's neck. "If I had known Bo was going the wrong way on the sweep," he said, "I would've gone for the field goal." He later added that the ball should have gone to Jackson in the first place, not exactly a bold affirmation of his offensive coaches' strategy.

Auburn ended the year with an anticlimactic trip to Memphis for the Liberty Bowl and a 21–15 defeat of Arkansas, for what that was worth. But Dye became the butt of plenty of Alabama jokes.

Know how to get to Memphis? Go to the 1-yard line at Legion Field and turn left!

Here's another one: Pat Dye prayed to God after the game and asked, "Lord, why'd you tell me to go for that touchdown instead of the field goal?"

"Hmm, I don't know, Pat," the Lord replied. "Why *did* we tell him to do that, Bear?"

So 1985 came around, and Jackson was starting to consider whether football was the right sport for him, even though he was Auburn's best Heisman candidate since Pat Sullivan in 1971. He'd single-handedly spurred a run on sales of No. 34 jerseys at the school bookstore, and he'd been at least partly responsible for the university's exponential growth in applications. The Auburn Board of Trustees signed off on a $15 million expansion of Jordan-Hare Stadium to increase the capacity from 72,169 to 85,214.

To keep Jackson in uniform, Auburn shifted its entire offense to focus on him. Bo was healthy, with a veteran team around him and a new offense—the I formation—built to maximize his skill and production.

Jackson scored twice in the opening minutes of Auburn's first game against Southwestern Louisiana, and never looked back. By the fourth quarter, he was out of his pads, signing autographs for fans along the sideline.

Once again, Auburn was No. 1. Once again, it wouldn't last.

In Week 3, Tennessee beat the hell out of Auburn, and Jackson removed himself from the game halfway through the third quarter. The blowback on both player and team was fierce. Auburn fell all the way from first to 14th. Jackson got torched in the national media as a quitter, his Heisman prospects apparently dead.

And then over the course of four games, Jackson ripped off nearly a thousand yards and seven touchdowns in four dominant Auburn victories that marked the end of any Bo's-a-quitter stories. In a 59–27 victory over Florida State, Jackson swatted the Seminoles' Deion Sanders out of the way like he was clearing a cobweb.

Alas, fate didn't see fit to bless the Tigers that year. An early-November loss to Florida ended Auburn's national title hopes. The Gators knocked Jackson out of the game, upending the Tigers' offensive scheme.

"Bo didn't have anything to do with us not beating Florida," Dye said, but he was flat-out wrong. The entire Auburn offense was built around Jackson, so if he was out, the offense sputtered.

As always, the Iron Bowl loomed. Auburn had one last chance to salvage some pride, one last opportunity for Jackson to take out the hated Tide, one last moment for Bo to burnish his Heisman credentials. An unranked, two-loss Alabama should have been easy pickings for the Tigers.

Should have been.

IRON BOWL 1985: THE KICK

Not every Iron Bowl carries greater significance beyond the game; not every Iron Bowl serves as a precursor to an SEC or national championship. Sometimes, the game's just a good ol' backyard brawl from which miracles erupt.

The 1985 Iron Bowl marked the 50th anniversary of the game, thanks to the long early-20th-century layoff. Alabama arrived at the matchup with a 7-2-1 record, having dropped games to Penn State and Tennessee. The Tide's losses were by a combined four points, but in the pitiless world of college football polls, they may as well have been by 400 points. Auburn, meanwhile, was only marginally better at 8-2, having dropped games to Tennessee and Florida.

Nothing was at stake in 1985 but pride. Of course, that was more than enough to guarantee the potential for brilliance.

No Iron Bowl is ever truly "routine," but the first three quarters of the 1985 edition seemed to run that way. After three quarters, Alabama led 16-10. Nobody was particularly comfortable anywhere in the stands, but still, there had been little to hint at the chaos that was to come.

The lead changed hands four times in that frenetic fourth quarter, which began with Alabama's Mike Shula throwing an interception in the end zone. Auburn turned the interception into an 80-yard touchdown drive that ended with a vintage Jackson dive across the goal line. Later in the quarter, Gene Jelks, playing in his first Iron Bowl, tore off a 74-yard run that gave Alabama a brief lead once again. Right after that, Auburn took a 23–22 lead with just 57 seconds remaining.

But Alabama still had one last chance to drive 80 yards down Legion Field. This wasn't unfamiliar territory for the Tide; Alabama had gone 71 yards in 50 seconds to win their season opener against Georgia. But then again, this was Auburn, and nothing was expected or guaranteed.

Alabama had a lot going in its favor. The Tide had Shula, calm and confident in the pocket. They had that record of success. And they had one hell of a kicker in Van Tiffin. If they could get into Tiffin's prodigious range, then they would be in business.

But the drive began ominously. Shula started out by throwing into quadruple coverage to tight end Thornton Chandler. The pass fell incomplete, and it was Alabama's good fortune that the ball didn't end up in Auburn hands. The very next play, Shula took a sack for an 8-yard loss that devoured 13 seconds, forcing Alabama to use their final timeout.

Thirty-seven seconds—and 80 long yards—remained.

All the confidence of the previous two plays had nearly evaporated. But the game wasn't quite over. Senior guard David Gilmer looked around the huddle and spoke two words.

"Remember Georgia," he said, and that was enough.

Shula found Jelks on a touch pass that Jelks turned into a 14-yard reception, converting a vast desert into a fourth and four. Alabama specialized in the sweep that year, and the expectation was that the Tide would try the sweep once again. For a moment, that looked like the plan—Shula took the snap and tossed to Jelks sweeping to the right. But then Jelks pulled an unexpected move, handing off to Al Bell on a reverse.

Shula threw a key block, and Bell rounded the corner to find daylight and 20 yards. That was enough to restore hope to the Alabama huddle. The Tide needed probably another 20 yards to get into Tiffin's range, but suddenly that didn't seem quite so daunting.

"It's pure confidence now," center Wes Neighbors would later recall to AL.com. "We know we're going to win the game. It isn't 'believe.' We *know*. We're going to make a play, and we're going to win this game."

Tiffin had a leg—he'd already made three field goals on the afternoon, and drilled a 57-yarder against Texas A&M on Legion Field earlier in the year—but he'd also missed a 52-yarder with the wind at his back in this game. And on this drive, he would be kicking into the wind.

Alabama had a drill for last-second field goal attempts—the unit was under a "white" formation, which meant every member of the kicking team had their helmets on and was ready to sprint onto the field without delay.

Out on the field, Shula threw another incompletion that cost the Tide six more seconds. Down to 15 seconds with no timeouts and another 20 yards to clear, Alabama had just one more play.

The call was to "Little Richard"—5-foot-9 receiver Greg Richardson, who hadn't yet caught a pass this game. Shula—thanks to the brick-wall blocking of his line—found Little Richard in stride at the Auburn 45-yard line. Richardson carved out a crucial extra 10 yards before he stepped out of bounds, stopping the clock.

Tiffin raced onto the field and put his kicking tee down on the right hash mark at Auburn's 42-yard line. This would be a 52-yarder, long but not impossible.

Up in the ABC booth, color man Frank Broyles nearly hyperventilated as Keith Jackson made the call. "My heart won't stand it, Keith," he said.

The snap and the hold were perfect, and Tiffin stepped into the kick and drove it through the uprights. The offensive unit barely had time to clear the field before the ball was in the air, and then the celebrations began.

Alabama fans rushed the field, and Perkins had to fight his way through a knot of them to get to his kicker. "Van!" Perkins shouted in the din. "Van Tiffin! I love ya, Van Tiffin! I love ya!"

Exultation on one sideline means despair on the other. "A game like this, Alabama players will remember the rest of their lives," Dye said after the game. "Auburn players... it'll eat their guts out the rest of their lives."

In the locker room afterward, Perkins, his seat finally cool, looked out at his exuberant team. "This feeling is why you came to Alabama," he told them. "You will remember it for the rest of your life."

That game would mark Jackson's final Iron Bowl as a player. "It's like you're at the top of a ladder and at that last step before you get to the top," he said, "somebody pulls the ladder from under you."

This might have been the most painful loss—in terms of what was expected and what was delivered—in Auburn history, certainly for the 1980s. Bo Jackson is on your team and you lose *two straight* Iron Bowls? Ray Perkins is stumbling his way through his tenure, and you let him win *twice*? It was a dark moment in Auburn history, to be sure, and the Tigers' pride at having the upper hand in the rivalry took a severe hit that day.

Jackson's Heisman Trophy prospects started leaking oil thanks to that Iron Bowl, with *Sports Illustrated* even heralding an unknown quarterback named Joe Dudek for the honor. (The fact that Jackson is Black and Dudek isn't did not escape the notice of many *SI* critics.)

What no one knew was that Jackson was in fact suffering through severe injuries. He'd cracked ribs against Georgia. A thigh bruise he suffered against Florida had continued to bleed internally. And he got kicked in the shin by a horse just before the Iron Bowl—with Bo, no injury was ever normal—and suffered a hairline fracture.

What was supposed to be a Bo Jackson coronation was instead the closest vote to that point in Heisman history—Jackson won by just 45 votes over Iowa's Chuck Long—and only Mark Ingram's narrow 2009 victory over Stanford's Toby Gerhart has since eclipsed it. Back in Auburn, the town exhaled and toilet paper filled the trees.

Jackson would play baseball for another season at Auburn, and he left The Plains as one of the greatest Auburn football players of all time. He passed from the Auburn football roster straight onto the school's Mount Rushmore, an unquestioned superstar who remains one of the most beloved figures in the history of the program.

1985 IRON BOWL

Final Score: Alabama 25, Auburn 23

IRON BOWL 1989: THE FINAL BRICK

There's a point in every stadium's life when it's simply too old to handle the modern, expanding game. Maybe there are too many fans wanting to get in, necessitating the construction of a new deck. Maybe high rollers want private boxes that allow them to network in air-conditioned comfort, enjoy sushi and craft cocktails, and perhaps glance at the game every once in a while. Or maybe a team just wants to reward its loyal fans by asking them to drive five minutes to the game, rather than two hours.

Pat Dye and Auburn won one of the most important Iron Bowl victories in the series' history long before toe ever met leather in 1989. By wrangling the Iron Bowl out of Birmingham and onto The Plains, Auburn established itself as a formidable, face-to-face, eye-to-eye rival with the Tide. No more "little brother" nonsense; this was Auburn flexing its muscle, claiming its own share of what it deserved.

And wow, did the idea of moving the Iron Bowl out of Birmingham go over badly in Tuscaloosa. "It won't happen," Ray Perkins had flatly declared just four years before. It did happen, in part because of Dye's pressure, in part because of the determination of Bobby Lowder and other

Auburn trustees, and in part because Alabama's own house was as fractured as it had been since the woeful days of Ears Whitworth.

As early as 1981, Dye and Bryant had discussed the idea of moving the game to Auburn. The move appealed to many at Auburn because of the revenue windfall it would provide, and because Legion Field was, in the words of 1957 Auburn player Morris Savage, "as neutral a location as Normandy was on D-Day in 1944."

After Bryant's passing, Dye and the Auburn trustees increased the pressure on Alabama and the city of Birmingham. Dye met with Alabama officials in Atlanta during the SEC basketball tournament in 1987, stating his case defiantly: Auburn had the right to move its game to its home stadium. Alabama fought the move, but in the end, there was nothing that could legally be done; if the Tide failed to show up for their 1989 date with Auburn, the Tigers would simply declare a forfeit and claim the victory. When the move became inevitable, Alabama students worked up a taunt—"Your ass on your grass"—that would prove easier to say than to do.

The city of Birmingham worked out a face-saving deal requiring Auburn to play one last home game at Legion Field in 1991. (Auburn wisely held fast to its plan to have the first home game at Jordan-Hare in 1989 and agreed to that throw-them-a-bone game in 1991, rather than the reverse.) Ever since, Auburn's so-called home games have actually taken place at Auburn's home.

Dye strong-armed Alabama down to Auburn for a few reasons, starting with pride and money. Auburn had pride in its newly expanded stadium, yes. But there was also the financial motivation: an Iron Bowl at home would bring in *so much more* season ticket revenue. For instance: An Auburn fan couldn't just dip in and expect to buy tickets to the Iron Bowl alone. No, you had to hold onto your season tickets if you wanted to see the Tigers humble them sumbitches from Tuscaloosa.

The Jordan-Hare Iron Bowl was an efficient way to pay for all those phenomenal improvements that had turned the stadium into one of the

SEC's marquee coliseums. Dye termed the 1989 game "the final brick," as in the last task necessary to rebuild Auburn into a national power.

Alabama, meanwhile, was suffering through more uncharacteristic upheaval. New head coach Bill Curry was trying to keep the ship afloat, but he was losing allies. President Joab Thomas, who had hired Curry, retired in 1988, and his replacement, Roger Sayers, effectively sent Bryant-era legend and current athletic director Steve Sloan packing, in part because of the Iron Bowl's relocation. In came Cecil "Hootie" Ingram, and although Ingram had impeccable Alabama credentials, there was plenty of suspicion that his recent Florida State tenure was a pretext to hiring Bobby Bowden to come coach the Tide.

A lot was happening behind the scenes, and Curry—who had already lost to Auburn in 1987 and 1988—knew that he had no room to maneuver. He needed to get a win over Auburn, or at least an SEC title ... anything to hold off the hungry dogs.

"If you want to be a successful coach at Alabama, you've got to beat Auburn," former Alabama head coach Gene Stallings said in 2013. "You don't have to beat them every year, but you have to beat them more than they beat you."

For a while in 1989, everything went right for Curry. The Tide stormed through the early part of the schedule, throttling Tennessee and beating Penn State on a memorable last-second field goal block by Thomas Rayam. Alabama was looking at a chance to claim the SEC title, and only a trip to Auburn awaited. "Only" a trip to Auburn.

Alabama worked out for the first time in Jordan-Hare Stadium the Friday before the game, and Curry clearly was impressed. "This is a beautiful place, isn't it?" Still, all wasn't quite smooth in the transition from Legion Field to Jordan-Hare. Curry made the unwise suggestion that Alabama fans without tickets come to Auburn and surround the stadium; local law enforcement, knowing exactly what could happen, quickly shut down that idea. Also that week, two Alabama players, Siran Stacy and

Charlie Dare, received death threats concerning enough that Curry called in the FBI.

Some less criminally minded Auburn students held a pep rally at nearby Plainsman Park, the baseball stadium, where Dye and the Tiger starters offered up a new hand signal: four fingers up, not for the start of the fourth quarter, but for four wins in a row against Alabama.

After the pep rally, Dye loaded his team onto buses to hide out at hotels in LaGrange, Georgia. All these years wanting the game to come to Auburn, and the Tigers had to get out of town to get some sleep.

And then, maybe around the time Auburn took the field in front of 85,319 fans, the largest crowd ever to watch a football game in the state of Alabama up to that point, came the realization that this game still had to take place.

"We moved it," Dye wrote. "We still had to play it."

In the hours before the game, the Tiger family gathered along Donahue Drive, named for that long-ago Auburn coaching legend, massing from Sewell Hall to the stadium. An estimated 30,000 people congregated around Jordan-Hare for the first Iron Bowl Tiger Walk, and Dye would later draw a parallel to another momentous gathering of joyful crowds that happened that fall.

"To see the look in the eyes and the faces of those fans, it must have resembled what happened the night the Wall came down in Berlin," he wrote. "It was as if they had been freed and come out of bondage." Too much? Perhaps. But at least one player was apparently so overcome with joy and emotion that he began hyperventilating and needed to be given oxygen before the game.

Auburn came out throwing, with quarterback Reggie Slack connecting with Alexander Wright for a 44-yard completion on the Tigers' first drive to set up a touchdown. Soon afterward, the rout was on: Auburn extended its lead to 17–10, then 24–10, then 27–10. Alabama rallied, but far too little and far too late, and the Tigers claimed a 30–20 victory over the Tide in their home stadium for the first time in school history. The blue-and-orange haze that hung over the stadium, dust from thousands of paper shakers, was the perfect complement to a most memorable day.

"All you people that said Alabama was going to beat us," Auburn play-by-play man Jim Fyffe gloated on air, "where are you now?"

Dye's postgame speech is one of Auburn fans' favorites. "I wouldn't swap this year for any year that I've been at Auburn," he said. "I wouldn't swap it, men, because I've watched you struggle, and I've watched you wrestle with them angels. But I've watched you grow up and become men." Overcome with emotion, he could manage only five more words: "I've watched you become men."

Auburn would go on to annihilate Ohio State in the Hall of Fame Bowl, ending the year 10–2 and ranked sixth in the country. Alabama lost to Miami in the Sugar Bowl, a game best remembered for Curry grabbing the face mask of Alabama's Prince Wimbley over a bit of showboating. The show of discipline would have been barbecued in the 2020s, but in 1990, it won Curry praise.

But that and two bucks might buy you a cup of coffee at The Waysider in Tuscaloosa. After the Sugar Bowl, Curry decided he'd had enough of Alabama, and made a shocking move, jumping ship for Kentucky. The Tide, humiliated and enraged, decided to turn to a familiar face.

Auburn, meanwhile, was feeling just fine, at home in its own stadium and riding high. But, like so many of the good times on The Plains, it wouldn't last. And when the good times ended, they ended spectacularly.

1989 IRON BOWL

Final Score: Auburn 30, Alabama 20

Chapter 24

THE SUN SETS ON THE PLAINS

Auburn fans aren't quite like Alabama fans. The Tide claims fans all over the country, a bandwagon as big as the whole South. You're either a part of them, or you're secretly jealous of them, no middle ground. You don't even have to be able to spell *Tuscaloosa* to be an Alabama fan. To paraphrase Bob Dylan, you just have to want to be on the side that's winning.

Auburn, meanwhile, doesn't have the same mindset. They refer to their fan base as "family." They pronounce their words the way they want. (In honor of ol' Shug, the first part of Jordan-Hare Stadium is pronounced "Jerr-dn," not the way Michael says it.) They often bumble their way into greatness, and then bumble their way right back out of it. But they're a family, and family is unbreakable . . . especially when family screws up righteously.

Even as Dye was piling up the wins throughout the 1980s and establishing himself as the preeminent coach in the state of Alabama, the hellhounds were on his trail. Sometimes that was because of bad behavior by those around him, sometimes it was because of his own mistakes, and sometimes it was because he poked the NCAA bear. But he never stopped fighting, and he never stopped throwing haymakers. In the midst of one of the many mini-controversies swirling around The Plains, he hinted not-so-subtly that Alabama's Curry was behind his woes. "If Bill didn't take it to 'em," Dye said, "he damn sure endorsed the investigation."

"It was difficult back then, because if there was any sense of an [NCAA] investigation, any sense at all, well, that meant you were busted," former Auburn quarterback Stan White recalls. "That meant they had something on you, because if they come crawling, you had to actually prove your innocence. You were already guilty."

As the scandals began to mount and the investigations started to overlap, Dye raged like a caged animal. "When I leave Auburn, they are going to carry me out feet first," he once snarled. "And there are going to be dead sons-a-bitches laying everywhere."

There were lighter moments. In the 1988 Sugar Bowl, Dye played for the tie against Syracuse, kicking a field goal on fourth down on the Orangemen's 13 with time running out. He remained resolute that he'd taken the prudent approach.

"My decision was not to get beat," Dye said afterward. "If Syracuse wanted to win, they should have blocked the field goal. I'm goin' huntin'."

Auburn fans, expecting either victory or glorious defeat, were incensed, calling him "Pat Tie" and "Tie Dye." A Syracuse radio station sent a boatload of old ties down to Dye as a stunt; he simply wrote the score on them, signed them, and sold them for charity.

But as the '80s wound down, Dye found himself putting out fires all over The Plains. Quarterback Jeff Burger got popped with allegations of plagiarism during the summer of 1987, and set off a cascade of academics-versus-athletics debates. An academics honesty committee recommended a two-quarter suspension, among other punishments. The school's vice president of academic affairs overruled the committee, the committee accused the administration of buckling to pressure from football backers, and so it went. At another point, academic officials were incensed that Dye played Brent Fullwood in the 1987 Citrus Bowl even though the running back hadn't bothered to attend class for the last two months.

In the end, though, academics would bring down the Dye regime. The first domino that fell was a paper in a sociology class. Eric Ramsey, a fifth-year senior defensive back from Birmingham, claimed that Auburn was running a racist program in a paper he wrote for the class in early 1991. Ramsey said his professor leaked the paper to the media, and from there, all hell broke loose.

The *Montgomery Advertiser* printed Ramsey's paper on June 12, 1991, and other Alabama papers quickly ran quotes from the essay without authenticating them, much to the fury of Dye and the Auburn faithful. In his paper, Ramsey alleged that the team was divided along racial lines in their rooms, dining halls, and parties.

When challenged, Ramsey released a series of tapes he claimed contained incriminating conversations with Auburn coaches and boosters about both racial incidents and improper payments. Ramsey later said he was stunned when a booster told him that the same fans who cheered him from the stands were also calling him racial epithets away from the field. "Eric," he said the booster told him, "that's the real world."

"The reason I brought the tapes out is because the backlash was so intense," Ramsey told the *New York Times* in 2010. "I just felt like, O.K., if they don't believe me, then I know they are going to believe this, because I have proof."

Dye's book *In the Arena*, published after the Ramsey scandal broke but before Dye would resign, is a full-on broadside at the idea that he could have cheated or maintained a racist program. He fired right out of the gate in the book's opening pages at Ramsey, his attorney, and everyone who publicized their charges. "You might imagine I hate Eric Ramsey," Dye wrote. "No, I don't. I hate what he said, the unfairness of it, and what it did to our kids and our coaching staff and to our program and to our 1991 season, and I hate what it did to Auburn."

Dye vehemently denied making any payments to Ramsey, and distanced himself from anyone who might have done so. "I never gave Eric Ramsey a dime, and I never knew of anybody who did," he contended. "And I didn't get him a loan or deny him one. Nor have I illegally given any player money or a loan."

Ramsey countered that Dye *had* loaned money to him, and had helped smooth the way with a loan officer at a nearby bank. According to Ramsey, boosters gave him $1,200 toward a car and a monthly stipend of $300, along with bonus payments for his performance in games—$100 for a big hit, $500 for a touchdown, and so forth.

Dye, in turn, claimed that Ramsey's wife, Twilitta, came to him and made some shocking allegations about another player—allegations that would have landed the player in jail if proven true. Twilitta was later accused of trying to sell the tapes to *Sports Illustrated* and other publications, requesting as much as $10 million and going as low as $360,000. No one paid.

Ramsey's allegations were serious enough to bring the NCAA's investigators back to Auburn... and that was when Dye suddenly had a real problem. Because there was, apparently, plenty the program wanted to keep hidden... whether Dye knew the specifics or not.

"We'll face the truth of our own investigation," Dye wrote, "and we'll get on with the job of putting Auburn football back where it ought to be."

Or not. A few months after making that statement, Dye was out of a job. Following an abysmal 1991 season, the Tigers collapsed at the end of the 1992 season, losing to both Georgia and Alabama to finish out a ghastly year. But even as the wolves neared the door, Dye remained resolute. "If the tapes are true and the allegations are true," he said, "then what I'm guilty of is doing a damn poor job of management."

Dye resigned the head coaching position the night before the 1992 Iron Bowl, citing his health rather than the mounting controversies. He had been facing health issues—in addition to having a tumor removed the previous summer, he suffered from hemochromatosis, an ailment caused by an excess of iron in the blood. Plus, there was the looming NCAA investigation into Auburn.

"There is a time to fight," he allowed, "and there is a time when to fight would cause more destruction than the other."

―――――

But destruction came regardless. In 1993, the NCAA's infractions committee served Auburn with one of the most punishing penalties it had meted out in many years, hammering the school with two years' probation, along with a two-year ban on postseason play and a one-year ban on televised games for the football program. Auburn, for all intents and purposes, would drop off the collegiate map for a year.

The NCAA's 1993 report indicated that Dye ignored Ramsey's allegations of a pay-for-play scheme because he didn't want to give credence to the player's simultaneous charges of racism throughout the program. You can debate the merits, or sins, of admitting to improperly paying players versus conceding that a racially charged environment existed, but by trying to conceal—or deny—both, Dye and Auburn ended up on the wrong end of the NCAA's enforcement barrels.

"Had there been a commitment on the part of the athletics department staff to investigate possible violations of NCAA rules when they came to light, this case might never have occurred, or it possibly would have been only a secondary violation," the NCAA said in its 1993 report. "Because that did not occur, very serious major violations were committed by members of the football coaching staff and representatives of its athletics interests."

The NCAA accused Dye of failing to control his program, but investigators couldn't find evidence that he knew of the cash payments. What the investigation did uncover, however, was that coaches and boosters had a significant and deeply damaging effect on the football program. The only reason the NCAA didn't drop the hammer even harder was that investigators were pleased that new Auburn president William Muse worked to aid them in their efforts.

"We have to be committed to not only success on the field but to preserving our integrity," Muse said at the time. "This is not an optional decision. If this program is going to survive, we can't have any more days like this one."

"This case is a very unfortunate one," the NCAA wrote. "The violations of NCAA rules that were committed at Auburn are indicative of what can occur when, in the minds of members of the university's athletic department staff and representatives of its athletic interests, the athletic program becomes more important than the university."

Those final nine words would be both an ethos and, for a few years, an epitaph for Auburn University. The next man in charge would have a whole lot to clean up . . . and that was assuming he didn't unearth more buried secrets.

TIMEOUT: AUBIE, BIG AL, AND THE BANDS

Few mascots in college football can match Auburn's Aubie the Tiger, a member of the inaugural class of the Mascot Hall of Fame, for name value, manic energy, and sheer ubiquity. Aubie began life as a four-legged drawing of a tiger on a game program, done by Birmingham cartoonist Phil Neel in 1959. He first stood upright three years later, and started wearing clothes—initially, just a blue tie and a straw hat—the next year. Finally, in 1979, Aubie came to life as a full-fledged sideline-worthy mascot.

Barry Mask, the first student to don the Aubie costume, said the mascot should have three traits: "Be a good dancer, have the cool persona of Pink Panther, and . . . be a ladies' man." Aubie must also be good with kids, since they're the Tigers of the future, after all.

Tryouts to don the Aubie suit are fierce and competitive. Aubie makes an estimated 300-plus appearances a year, and remains a motivating force along the sidelines at every Auburn football game. When you put on the stripes, you're all in.

Aubie first won nationwide acclaim at the 1979 Iron Bowl. Bear Bryant had declared that if he lost that game, he'd go back to his plow in Arkansas. Aubie showed up for the game sporting a houndstooth cap and pushing a plow. Auburn lost, but Bryant allegedly got a look at Aubie in the newspaper the next day and declared that Alabama needed a mascot like that.

Aubie's rival is Big Al the elephant . . . which makes perfect sense when you consider that Alabama is the Crimson Tide, right? The elephant motif dates to 1930 and Coach Wallace Wade's battleship of a team. Assessing the squad in the wake of Alabama's beatdown of Mississippi, *Atlanta Journal* writer Everett Strupper wrote, "That Alabama team of 1930 is a typical Wade machine, powerful, big, tough, fast, aggressive, well-schooled in fundamentals . . . At the end of the quarter, the earth started to tremble, there was a distant rumble that continued to grow. Some excited fan in the stands bellowed, 'Hold your horses, the elephants are coming,' and out stamped this Alabama varsity."

The "Red Elephants" of 1930 went undefeated, outscoring opponents 217–13 and claiming Wade's third national championship. The "Red Elephants" name faded, but the elephant's presence remained. Right up through the 1950s, Alabama would even welcome actual elephants to campus.

The first attempt at an elephant costume was an abject failure. At the 1964 Iron Bowl, someone—almost surely a student—strode onto the field wearing a red elephant suit with a ghastly papier-mâché elephant mask. As Auburn's band played, the "elephant" swung a live, wing-flapping chicken over its head to mock Auburn's War Eagle chant. The crowd in the stadium loved it, but the broadcast audience was horrified, and Alabama president Frank Rose rushed to the field to dispatch the overeager mascot.

In the wake of the 1979 Iron Bowl plow incident, Alabama secured an improved, more photogenic mascot. Big Al debuted at the Sugar Bowl, and he's been part of Tide lore ever since.

On game days, both mascots cavort to the backing of their respective bands. Alabama's Million Dollar Band begins its Saturday Tuscaloosa festivities on the steps of Gorgas Library on Alabama's Quad, within sight of Denny Chimes, and continues filling the air with the school's theme songs until long after the game clock reaches 0:00.

The Alabama marching band dates back to 1913 when 14 members gathered to play their instruments, and it gained its name nine years later. Trying to raise funds to get to a Georgia Tech game, the band sought donations from local merchants. They pulled together enough money to secure a sleeper car on the train to Atlanta, impressing booster Champ Pickens with their fundraising abilities.

Alas, the band witnessed a 33–7 stomping at the hands (stingers?) of the Yellow Jackets. An Atlanta sportswriter asked Pickens, "You don't have much of a team; what do you have at Alabama?" Pickens, who would go on to champion the cause of the 1926 Rose Bowl team, replied, "A million-dollar band."

Auburn's band, meanwhile, prefers a lower-key approach. Former Auburn president Harry Philpott issued the declaration the band lives by to this day: "Some other institutions need to give descriptive names to their bands in order to praise them. The quality of the music, the precision of its drills, and the fine image that it portrays have made it unnecessary for us to say more than, 'This is the Auburn University Band.'"

Yes, the rivalry extends everywhere.

Chapter 25

JUNCTION BOY MADE GOOD

Fire *him*, the demands came.
Enough is enough.
This won't do.
This is Alabama, for heaven's sake!
We have standards!
Fire this man!

The new coach at Alabama was Gene Stallings, and he had gone all of 0-3. That's how little patience Alabama fans had left by 1990.

It had been a long, long fall from the days of the Bear. Ray Perkins had flamed out, heading back to the safety of the NFL and the Tampa Bay Buccaneers. Then his successor, Bill Curry, had left Alabama to take the head coaching job at Kentucky. *Kentucky? Unbelievable! Alabama is no coach's stepping stone!*

The Alabama Powers That Be knew that a complete course correction was necessary. They had tried their hand with an outsider, and that had failed. Curry was the first coach since Frank Thomas in 1931 to come to the Alabama program without prior Tide ties. Worse, he lost to Auburn all three times he played them, including that humiliating 1989 Iron Bowl on The Plains.

So in 1990, Alabama once again turned to one of their own. Much to the alumni's dismay, not even the Tide could raise the Bear from the dead, so they attempted the next best thing: bringing aboard Stallings, an imposing figure with the same deep, rumbling baritone as Bryant. Surely someone who'd flowered under the Bear's tutelage had absorbed some of his greatness, right?

At A&M, Stallings had struggled with the same problems Bryant had faced decades before—top recruits didn't want to attend a male-only military school in the heart of the Vietnam War. He'd then spent years on the sidelines of the NFL's Cowboys and Cardinals, right up until Mama came calling for him too.

The ol' Junction Boy's first year didn't begin on an auspicious note. He lost his first game to lightly regarded Southern Miss—the same team that had bedeviled Bryant in his final days, a team now quarterbacked by a young gunslinger named Brett Favre—and then dropped two more, to Florida and Georgia. Tailback Siran Stacy, the SEC's reigning leading scorer, tore ligaments in his right knee in the Southern Miss game and was lost for the season. Nothing was working, nothing at all.

But the offense got itself together, dropping 59 points in a win over Vanderbilt—the Commodores were (almost) always good for what ailed other SEC teams—and upset No. 3 Tennessee, eventually finishing the 1990 season at 7-5. The next year, Alabama posted an 11-1 record and closed the year at No. 5 after knocking off defending national champion Colorado in the very-1990s-named Blockbuster Bowl.

And then came the 1992 season, which gave the Tide faithful hope that the good ol' days were here again. Alabama ran the table, outscoring opponents 366-122, including its first shutout of Auburn since 1975. That Iron Bowl was Pat Dye's last game before his "retirement," and the Tigers had hoped to send him off with a win, but Alabama had other ideas.

"If you need emotion to win a big game, you're in trouble," Alabama senior fullback Martin Houston said after the game, summarizing the entire Stallings ethos. "Emotion doesn't win it. It's who hits. Everybody said

Auburn had all the emotion, but everybody forgot that we wanted to get to the SEC championship game undefeated and keep our national championship hopes alive. We had a lot more to play for than they did, in my opinion."

Alabama met Miami in the Sugar Bowl, and one fact distinguished the two schools: Alabama had an 11:00 p.m. curfew in New Orleans, and Miami's was 1:00 a.m. A lot can happen in those two hours, and a lot did, none of it good news for the Hurricanes.

Miami players conducted a theatrical trash-talking performance that lasted right up until kickoff... when the Alabama defense offered its rebuttal. Alabama swarmed Miami quarterback Gino Torretta, sometimes bringing all 11 men up to the line and daring him to beat them deep. He couldn't, and Alabama won 34–13, despite the fact that Tide QB Jay Barker completed just four of his 13 passes for 18 yards. Alabama celebrated its latest national title and a restoration of the natural order in college football.

The future seemed bright for Alabama. That bright future wouldn't even last hours.

Antonio Langham, Alabama's star cornerback, sat in a hotel room in New Orleans on the second day of 1993, hours after that national championship victory, and, according to a report in *Sports Illustrated*, made a decision right then and there that would ripple throughout the college football universe. The junior, fresh off the stunning upset of Miami, decided he wanted to turn pro, and wanted an agent to represent him.

But Langham had immediate regrets, and days later, he called Stallings to see if there was a way to back out of his decision. Stallings asked whether he had signed with an agent, and whether he'd received any money. Langham said no, and Stallings had no reason to disbelieve him.

"Here's a guy I've coached for three years, and he's never misrepresented anything to me," Stallings would later say. "I don't think he thought there was an agent involved. He thought what he was doing was filling out papers to go to the NFL."

The problem for Alabama was Langham had signed with agent Darryl Dennis and was already immediately ineligible for the 1993 season, and in attempting to dig its way out of the situation, the Tide hit a gas line. If the school had declared Langham ineligible and applied for his reinstatement, he would have likely missed a couple games, and that would have been that.

Alabama chose a different option.

When the NCAA began looking into the matter, Alabama's bureaucracy immediately took on an air of outraged grievance over the governing body's audacity to investigate the school. Bumper stickers around Tuscaloosa at the time read "IT'S HARD TO BE HUMBLE WHEN YOU'RE FROM BAMA," and that was exactly the attitude that enraged the NCAA.

Tom Jones, Alabama's faculty chairman of athletics, attempted to tie a bow on the Langham case in November by saying Langham didn't know he was signing with an agent, but the NCAA wasn't swayed. Its infractions committee accused Jones of "providing incomplete and otherwise false and misleading information," especially pertaining to what the school knew about Langham's connection to Dennis. The infractions committee recommended a lengthy probation among other sanctions, one of the toughest penalties handed down short of the "death penalty" the NCAA had dealt SMU in 1987.

After a three-year investigation, the NCAA dropped an absolute boulder on Tuscaloosa: three years' probation, the forfeiting of 11 games Langham had played in during the 1993 season—transforming a 9-3-1 record into 1-12—and giving up the chance to play in either the SEC championship or a bowl. Worst of all, the NCAA crippled Alabama with the removal of 26 scholarships—including 22 freshman and transfer scholarships—in both 1996 and 1997.

The Langham situation was part of the problem, but so was the case of cornerback Gene Jelks, who received improper loans in 1989 and 1990. Yet another facet of the mess was Alabama's how-dare-you attitude, exemplified by school president Roger Sayers, who thundered that the NCAA's actions were "excessive and inappropriate," adding that "I categorically reject the one instance of unethical conduct they allege. We will appeal." That was exactly the kind of attitude that incited the NCAA into bringing the heat.

The reaction from the eastern side of the state was unmitigated joy, at least among the fans. Auburn's coaches had a more muted response. "It used to be, from a moral standpoint, that you believe in fair play, honesty, being a role model," new Auburn head coach Terry Bowden said. "Now, it's a matter of survival. You make one mistake, and your career could be over. That scares me."

Bowden understood what a tenuous line both schools were walking, and how precarious everyone's job security was, especially when rambunctious alumni decided to get involved. "This is a situation that needs to stop," he said. "This has got to be the end. No one wins from this attack on each other. If something happens in the next three years, we're dead. Both of us."

That national championship celebration on the field in New Orleans would turn out to be the last high point of Stallings's career at Alabama. He would coach through the 1996 season, stepping away after a dramatic 24-23 Iron Bowl win keyed by quarterback Freddie Kitchens's pass to running back Dennis Riddle for a touchdown with just seconds remaining. That same day, Stallings announced his retirement. As he would later put it, "I just wasn't on the same page as the athletic director and the president of the university at that time."

Stallings wanted to get to 70 wins, and in his final game—the Outback Bowl against Michigan on New Year's Day 1997—he got there, in the eyes of his fans and players, if not the NCAA. Alabama would not see his championship-winning likes again for many—*many*—years to come.

Chapter 26

THE MOST AUBURN YEAR EVER

There may be no more Auburn year in Auburn history than 1993, a season in which the Tigers went 11–0 but didn't even sniff the national championship, prisoners and victims of a prior regime. Bringing the best talent to bear at the absolute worst possible time . . . could there be anything more Auburn than that?

The Eric Ramsey scandal had cost Pat Dye his job, and had also exposed the significant degree to which trustees and boosters influenced the direction of the university and the athletic department. Later reports would suggest that board of trustees members, including, most notably, Auburn kingmaker Bobby Lowder, met with Dye and asked him to resign, a move they made without the involvement of the administration.

Lowder, a Montgomery banker, was the most powerful man at the university, freely exercising his relentless will over the administration, the school, and the athletic department. He was the leading figure in a collection of trustees and boosters that was a continual source of controversy and frustration for Auburn throughout the 1990s and the 2000s. Many associated with the school, from faculty to officials to students, accused Lowder and other trustees of marshaling too much power for their own ends—whether they were selecting a football coach or determining which academic departments merited more funding.

"The manipulative Auburn Tiger," ESPN's Mike Fish wrote in 2006, "is the most hands-on alumnus in college sports."

"The board [of trustees] exercised final authority in running the university," Dwayne Cox wrote in the Auburn history *The Village on the Plain*. "If they chose, the trustees could ignore the administration, faculty, students, and alumni, who often possessed greater knowledge than the board in specific areas."

Still, Lowder had his defenders, who noted that whatever his means, the ends were always in service of Auburn University. "During the lean years at Alabama," Paul Finebaum wrote in 2009, "I heard several prominent Alabama boosters say, 'I wish we had a Bobby Lowder running our program.'"

"He's keenly interested in all aspects of Auburn university—the football program and basketball, facilities and the upkeep of the physical plant, and the business school," former athletic director David Housel said in a 1999 book. "People may agree or disagree with Mr. Lowder—that's the American way—but nobody can say that he doesn't want to be helpful to Auburn."

"That [the role of the boosters at Auburn] gets misconstrued so much," Auburn broadcaster and former quarterback Stan White said in 2024. "Somebody wants to have someone to blame, and it's easy to blame someone with the biggest checkbook, right?"

To replace Dye, Auburn president William Muse suggested Terry Bowden, head coach at Samford University in Birmingham and son of legendary Florida State coach Bobby Bowden. After surveying six candidates, the search committee universally approved of Bowden's hiring, and he immediately paid off their trust... even if he had to walk in some deep footsteps.

On his first day in the office at Auburn, Bowden found a package containing a pair of size-20 shoes and a note that read, "These are Coach Dye's. They're going to be hard to fill."

Bowden, who carried the most famous surname in 1990s college football, wrote back, "I've been filling big shoes all my life." He wanted to add, "Bigger shoes than those," but that would be a bit much for his first day on the job. However, that didn't stop him from voicing, early in his Auburn career, the goal of matching Bear Bryant's NCAA-record 323 victories. He arrived at Auburn trailing Bryant's Division I total by just... 323 victories.

Bowden had been the youngest head coach in the nation when he led Salem College's football program in 1983 at just 26 years old. Even though he still looked, in *Atlanta Journal-Constitution* columnist—and old Bryant nemesis—Furman Bisher's words, "like a Boy Scout who'd just made Eagle," the 36-year-old, 5-foot-6, 160-pound Bowden did something that no one had ever done before in major college football when he arrived at Auburn: finished his first season undefeated and untied at 11-0.

The perfect Bowden team was in part the product of Dye's recruiting and development, and Bowden made sure to keep a significant measure of continuity in-house. He held onto many of Dye's former coaches. He also simplified the offense—down to six running plays and 12 passing plays—and developed a lean, mean Tiger machine.

The team had to bond in unconventional ways ... like over the disrespect of being named the homecoming opponent for Arkansas. "You hear about how we were getting beat by Arkansas, and Terry Bowden delivered this rousing halftime speech, and it got everybody going, and we came out and beat the Razorbacks," recalls Ace Atkins, a member of the 1993 team and now a celebrated crime fiction writer. "The reality of it was, we were getting beat because our equipment manager forgot to pack our cold weather gear and it was cold."

Arkansas's homecoming queen was trashing the players with unrelenting venom. But, Atkins recalls, when safety Otis Mounds told her to pipe down—in more colorful language—the fired-up Tiger team went out and won the game ... and every other one that year besides. Probation meant no postseason play, but Auburn was the only major college program to go undefeated that year.

"The players had so much adversity that they were doubting themselves," Bowden said early in his first year. "They no longer had faith in the truism that 'if I do the little things and I work hard, I'm going to be successful,' because they played so hard and they wanted to win so bad and they lost. But I'm a pretty confident person. And I have this undying belief that things will work out."

Well, yes and no. Bowden also learned that there was a certain way of doing business at Auburn.

Bowden led Auburn to 20 straight wins in 1993 and 1994. But as the Dye pipeline started to run dry, the win-loss records started to slip, and Auburn began losing ever more SEC games in 1995 and 1996. After a brief bounceback in 1997, the wheels came off completely in 1998. Recruiting challenges, injuries, and disciplinary problems combined for a perfect storm, with Bowden at its center.

Following a 1–5 start to the 1998 season that ended with a blowout loss to Florida, Bowden walked away from the Auburn job the night before the team's seventh game of the season, against Louisiana Tech. After a conversation with Housel, it became obvious that he wouldn't have the opportunity to right the ship for another season, and so that, to him, was that.

"It became so very apparent to me that this was not a dying issue, and that my continued stay at Auburn was going to be a central issue for the remainder of the year," Bowden told Montgomery's WSFA-TV. "Every week, that would be the only thing discussed. And our players don't deserve it."

At the same time, ugly rumors about Bowden's personal life swirled, so much so that he and wife Shyrl had to issue a press release refuting and condemning the allegations. In Auburn, the professional is personal, and vice versa.

Bowden later issued a statement that hinted at the behind-the-scenes strife between him, university administrators, and Lowder and other trustees.

"There continues to be a very serious and divisive public debate about the certainty of my status at Auburn University," Bowden said in the statement. "I cannot allow this painful controversy to continue. Someone must be willing to step up to the plate and put closure to this endless debate if Auburn is going to move forward. I believe that someone must now be me."

Whether he jumped, was pushed, or was pushed as he jumped was a matter of perspective, but Bowden's departure indisputably offered a peek at an ugly, simmering Auburn power struggle. The real problem was that he had apparently run afoul of Lowder, who made his few public utterances with care . . . and devastating precision. "Bowden's decision is hard to understand," Lowder said at the time. "Auburn people everywhere are trying to understand it, and they are looking for reasons for his resigning and some of them are blaming me."

Columnists outside the reach of Auburn had no problem savaging the university. A column in *The Oklahoman* mocked the culture of The Plains, "where gossip is as much a part of the lifestyle as fried chicken," and said the entire affair "stinks." An *Orlando Sentinel* column, citing "sources," charged an even darker conspiracy involving the trustees and several past and present members of the coaching staff.

Lowder emphatically denied that he had anything to do with Bowden's departure. "I did not ask coach Bowden to resign, I did not tell him to resign and I did not advise him to resign," he told the *Mobile Register*.

Still, Lowder did offer up one final twist of the knife. "Even if someone had told him he had to win three or four games to keep his job, I would like to think he would have taken up the challenge and really tried harder, not just quit," he told the *Montgomery Advertiser*. "It's a good thing we never gave him that challenge, looking back on it."

"I don't think the whole truth will ever come out because it would hurt both sides," Dye said, a fascinating comment given the fact that both sides were professing baby-faced innocence.

Bowden unloaded on Auburn in a wide-ranging 2001 interview, in which he claimed in recordings that players received bonuses of $12,000 to $15,000 for signing with the team, and subsequent monthly cash stipends of $600. These perks were allegedly funded by several dozen boosters who contributed $5,000 each per year. In the 2020s, this sort of payment would be legal—even sanctioned and encouraged—under NIL rules, but in the 1990s, it was completely forbidden.

So Auburn was, as usual, in turmoil. If there was any consolation, though, it was this: things were worse over in Tuscaloosa.

Chapter 27

THE TIDE RECEDES

Two months after September 11, with the nation still in shock and attempting to find some semblance of normality in a world that had been turned inside out, the members of the NCAA's Division I Committee on Infractions sat around a conference room table in an Indianapolis hotel and stared at one another. Before them was a massive challenge—though, granted, it wasn't anywhere near the one facing the rest of the nation at that moment.

The NCAA had to decide whether to snuff out football at one of the nation's elite institutions. The evidence was overwhelming; the guilt was obvious.

All that was left was leveling a punishment. Would Alabama really get the death penalty?

Alabama experienced its own power struggles in the immediate post-Stallings era. School officials wanted Virginia Tech's Frank Beamer to replace Stallings in 1997. But the alumni favored Mike DuBose, who'd played for Bryant in the early 1970s and then went on to coach with the Tampa Bay Buccaneers. The alumni won the fight, and DuBose got the job.

His tenure began badly—Alabama won only four games that 1997 season, the Tide's lowest win total since 1957, back in the days of Ears Whitworth. DuBose managed in 1998 to return Alabama to a winning record—7–5 is a winning record, if only barely—and a spot in the Music City Bowl. But that would be as good as it got for him.

In the spring of 1999, rumors began to circulate that DuBose had had an affair with his secretary. In early May, he released a fiery statement that read, "There is absolutely no truth or factual basis to any of these rumors that you have heard involving me or other university employees. They are unfounded and hurting innocent people." That statement held up until August, when Alabama paid $350,000 to "an employee" to settle a potential sexual harassment and discrimination lawsuit against DuBose.

"My statement misled all of you, and I am truly sorry," DuBose later conceded. "I made a mistake, and made the situation worse with my response."

The scandal cost Alabama athletic director Bob Bockrath his job. DuBose had to pay the $350,000 out of his own pocket over three years, and he lost two years off his five-year contract. He managed to lead the 1999 Tide to the Orange Bowl, but they fell in overtime to Michigan and its quarterback, a senior named Tom Brady who threw four touchdown passes in the second half.

In October 2000, following a 40–38 loss to Central Florida at home, DuBose was shown the door. Alabama lost ugly games to LSU and Auburn and finished the season 3–8. The days of Bear Bryant seemed a long way away.

And yet, it was about to get worse. So much worse.

DuBose had been laboring under the effects of the NCAA's penalty of three years' probation, the result of the Gene Jelks pay-for-play and Antonio Langham ineligibility scandals. Alabama's five-year clock for avoiding future major penalties started on August 2, 1995. But then, in 2000, investigators again began sniffing around the program, and it didn't take them long to hit pay dirt.

For years, allegations had swirled that overactive and well-heeled boosters had been juicing the high-school-to-Alabama pipeline. (This was, of course, not limited to Alabama, but Alabama was in the crosshairs in this particular instance.) Investigators found that Alabama boosters had offered two high school coaches $100,000 and an SUV apiece if they got 6-foot-6, 310-pound defensive lineman Albert Means of Memphis to sign with the Tide. Boosters had also paid a total of more than $150,000 to various recruits. And at least two Alabama coaches had had "frequent contact" with the boosters.

This was bad. Extraordinarily bad, given Alabama's previous dances on the wrong side of the NCAA's rules. And there was precedent for the absolute worst-case scenario in terms of punishment.

In 1987, the NCAA hit SMU with the "death penalty" for a pay-for-play scheme that cost the school two years of football—one mandated, one self-imposed—and it took nearly two decades for the program to even faintly recover. By 2001, a school had faced the maximum sanction in 20 cases, including Alabama, and in 18 of those instances, the NCAA had shown mercy. Would the streak continue for Alabama?

Tom Yeager, commissioner of the Colonial Athletic Association and a former NCAA enforcement investigator, indicated in 2002 that the Tide was staring down the barrel of oblivion. "Alabama came as close to SMU as anyone ever has," he said. "We seriously considered the death penalty."

But the NCAA ended up showing mercy, in part because the school convinced its investigators that the violations were the work of "rogue" boosters and coaches, in part because of the administration's willingness to assist the investigators, and in part because the NCAA realized just how badly the death penalty harmed a program.

"SMU represented a broad-reaching conspiracy," Yeager said at the time. "This did not."

The penalty was announced on February 1, 2002, a gray and ugly day in Tuscaloosa that matched the tenor of the news. The Tide got a five-year probation, a two-year ban on postseason play, and 21 lost scholarships over three seasons. What saved Alabama? According to the NCAA, the university saw the light at the last possible moment and started cooperating with investigators.

The Tide also may well have been saved by what happened to SMU, which was nearly crushed by the penalty. "It's like the atomic bomb," SMU coach Phil Bennett said in 2002. "The NCAA did it one time and created devastation beyond belief—and it's never going to be done again."

"If the death penalty was intended to forever change a place, then it has succeeded," *Sports Illustrated*'s Tim Layden wrote in 2002. "SMU is chastened and fearful, with modest expectations. There is no place quite like it in college football. Probably never will be again."

Still, the NCAA sanctions against Alabama ripped away scholarships, bowl appearances, and swagger. Dennis Franchione, brought in following DuBose's firing, bailed on the Tide after just two seasons, lighting out for Texas A&M without telling his players he was leaving. Franchione's replacement, Mike Price, didn't even coach a single game, getting fired following offseason indiscretions in Pensacola, Florida. A third—Mike Shula—also struggled and was gone less than four seasons into his tenure. (Shula very nearly brought a quarterback named Tim Tebow to Tuscaloosa, which would have altered the Tide's future indeed.) The lone real highlight of that era: Tyrone Prothro making one of the most magnificent catches in football history, a Hail Mary that he caught by reaching around the back of the Southern Miss player guarding him, then holding the ball to the defender's back. It was ESPN's "Play of the Year" for 2005, and it remains spectacular two decades later.

In all, five men coached at Alabama in 10 years, with DuBose, Franchione, Shula, and interim coach Joe Kines going a combined 51–55 (after sanctions). Their bowl record: 1–4.

No one was innocent in this mess. Boosters ran wild, unchecked by the administration or the various impotent coaching staffs. The administration gave two of the coaches significant raises and extensions before firing them, costing the school millions in buyout money. Fans were throwing around death threats—a serious escalation in their expressions of ire since the time, if an oft-told story is to be believed, someone threw a brick through head coach Bill Curry's office window.

The entitlement mentality of those fans was a problem too—the Bear's monstrous shadow still loomed over the program and existed in the memories of all but the youngest Tide fans, and there was a presumption that Alabama deserved prominence. And if that meant special treatment, well, so be it.

After the NCAA's sanctions, though, the Tide were broken, despondent, without hope. They needed someone to rescue them. And, miracle of miracles, they found him.

Chapter 28

THE MAN FROM MONONGAH

Mine deeply enough in the legend of Nick Saban, and you find the elements of the coach he would become even in his earliest days.

Saban grew up in Monongah, West Virginia, atop a bed of coal that runs from Pennsylvania to Alabama. Born on Halloween 1951 to Mary Conaway, the daughter of a coal miner, and Big Nick Saban, a service station (and, later, a Dairy Queen) owner, Nicholas Lou Saban Jr. learned the value of hard work early. As soon as little Nick was able to help out, he did everything around the service station—pumping gas, wiping windshields, checking oil, rotating tires, washing cars.

"The gas station and Dairy Queen consumed my parents' lives, and, since we lived directly behind both, there was no real distinction between work and home," Saban would later write. "The station opened at seven in the morning and closed at midnight."

Father and son bonded over football, a shared language that ran throughout the region. Big Nick and a friend started up the first youth football team in the area and named it the Idamay Black Diamonds, after anthracite, the most prized type of coal. They found a field near the Bethlehem No. 44 mine, leveled it out, and began practice on August 1, 1962.

Big Nick would send his boy out on recruiting missions to the elementary and middle schools all around Monongah, Idamay, Farmington, Carolina, and other nearby coal-mining towns. They double-teamed the players—Big Nick offering football, little Nick promising fun, cheerleaders, and food. Recruit 'em however you can get 'em.

Big Nick painted an old 20-seater school bus orange with black trim. Inside, Mary used a marker to write motivational slogans like "When the going gets tough, the tough get going" and "Practice makes players." Big Nick drove the bus everywhere, since some of the kids lived as far as five miles away from the field. It gave him a level of control over practices. It gave him a level of control over *everything*.

Big Nick was a demanding taskmaster, never missing an opportunity to teach through criticism. "Even after I threw touchdown passes (and we scored a lot), there was always something to improve on," Saban wrote. "Poor throwing form. Made the wrong read on the play. Didn't put enough spiral on the ball."

One of the most dramatic moments of Saban's young life took place when he was in eighth grade. A shy kid, he didn't like getting up in front of class, and when he refused to sing in front of his music class, his teacher gave him a D. Big Nick was livid, and dropped a fierce lesson on young Nick's head. He drove his boy to the No. 44 mine—the one beside the Black Diamonds' field—and had some friends take them deep into the mines, 550 feet below the surface.

"If you don't do better in school, if you don't get a college education, this is where you will end up," Big Nick said. (The reactions of his friends went unrecorded.) "Is this what you want? Do you want to end up down here for the rest of your life?" As with Dale Earnhardt, who would get the exact same lesson amid the cotton plants of Kannapolis, North Carolina, a few hundred miles south, the message stuck.

Saban met a young lady named Terry Constable that next summer at a 4-H science camp. Terry was immediately sweet on Nick, and invited him to go bird-watching with her. He said yes, but later remembered he had a softball game and stood her up. Not a great beginning to what would become one of college football's most enduring marriages.

Saban would play for the Black Diamonds through the ninth grade. Father and son would go over plays, watch West Virginia games and practices, talk football long into the night. It was the kind of priceless bonding that few sons get with their fathers. And when Saban left for his high school team, Big Nick kept the Black Diamonds going. They would go on to defeat teams all over the region, including one from Monongahela, Pennsylvania, quarterbacked by a lad named Joe Montana.

The Black Diamonds still exist to this day.

Saban attended Monongah High School, where he took over as quarterback of the football team. He was smaller and weaker than most of his teammates, but he had an indomitable will, a serious demeanor, and a brilliant mind that allowed him to see the possibilities in any situation on the field, before or during a play.

Saban led the team to two state championship games, losing in his junior year and then winning his senior year. He was a diligent student, too, and a member of the National Honor Society. Sometime during his senior year, he worked up the courage to redeem himself for his softball gaffe and asked Terry out to a showing of *Gone with the Wind* at the Lee Theatre. They've been inseparable ever since.

Saban had wanted to play football for West Virginia. But like Shug Jordan before him, he was too short, too small, and too slow to play college ball at a big-time program. He eventually accepted a scholarship offer from a nearby school that had gone 1–9 the year before.

The school's name was Kent State, and Saban was about to walk into history there.

On May 4, 1970, Saban was walking with a friend near Kent State's Commons. It was a magnificent late spring day in Ohio, the kind of day on a college campus that should feel full of hope and possibility. But Kent State was on edge. Protests over Nixon's invasion of Cambodia had been wracking campus. A major rally had been called at the Commons that day, and the Ohio National Guard was on high alert.

Despite their coach's warnings, Saban and teammate Phil Witherspoon wanted to check out the protest, but first, they grabbed some lunch. The protest began at noon. The Ohio National Guard tried to disperse the protesters, and got backed into a defensive position. At 12:24, they opened fire, shooting at unarmed protesters for 13 long seconds. Four students, two of whom weren't even involved in the protest, were killed. Nine others were wounded.

Saban and Witherspoon walked out to Blanket Hill and beheld a chaotic scene. Helicopters loomed overhead, and sirens wailed in the air. Years later, Saban would recall seeing "large pools of blood" from the dead and the wounded. Then just 18 years old, he knew one of the students killed, Allison Krause. She had been in his English class.

"There's not a May 4 that goes by that I don't think about it," he told *USA Today* in 2010.

After graduating from Kent State, Saban signed on with the football team as a graduate assistant, meaning he did all the work around the program for little of the money and none of the credit. He took on the job with joy, and in the first game, Kent State upset Louisville. Saban excitedly called his father to tell him about the win. As it turned out, it would be the last time the two ever spoke.

Big Nick's heart had started to go out on him. He needed to dial back his work, but he refused to. On a jog home from football practice, he suffered a major heart attack and fell over dead. Big Nick Saban was 46 years old. He's buried at Mount Carmel Cemetery in Fairmont, under a tombstone that reads, "No man stands as tall as when he stoops to help a child."

There's a path that coaches must follow if they want to succeed. They can't stay too long at one place, lest they lose control of their own career and become too tied to one organization. Still, few coaches have wandered quite like Saban did in the 13 years after 1976, rolling through six different assistant coaching jobs—an average of just over two years per stop.

After turning down an offer from Bobby Bowden to join the West Virginia staff, Saban stuck around Kent State for two more years. Saban then moved to Syracuse for a year, and then leaped to old familiar West Virginia. The move didn't sit well with Syracuse, starting yet another Saban trend—leaving behind a string of former employers dissatisfied with his decision to leave. He enjoyed his time at West Virginia, but it wasn't long before a better offer came in: Ohio State. But Ohio State didn't last, and he was fired on December 31, 1981, for the first and only time in his career.

Saban moved to Navy in 1982, a clear and obvious step down. He was there for only a year; a member of the Navy athletic department claimed he left without even saying goodbye, and Paul Evans, the basketball coach, replied, "That's all right, he never said 'hello.'" But the Navy job had its perks—there, Saban met a fellow coach by the name of Bill Belichick.

Saban next went to Michigan State, where he truly fell in love with the college world. From Michigan State coach George Perles, he adopted the "24-hour rule"—in other words, celebrate every win or mourn a loss for no more than 24 hours, and then move on.

In January 1988, Saban, then 36, won the job of Houston Oilers defensive coordinator over candidates that included Pete Carroll. Saban didn't change his approach to his players in the least, tearing into NFL pros like they were little kids back on the field in Monongah. But these players didn't much care for being treated like children and lectured all the way through practice. Meanwhile, head coach Jerry Glanville was running practice like he was a jovial uncle at a Thanksgiving Day Turkey Bowl game, seemingly making it all up as he went along. Midway through his second year in Houston, Saban got itchy feet again, eventually landing a head coaching job at the University of Toledo.

"A lot of people want to know why I want to come back to college football," Saban said at his introductory press conference at Toledo. "I think college football is a lot more fun. The involvement you have with the players, the influence you have on their lives at a time in their lives which is critical to their development, is a lot more fun and a lot more rewarding than the professional athlete." It's a philosophy he would carry forward for the rest of his college career—and it's not hard to see how it contributed to the end of that career as well.

Toledo went 9-2 on the season, suffering its two losses by a total of five points. Things looked bright for Saban and for Toledo. And then Bill Belichick got involved. Just weeks after Toledo's season ended, Belichick was responsible for crafting a defensive plan that shut down the mighty Buffalo Bills in Super Bowl XXV. That propelled him to a head coaching gig in Cleveland, and he wanted Saban as his defensive coordinator.

Belichick proved to be the most demanding coach Saban had seen since Big Nick. Saban spent four years under Belichick, four of the most relentless, difficult years of his professional life—grinding through film, always digging in more and more and more for 18-hour days. When another head coaching gig came open—this one back at Michigan State—Saban again hit the road.

Saban's five years at Michigan State would be the turning point in his career. It was here that he truly instituted his vicious Fourth Quarter program, designed to break players down to their component parts and rebuild them stronger. The idea was to prepare them for any challenge they might face on the football field, because they had already faced so much worse in practice.

At Michigan State, Saban met Lonny Rosen, a psychiatry professor who helped him form the basis for what would become his mantra: The Process. At its heart, Rosen preached "process thinking"—the breaking down of larger tasks, like game plans or entire seasons, into smaller steps that can be executed without as much drama.

The Process was implemented as Michigan State prepared to play Ohio

State, then ranked No. 1 in the country. Rosen noted that plays in football games take only about seven seconds, so players and coaches should focus on those seconds, and then take a break between them. Michigan State won the game 28–24, a stunning upset, and Rosen has been a confidant of Saban's ever since.

Like Bear Bryant, Saban was motivated by snubs. In 1999, Michigan State knocked off Michigan, and the teams finished the season with an identical 9–2 record. Saban believed his team worthy of a New Year's Day bowl, but Michigan got the invitation instead, despite losing the head-to-head matchup. Saban would later point to that snub as one of the reasons for his departure—he knew he'd be fighting an uphill battle for top-dog status in the state forever.

So when a vacancy opened up in Louisiana, Saban and LSU began a dalliance that neither had expected or anticipated. That flirtation led to yet another awkward Saban exit, yet another last-minute decision, yet another set of frustrated administrators left in his wake.

Saban arrived at LSU in 2000 with a five-year deal that paid him $1.25 million a year, making him the third-highest-paid coach in the country behind Steve Spurrier and Bobby Bowden. He needed to rebuild the program from below the ground up, and that meant patching up relationships with high school coaches in the area. He got to know their names, sent them congratulatory messages when they won, visited their games and their schools.

Saban also began to flex his muscle with alumni. He brought in Jesse Jackson to speak to his players, even though the move drew criticism from some of LSU's conservative white alumni. But it went over well with his Black players.

LSU squeaked out Saban's debut against Western Carolina by a score of 58–0, a game mostly notable for the fact that Saban was irritated by his team's effort in the pregame walk-through and ordered them to hit each other. *Pregame.*

Some mild success followed, but in 2002 came the first of many Saban-related games that earned its own nickname: The Bluegrass Miracle. At Kentucky, the Wildcats kicked a field goal with 11 seconds left to go up 30–27, and the Kentucky players dumped Gatorade on their head coach, Guy Morriss. Fans flowed down from the stands onto the sidelines. LSU was left with the ball on its own 25 with just two seconds remaining.

LSU offensive coordinator Jimbo Fisher sent in a Hail Mary play called Dash Right 93 Berlin. As the ball was snapped, the students began storming the field and tearing down the goalposts behind LSU. Quarterback Marcus Randall threw the ball 57 yards downfield, where multiple players tipped it until it ended up in the hands of Devery Henderson, who managed to break a tackle and scoot into the end zone for a stunning victory and a play that lives on in LSU lore.

"We won the game, but we didn't defeat the team," Saban grumped afterward. "If you want to be happy with the results, I'm happy with the results. If you want to be happy with the process, I'm not."

The next season, despite losing in October to Florida, everything fell into place for 11-1 LSU—the Tigers annihilated Georgia in the SEC championship game, while undefeated Oklahoma lost to Kansas State and USC beat Oregon State in its final game. The AP ranked USC number one, LSU two, and Oklahoma three. But the Bowl Championship Series computers—a relic of a bygone era—put Oklahoma at No. 1 and LSU at No. 2, so the Sooners and the Tigers played for the title. LSU used a punishing defense and a grinding running game—two Saban hallmarks—to post a 21-14 victory for Saban's first national title.

The 2004 season began with high expectations and one small but significant addition to Saban's coaching staff: a bright young defensive mind from Georgia named Kirby Smart. But the team showed up out of shape, overweight, and complacent, losing two games early on. The combination of displeased fans and disconnected team started to weigh hard on Saban, and Miami Dolphins owner Wayne Huizenga took advantage, putting on a charm offensive. Huizenga flew to Baton Rouge in December, arriving ostentatiously on a private plane with the Dolphins logo on it.

Soon afterward, Saban was gone, off to his first head coaching job in the NFL. In Miami, he got everything he wanted—a practice field, virtually unlimited assistant coaches, final say on personnel matters. He should have been happy, right?

The problem was, the team was penned in on all sides—high-priced veterans took up cap space, and deals from prior regimes had cost Miami precious draft picks. Moreover, Saban made an unfortunate—but defensible—personnel choice that may have cost him his NFL career. Miami needed a quarterback, and had the opportunity to sign either Daunte Culpepper or a career backup for the San Diego Chargers . . . a guy named Drew Brees. Both players were recovering from injuries. Saban went with Culpepper because his injury was deemed less severe and more likely to allow for a long-term comeback than Brees. Saban made the prudent decision . . . it just ended up being one that cost him a Hall of Fame quarterback.

The Dolphins were a trendy Super Bowl pick in 2006. But the season went sideways when Saban benched Culpepper without warning and Culpepper stormed out of the Dolphins' practice facility, cursing Saban the entire way. The coach had lost the team, and at that point, the obvious change was inevitable. Nick Saban would be on the move yet again. But where would he go this time?

Saban's last win in the NFL came at the expense of Bill Belichick, when the Dolphins beat the Patriots 21–0 in Week 14 and held Tom Brady to only 78 yards passing. (Belichick and Saban were 2–2 against one another, with Saban's Dolphins scoring 75 points to Belichick's Patriots' 69.) Saban finished the year 6–10, the only time in his head coaching career that his team had a losing on-field record.

Over in Alabama, the Crimson Tide brain trust had just fired Mike Shula after another loss in the Iron Bowl. As was customary when a job came open, Saban's name came up, so much so that he had to issue a statement saying he was "flattered" by the attention, and asking, "Why would I have left [LSU] if I was going to be interested in other college jobs?"

Chapter 29

FEAR THE THUMB

The football program at Auburn University and the US Senate—you can decide for yourself the order of importance of these two institutions—both very nearly missed welcoming one of their own thanks to, of all things, fried catfish. The story of Tommy Tuberville—Auburn head coach, US senator, thorn in the side of both Alabama fans and supporters of the military—is a genuine American folktale, even if a whole lot of people haven't much cared for its twists and turns.

Tommy Tuberville was born on September 18, 1954, one week to the day before Auburn kicked off Shug Jordan's fourth season. His parents, Charles and Olive Tuberville, raised young Tommy in Camden, Arkansas—the home territory of a gentleman by the name of Bear Bryant. Young Tommy quarterbacked the very first iteration of the football team at Harmony Grove High School. It went about as well as expected, given that Tuberville's senior class had a total enrollment of about 60. Still, that was enough to encourage him to get into coaching, and he began his college coaching career with a job at Arkansas State, a school in what was then known as Division I-AA.

But progress upward through the coaching ranks was slow, and

Tuberville found himself frustrated. When he turned 30, he vowed to be a head coach at the Division I-A—what's now called FBS—level by the time he turned 40. The trick about that, though, is that it's exceedingly tough to campaign for a coaching job while you've already got a job. So Tuberville decided to take a year off from the sideline and begin networking.

"I wasn't making any headway," Tuberville said in 2001. "I decided to take a season off. I said, 'I've got to take a chance.' That's what I did."

Still, the 30-year-old assistant coach hadn't quite saved up enough of a nest egg that he could go without a job. A friend had operated a catfish restaurant with great success in Arkansas, so Tuberville talked his sister into going in together on a restaurant in Tullahoma, Tennessee. And so was born Tubby's Catfish. House specialty: Tubby's Pond Platter—two catfish fillets, two catfish steaks, two frog legs, hush puppies, and a splash of Tubby's Pond Water (fruit punch), all fried, for the bargain price of $6.99.

Tuberville lasted barely six months at Tubby's. True to his word, in January 1986, he traveled to New Orleans and plunged into the murky waters of the coaching job search, visiting the American Football Coaches Association convention—the nexus of all college football job openings—and got a bite from one of the biggest fish in the pond.

Jimmy Johnson, then the coach at the University of Miami, needed a graduate assistant. It was a huge step down for Tuberville title-wise, but professionally, it gave him the connections he needed to begin working his way up the ranks. While at Miami, Tuberville coached on three national championship teams, which put him on the radar far better than slinging catfish ever could.

From Miami, Tuberville jumped to Texas A&M, where he served as defensive coordinator for a team that went 10–0–1. Then, with his 40th birthday looming, he made the decision to take a head coaching job at Ole Miss in 1994. He'd achieved his goal, and he was about to achieve a whole lot more.

At Ole Miss, Tuberville found himself smack-dab in the middle of a vicious controversy over the use of the Confederate battle flag at Vaught-Hemingway Stadium. University chancellor Robert Khayat was facing gale-force headwinds in trying to remove the flag from the stands. Harold Burson, an Ole Miss alum and founder of public relations giant Burson-Marsteller, was the strongest advocate for the change. But it was Tuberville who lit the fire that finally got the flag banned once and for all.

The Egg Bowl, the annual Thanksgiving weekend battle between Ole Miss and Mississippi State, doesn't have quite the majesty, pageantry, and national significance of the Iron Bowl. But it means every bit as much to the citizens of Mississippi, and when Mississippi State blanked Ole Miss 17–0 in 1996, Tuberville had had enough.

"We can't recruit against that flag," Tuberville told Khayat. Consciously or not, he was echoing the arguments of Bear Bryant nearly 30 years before. The policies and traditions of a South with Civil War–era grievances still on its mind were fine if the region wanted to stay in a sociological cul-de-sac, but if Ole Miss wanted to win some damn football games, things would have to change.

Burson began a public relations investigation, talking with key players in Oxford. When he asked Tuberville about the flags, the coach replied simply, "They're killing us." According to Burson, Tuberville went on: "In the state of Mississippi, the best football players are Black. With the flags on campus, we're not getting our share of Black players that are going to other schools."

Over in Starkville, on the other side of the state, Mississippi State head coach Jackie Sherrill used the Confederate flag as a deterrent, telling Black recruits how unwelcome they'd be in Oxford. Oppositional recruiting is a tradition as old as recruiting itself—part of a recruiter's job is to tell a targeted athlete how miserable he'll be if he chooses to play for a rival school. But it's one thing to hint about depth charts or the age of that coach over there. It's quite another to suggest that the rival school hates you for who you are, and is using you for your labor alone.

Complaining is easy, though; doing something is much harder. Burson informed Tuberville that—much like Bryant in the 1960s—he was the man who could get this change through. Tuberville, according to Burson, was hesitant to take an active role in the controversy, but finally issued a statement before Ole Miss's 1997 homecoming game, urging fans to leave their flags at home and "discontinue waving the Confederate flag at home sporting events."

The message worked pretty much as expected. Older alumni with more perspective largely went along with the program, leaving the Stars and Bars at home and switching over to the university's red-and-blue block-M flag. But the you-can't-tell-me-what-to-do students and the non-alumni fan base doubled down on the Confederate flags, waving them with even more vehemence and gusto.

"Over time, people began to see that the benefit of not having that flag tied to our university, or vice versa, was far more valuable than the enjoyment that anybody received from waving that flag," Khayat said in 2013. "It was measurably destructive to the university."

Tuberville did not, however, extend his opposition to other elements of Confederate iconography at Ole Miss. The Colonel Reb mascot cavorted on the sidelines of Ole Miss football games until 2003, and the band played "From Dixie with Love" until 2016.

The Tuberville era at Ole Miss was notable for its sweeping break with the past ... and for the way it ended. After the 1998 season, while still head coach at Ole Miss, he said the only way he'd leave that job was "in a pine box." A few days later, he took the job as Auburn's head coach, doubling his salary to $900,000 a year.

It was the right move for Tuberville, but it was a gut punch to Ole Miss fans, who had spent years hearing Tuberville make pronouncements like "I'm a Rebel at heart. I want to be where people want you, where you have a chance to win, where your players are giving all they can and where it's a great place to live. That's exactly what we have in Oxford." But according to several of his players, he left without even saying goodbye. It wouldn't be the last time that charge was leveled at Tuberville.

At Auburn, Tuberville quickly added to his growing reputation as a gambler, willing to throw some genuinely weird plays into the mix. One specialty: the Globe of Death, employed during the 2000 SEC championship game. After the kick recovery, half the team ran into a mock huddle, and Roderick Hood came out with the ball and rushed for 25 yards. Teams now regularly go for it on fourth down, but Tuberville was one of the earliest innovators of the aggressive practice.

He was also aggressive off the field. "The program is down," Tuberville conceded shortly after he was hired. "People are looking for somebody to be honest." At the end of his first spring practice, he took away scholarships from six players, dismissing them with a cruel line: "Some of these guys we wouldn't have recruited." (The six players were later offered nonathletic scholarships after public criticism.)

The 2003 season began with Auburn ranked sixth in the nation. That didn't last, as the Tigers lost first to USC and then to Georgia Tech. Auburn president William F. Walker was ready to fire Tuberville immediately—he apparently was headed to the locker room right after the Tech game—but trustees talked him down.

The Auburn administration as a whole didn't exactly cover itself in glory during the early 2000s, especially with incidents like JetGate in November 2003. Walker, athletic director David Housel, and two board members took a plane furnished by trustee Bobby Lowder's bank to a small airfield outside Louisville. (The Colonial Bank logo on the plane wouldn't arouse suspicions; the Auburn-logo private plane most certainly would.) There, they met with Bobby Petrino to discuss the idea of the itinerant coach, and onetime Auburn offensive coordinator, replacing Tuberville.

Once the news of the meetup came to light, everyone involved backed away in a hurry. Tuberville remained on the job at Auburn, Petrino stayed at Louisville—for a few more years, at least—but everyone involved ended up looking a little worse for the experience. Housel, in particular, took undeserved heat, and although he later left the athletic director post, he remains a university stalwart to this day.

"I truly believe a majority of fans probably shared some of the same opinions [of Tuberville] as those in charge," Auburn radio announcer Rod Bramblett later wrote, "but after word got out of this meeting, the fact that it took place the week of the Iron Bowl, and the way it appeared the whole situation was being handled, completely changed the emotional tide (sorry for the pun) of the Auburn fan base." Bramblett praised Tuberville's "calm professionalism" as the key to getting Tigers fans in his corner.

Around this same time, the university faced an existential challenge. The Southern Association of Colleges and Schools had begun an investigation after an ad hoc faculty committee sought "an external, objective, and independent assessment of Auburn University—with special attention to the performance of the Board of Trustees." After two reviews, SACS issued a stunning condemnation over the outsize role of trustees in university operations, and mandated probation for the university, one step short of revoking its accreditation. Had that happened, Auburn would have lost hundreds of millions in federal funding, as well as its reputation.

Between the Bowden affair, JetGate, and the SACS inquiry, Auburn was navigating treacherous straits. But on the positive side, the football team was beating Alabama on the regular. And even the university's fiercest critics had to concede that counted for a whole lot.

Despite the early bumps, Tuberville started his Auburn career seeming like he was headed to Jordan-Dye heights. He led Auburn to eight straight bowl appearances. His 2004 team finished the season 13–0, but missed out on a berth in the BCS national championship game thanks to the vagaries of computer-aided polls. To wit: Auburn got dinged in the polls because the Tigers didn't beat Alabama badly enough in the Iron Bowl—a game where any victory ought to count as a season-high triumph. The fact that voters (and the computer) couldn't comprehend that was yet another cruel jab at Auburn's gridiron reputation and hopes. (Oklahoma and USC played for the title that year; Auburn had to settle for beating down Virginia Tech in the Sugar Bowl.)

Ask Auburn fans whether they'd like to have one national championship or six straight wins over Alabama, though, and they'd have to think about it. Six straight is exactly what Tuberville delivered from 2002 to 2007, delighting the Auburn family and stoking the seething rage in Tuscaloosa.

Tuberville leaned hard into tweaking Alabama. In 2005, as Auburn was putting the finishing touches on a 28–18 Iron Bowl victory for a fourth consecutive win, Jordan-Hare Stadium cameras found Tuberville. He raised four fingers, and the Auburn crowd lost its collective mind. One month later, Tuberville was photographed wearing a "Fear the Thumb" T-shirt—thumb, fifth finger, five consecutive wins, get it?—and Auburn had a devastating, if rarely usable, catch phrase.

Auburn did indeed get that thumb, and a finger on the next hand too, which meant there were several classes of Auburn players who never lost a game to Alabama. "I can live the rest of my life here and never have to answer any questions about this rivalry," offensive guard Ben Grubbs said at the time. "I'll be the only one talking. I can tell my kids I never lost to Alabama."

There's an old saying about how everything ends badly, otherwise it wouldn't end. At Auburn, that saying goes a little further: everything ends badly and quickly. Coaches don't leave Auburn with dignified exits; they get handcuffed and thrown to the sharks.

The win streak over Alabama ended in 2008 with a decisive 36–0 defeat at the hands of the Tide, and Auburn hasn't posted consecutive Iron Bowl victories in the decade and a half following that loss. (Not coincidentally, that 2008 team was the second one coached by a gentleman named Nick Saban.)

The 2008 defeat was part of a seven-loss season, and seven losses at Auburn are enough to light a coach's seat on fire. Tuberville resigned after that 36–0 blowout, one of many coaches Saban pushed out the door. Tuberville managed to both walk away from Auburn and wrangle his entire $5 million buyout; he would take a year off, assume the reins at Texas Tech . . . and then, in 2012, engineer one of the more infamous exits in college football history. Out at dinner with recruits at the 50-Yard Line restaurant in Lubbock, he got up from the table to use the restroom or take a phone call (recollections vary) . . . and, according to at least one player, never returned. The next day, he announced he was going to coach at Cincinnati. (For his part, Tuberville in 2019 called the report that he never came back to the table "fake news," adding, "I left when everyone else did. I actually paid the bill.")

However he left Lubbock, Tuberville was gone, marking yet another strange turn in his career . . . and the most bizarre was yet to come. But that would be another few years in the future.

Chapter 30

THE PROCESS COMES TO TUSCALOOSA

At a press conference late in 2006, Nick Saban had had enough of the Miami media, and issued the declaration that would soon haunt him: "I guess I have to say it. I'm not going to be the Alabama coach."

On the first day of 2007, Alabama's undeterred athletic director, Mal Moore, flew to South Florida to try to land Saban. Bama had become its own version of the coaches' graveyard, declining to the point that big names weren't even considering the Alabama gig. Steve Spurrier turned down the job to stay at South Carolina. Moore thought he'd signed Rich Rodriguez to a contract, only to see Rodriguez turn around and stay at West Virginia. He'd merely used Alabama as a bargaining chip.

Saban understood a truism about the NFL: it's very, very tough to win, especially when you only get one first-round draft pick a year. In college, you can bring in the equivalent of four, five, six, or more, if you work at it. Plus, in the NFL, one season of success sets you back; the best teams one year get the worst draft picks the next. Saban preferred an environment where excellence could thrive without outside meddling or enforced parity. He also knew that Alabama was so desperate to return to football glory that it would give him everything he wanted.

But he had to make the decision in concert with his wife. After a game of telephone tag, Terry invited Moore to dinner to discuss Alabama possibilities. Shortly afterward, Saban called Terry and said he'd made a decision: he'd be staying with Miami. Terry replied by informing him that Moore would be coming over for dinner that evening.

Moore made his pitch—unprecedented power, a multiyear, multimillion-dollar contract—but Saban kept his cards close. He then met with Wayne Huizenga, the owner of the Dolphins, who advised him to go with what was in his heart. And it was very clear that what was in Saban's heart was a return to the college game. He called Moore and accepted the job, called his coaches and announced he was leaving, and by then the local media was on the story.

Helicopters loomed over Saban's home as the family packed suitcases into Moore's car. They followed the Sabans all the way to the airport, where a private plane was waiting.

Moore and Saban sat across from one another in the plane en route to Tuscaloosa. "Mal, let me ask you something," Saban said. "Do you think you've hired the best coach in the country?"

"Why, Nick, of course I do," Moore replied, silently praying he'd made the right choice.

"Well, you didn't. I'm nothing without my players," Saban said. "But you did just hire a helluva recruiter."

It was on.

The national media nailed Saban's hide to the wall for his deceptive "I'm not going" line. Legendary Dolphins coach Don Shula didn't hold back: "My reaction is that Saban in two years [at Miami] was 15–17. I don't think it will be any great loss. He has run away from a challenge." Worth noting: Saban would be replacing Shula's son at Alabama.

Saban attempted to walk back his own declarative statement, saying, "The circumstances changed and I made a different decision. That's not lying."

When he arrived in Tuscaloosa, a crowd of around 500—students were away on winter break—awaited his plane. "Thank you Jesus! Thank you Nick Saban!" yelled one woman. Dueling signs read "We've been Saban our hearts for you!" and "We've been Saban our money for you!"

Saban got an eight-year, $32 million deal, the highest ever for a college coach at the time. Alabama opted to fly without a net, writing no buyout provision into the contract to protect the school from yet another early Saban departure.

Saban, for his part, tried to gently, politely, but firmly burn all existing Alabama sense of entitlement to the ground. "I have respect for history and tradition, but none of that impacts what we do now," he said. "We cannot depend on the successes of the past to help us be successful in the future. That's the kiss of death."

"Saban's first and greatest victory in Tuscaloosa occurred when he brought its famously meddlesome, fractious booster corps to heel," Steven Godfrey wrote in *The Washington Post*. "This sounds like a logical first step when taking over a Tiffany brand such as Alabama, but it proved impossible to accomplish for the coaches who preceded him."

Saban hammered away at getting the very best for his team to ensure they could focus completely on the task at hand: developing into excellent players. In 2012, he won approval for the construction of a 30,000-square-foot football facility that included a $9 million weight room, a 212-seat theater-slash-meeting room, a hydrotherapy room with a waterfall, state-of-the-art training equipment, and various other amenities to help remove the sting of his demanding coaching style. The idea was to wrap the players in a bubble and keep them sheltered, away from anything that might cause any problems for them in any way.

But like Bryant before him, Saban established new expectations from the first day. "I heard Shula raise his voice twice in one year," former Alabama linebacker Alex Benson told author John Talty. "Whereas Saban, in the first five minutes of the first workout, dog-cussed every single one of us. It was night and day; that was obvious."

Along the way, Saban systematized The Process into a complete philosophy. The reason Alabama became so successful is because Saban had the mentality, the drive, and the vision to create a dynasty, to put his players and coaches in a position to succeed and get them focused on the process, not the results. Imagining holding a trophy over your head is nice. Focusing on the work it will take to get to that point is a much more effective way of ensuring it will happen. To Saban's mind, every single morning begins with a stark choice: You either get better or you get worse. Which is it going to be?

What's remarkable is how Saban's rebuilding of Alabama's football program is a reflection of what was happening in the state of Alabama at the same time. Even as the new coach was reshaping the state's namesake university, Birmingham was transitioning from a steelmaking hub into a destination for high-tech and medical corporations. Meanwhile, the state was welcoming in the likes of Mercedes-Benz and Amazon. The old "Bombingham" image from the civil rights era was slowly fading, but the football team remained an outsize source of pride.

Alabama fans were delirious with joy. They sported T-shirts with slogans like "Sabanation" and "Got Nick?" The spring practice intrasquad game—known as A-Day—drew 92,138 fans Saban's first year, with another 10,000 or so milling around outside Bryant-Denny.

But a college football dynasty doesn't become a dynasty without getting a little mud on the tires. The first scandal of the Saban era reared up just eight games into the 2007 season, when Saban suspended five players who had gotten free textbooks from the university bookstores. The scheme had begun under Shula but continued, briefly, under Saban.

The 2007 season included one of the most shocking runs of Saban's career: after losses to LSU and Mississippi State, the mighty Crimson Tide lost to Louisiana-Monroe... in Tuscaloosa, no less. It was a matchup of the college game's highest-paid coach against the lowest-paid one—ULM's Charlie Weatherbie was making just $130,000 at the time.

Saban referenced 9/11 and Pearl Harbor in a press conference, demonstrating how a catastrophic event can create a new mindset. But the idea of invoking such horrific tragedies in service of a routine college football season again didn't sit well with the national media, which by now was ready to pounce on every Saban utterance, no matter how innocuous.

And then came the Iron Bowl. Alabama lost 17–10, its sixth straight loss to Auburn. As he walked off the field, Tommy Tuberville held up those six fingers.

Meanwhile, the Dolphins finished 1–15, and LSU won the national championship with some of the players Saban had recruited still on the roster. But Saban was about to get his biggest prize yet, one that would set the stage for all the rest.

During the middle of the 20th century, the upper Midwest—coal country, the land where Joe Namath, Joe Montana, Dan Marino, and Saban himself hailed from—was a hotbed of recruiting, breeding a tough, hardy type of football player. In later years, though, the center of American football recruiting moved south, to the Gulf Coast, and there Saban began mining. He struck gold right off the bat on February 6, 2008, at Foley High School in Baldwin County, Alabama. There, a tall, lanky receiver by the name of Quintorris "Julio" Jones sat at a table with hats representing Florida, Florida State, Oklahoma, and Alabama before him. It's a now-familiar scene, but Jones was one of the first to do it live on ESPN. And when he lifted the Alabama hat and placed it on his head, the cheers nearly blew the roof off the gym.

Saban recruited Jones to a class that included Dont'a Hightower, Mark Ingram, and half a dozen other players who ended up in the NFL. He came within a fingernail of landing Andrew Luck, too, but Luck ultimately decided to go with a more academically minded school in Stanford.

In Louisiana, Saban had sought to put up walls around the state. He wouldn't be able to do that in Alabama—after all, Auburn was right there—but he again hit the high schools and began establishing relationships with local coaches.

Saban established a comprehensive recruiting system that accounted for all variables. He assessed recruits across at least 10 different categories, including size, speed, character, toughness, academics, flexibility of the ankle, knee, and hip, balance and body control, and explosive power. Each potential recruit got a dot. Green was for character problems. Red, academic problems. This ended up with a comprehensive ranking of 1 to 5, with 1 being the best. Few players ever got anywhere close to a 1; Jones was a 1.8. Anyone ranked around 2 was offered a scholarship.

By the mid-2010s, Alabama basically recruited itself, but just to be sure, Saban clearly laid out the value proposition for his possible recruits. He showed them how much they would make in the NFL. He showed them how many first-round draft picks he'd shepherded into the league. He won the title "Lord of the Living Room" for the way he managed to talk recruits and their families into signing with Alabama. The room in Bryant-Denny Stadium where Saban addressed the media was lined with the NFL jerseys of Alabama alumni, an indelible image of what awaits those who work hard.

"As much as we treat [football coaches] like gods, they're still having to call 15- and 16-year-old kids and beg them to come to their school," author John Talty says. "It's not the most enjoyable process. [Saban] realized early on that it's what powered the whole machine. And he was willing to go above and beyond in a way that I think a lot of other head coaches had no interest in doing. That allowed him to stack a lot of talent, at LSU and then Alabama."

But all that glory was down the road. In 2008, the NCAA put the brakes on his operation, passing what was quickly dubbed the Saban

Rule—a way to minimize in-person contact with recruits. Saban quickly deduced what the rest of the planet would learn all too well a little over a decade later: videoconferencing can be an effective way of looking someone in the eye and learning what you can from an almost-face-to-face encounter. Alabama's compliance pros signed off on it, and Saban once again had the edge on the competition.

Soon enough, Alabama came into its own. The new-look Tide absolutely beat the dog out of Clemson in the 2008 season-opening Chick-fil-A College Kickoff game. By November, the Tide was No. 1 in the BCS rankings. Shortly after Alabama beat Auburn in that year's Iron Bowl—ending the Tigers' run of six straight victories—Tuberville resigned. Tennessee's Phillip Fulmer was asked to step aside on the heels of a loss to Alabama. True or not, the prevailing wisdom—or the easy joke—held that Saban was slowly carving up the SEC, knocking off coach after coach who would pose any threat to him.

Alabama faced Florida in the 2008 SEC championship. The Gators were led by Tim Tebow, who, interestingly enough, was close to signing with Alabama during the Mike Shula years. The Tide lost to that Florida team, which would go on to win the BCS title. But Alabama didn't forget. And in 2009, they'd get the chance to right some wrongs.

In June 2009, the NCAA issued a ruling on the textbook scandal. Seven players were found to have obtained free textbooks for friends and others, worth as much as $4,000 in one case. The football program had to vacate 21 wins and was on probation as a "repeat violator"—any other major infraction in the next five years, and Alabama would again be looking at crippling penalties. Saban understood that the mistakes previous regimes had made simply wouldn't fly any longer.

If the 2008 team was about getting the pieces, 2009 was about putting them together.

Alabama stomped all the way through that season, and Mark Ingram won the Heisman—incredibly, the first time an Alabama player had received the award. The Tide's reward was a rematch with the Florida Gators in the SEC championship. Tebow had won 22 games in a row, and the Gators were the preeminent team in college football.

They were also in Alabama's way.

The Tide dissected the Gators in that matchup, slicing through what had been the college game's greatest offense. The victory symbolized the fact that Alabama had arrived, and there would be a new sheriff in town for the next decade. Tebow wept on the sideline, his tears flowing into his eye black, where he had written John 16:33. (The verse: "I have told you these things so that in me you may have peace. In this world you will have trouble. But take heart! I have overcome the world.")

Alabama would move on to face Texas in the Rose Bowl for the national championship, where another great what-if rose up. In that game, Texas quarterback Colt McCoy got hit by Marcell Dareus and lost feeling in his arm. He wouldn't play another down, and the emboldened Tide would go on to win the program's latest championship and its first under Saban.

In 2010, Alabama seemed prepared to run it back and contend for another title. The team stormed right through the schedule, so much so that coaches began worrying if they were taking things *too* casually. They would get their answer against South Carolina, when Spurrier caught Saban napping and stuck a loss on the Tide. Three weeks later, in the latest edition of the Saban Bowl, LSU upset its old coach, pinning the season's second loss on Alabama.

Still, when LSU later lost to Arkansas, Alabama still had a narrow pathway to a repeat national title. If they closed out their schedule with a victory, then won the SEC championship, they'd be back in the mix. There was just one more team remaining on the regular-season schedule: Auburn, of course. Auburn, and their new quarterback... a guy named Cam.

Chapter 31

SUPERMAN ON THE PLAINS

There are a few players who make such a massive, generational impact on college football that they literally reshape the fortunes of their university, players who define the history of their institution, players after whom nothing is ever the same.

Cam Newton is one such player. Without Newton, the 2010 Auburn Tigers would have been a .500 team at best. Bigger than anyone faster, faster than anyone bigger, stronger than pretty much anyone, he was a superhero in blue and orange, an Avenger who single-handedly overthrew the Alabama empire in the 2010 Iron Bowl.

Newton was a singular quarterback, and his race was an essential component to his success. Historically, white football coaches hadn't started Black quarterbacks, finding any number of reasons to discount their ability, their intellect, their preparation, or their decision-making. Newton obliterated every possible argument on the field . . . even if his decision-making off the field proved occasionally debatable.

Born in Georgia in 1989, Newton was always an exceptional athlete, both the youngest and the biggest on most of his youth teams. He started playing football at age 7, and added baseball to the mix around age 9. A big fan of Ken Griffey Jr., Newton loved to stalk center field and modeled his swagger after The Kid. Still, he quit baseball when he was 14 because he was afraid of getting hit by pitches. He switched over to basketball, but his football mentality—he started out as a linebacker—got in the way. He fouled out frequently, and realized his true destiny lay on a football field.

"My mom always wondered how I could be afraid of a little baseball when I always had these huge guys chasing me," Newton later said. "It's a good question."

Newton was a freshman at Atlanta's Westlake High School when his brother was a senior. The Westlake team was strong enough to draw attention from college scouts, and young Cam watched as scouts from Georgia Tech, Florida State, Auburn, Florida, USC, Texas, and other schools visited his south Atlanta campus. At that point, he realized that college might be in the cards. "Okay," he thought, "this pigskin can take me places."

Newton was simply spectacular in high school, grading out as a five-star prospect and catching the attention of Florida, Georgia, Ole Miss, Mississippi State, and several other colleges. He committed to Urban Meyer's Florida program at the start of his senior year, and suited up for the Gators starting in the fall of 2007.

At Florida, Newton was an understudy to Tebow, and made the most of his extraordinarily limited action. In five games, he threw 10 passes, completing just five for only 40 yards. But he also used his legs, rushing 16 times for 103 yards and three touchdowns. His sophomore season ended after just one game in 2008, when he suffered an ankle injury against Hawaii and redshirted the year. A few months later, matters turned much darker.

Newton's days at Florida were numbered once he was arrested and charged with burglary, larceny, and obstruction of justice surrounding the theft of a laptop computer from another Florida student. The student reported his laptop, valued at $1,700, stolen from his room on October 16, 2008. When University of Florida police searched Newton's room, they spotted the laptop, and Newton asked for a moment to call an attorney. When they returned to the room, the laptop was no longer there. An investigation of the area outside Newton's window turned up—surprise!—the missing laptop.

The charges were later dropped after Newton went through pretrial diversion, but the damage was done. He knew that his playing time would be limited to nonexistent with Tebow returning for his senior season, and thus made the call to leave Florida and find playing time elsewhere.

"I think I was left with no choice but to leave," Newton said at the time. "I felt like if he comes back for his senior year, I really wasn't going to get a chance to play, and that was another year washed down the drain." He announced his intention to transfer away from Florida in January 2009, just three days before the Gators beat Oklahoma for the national championship.

"I believe that a person should not be thought of as a bad person because of some senseless mistake that they made," Newton said several years later. "I think every person should have a second chance. If they blow that second chance, so be it for them."

However, there was another twist: in 2010, a Fox Sports report indicated that Newton had been facing substantial penalties for academic cheating. The Fox Sports report indicated that he had one instance of cheating his freshman year, and two more as a sophomore. In one of those two incidents, he was accused of putting his name on another student's paper and purchasing a replacement paper on the internet. He was scheduled to appear in front of Florida's Student Conduct Committee during the spring 2009 semester.

Multiple reports suggested that Meyer had been the source who leaked information about Newton. "For anyone to think that I or anyone on our staff may have leaked information about private student records to the media doesn't know us very well," Meyer said in a statement in 2010. "It's a ridiculous claim and simply not true."

"I'm not going to respond to every story or criticism that is reported by the media," Newton said in a 2010 statement about the cheating allegations. "I've talked on several occasions about my time at Florida."

What's clear is that Newton needed to get out of Gainesville. *Far* out of Gainesville. He wanted to play immediately, lying low while his legal woes dissipated. He had to sit out a year of Division I football if he wanted to transfer, but junior college provided a loophole that allowed him to continue to play.

He ended up in The Middle of Nowhere, Texas.

The Newtons connected with Brad Franchione, the head coach at Blinn College (and the son of briefly tenured Alabama coach Dennis Franchione). After some back-and-forth, and some hard questions on both sides, Newton agreed to attend Blinn, a two-year community college with an enrollment of about 2,400, for a year.

Blinn was nowhere near anything. Located on Highway 290 between Houston and Austin, it was exactly what Newton needed—a place far from the spotlight he'd drawn to himself.

"I don't know what I wanted to get out of Blinn," Newton told the *New York Times* in 2016. "I think I just wanted that opportunity. When I was in junior college, I was mentally hurt. I needed to regain some confidence by playing the quarterback position, let alone football, because I hadn't played important downs in so long."

The Newton family's offer was limited—one year only—and the demands were clear. Newton was capable of stomping everybody in sight, but his family didn't want him to just be a basic option quarterback. They wanted him to develop as a pocket passer as well, in order to unlock his next phase of development.

They had a three-hour dinner in Houston to hash out the final details: No interviews with the media. No option quarterbacking. Constant improvement of his leadership skills through daily talks with Franchione.

Newton traveled to Brenham, Texas, carrying nothing more than a Nike duffel bag. Unable to move into his dorm, he spent his first night on Franchione's couch. Once practice began, he immediately began challenging his teammates with lines like "Did you get better today? Did you get better that play?"

Newton threw himself into his days at Blinn, chafing at the usual rule that quarterbacks couldn't be tackled. When he believed that Franchione whistled plays dead too early, he barked his displeasure.

Newton had thrown only 12 passes at Florida. But it wasn't long before both his coaches and his teammates realized just how much he could do for all of them. He organized seven-on-seven games at the stadium, and nearly 60 players showed up.

Every morning, Newtwon would awaken in his first-floor apartment to the sound of cows mooing. He'd get up, sign in to the football offices at 7:00 a.m., head to his English comp class at 8:00 a.m., and then endure brutal practices and team-building exercises. He and his teammates once had to paint the bleachers at Spencer Stadium, a facility so unsafe that those bleachers were removed the year after he left. He had basic equipment, but anything special—visors or gloves, say—was at the player's own expense.

Newton was already one of the most touted junior college players in the country, and in the fourth game of the season, he proved why. Blinn traveled to Tyler, Texas, to play Tyler Junior College. Blinn ran up 60 points, and Newton accounted for 503 of the team's 601 total yards all by himself. In another game, he put up seven touchdowns and 369 yards of total offense against Cisco College in a merciless 71-point stomping.

All the while, Newton was using his year out of the limelight to learn leadership lessons. He'd pick Franchione's brain, expecting his coach to come prepared with a leadership lesson every day and calling him out when he didn't.

On the season, Newton was responsible for 38 touchdowns, including 16 on the ground, and had a 60.7 completion rate while throwing only five interceptions. Over one four-game stretch, Blinn outscored opponents 262–115, including that 84–13 demolition of Cisco.

In the junior college national title game, Blinn had a 31–26 lead late in the game over Fort Scott Community College. With only one Hail Mary play remaining, Fort Scott was down to its last chance. Newton went in on defense to help knock down a potential miracle throw. Blinn held on to win, and Newton wouldn't lose another college football game.

Before 2010, Newton had narrowed his choices to either Auburn or Mississippi State. "It was neck and neck," Newton would later say of the race. The tipping point: Auburn's 22 seniors and their ability to win immediately.

"I wanted to go to a school that could get me to a BCS (championship) game," he said, and Auburn appeared more prepared for that than Mississippi State.

There remained one task to resolve: notifying Mississippi State, and specifically head coach Dan Mullen, that he would not be coming to Starkville. Mullen had spent significant time with Cam while the two were at Florida in 2008, and clearly believed that gave him an edge in signing the mega-talented quarterback. Newton later remembered the conversation going something like this:

"How's my quarterback?" Mullen asked.

"Coach, I just wanted to be a man and call you and tell you and Ms. Megan that I am going to Auburn," Newton replied. "I didn't want you to hear it through the grapevine. I didn't want you to hear it on ESPN."

"But how, Cam?" Mullen asked. "I was going to do right by you. We need you."

Cam pointed out that Auburn only needed the right quarterback. "They ready to win," Newton said. "They just need me."

"I said to myself, 'If I can get a guy, not at 16, 17, but a guy at like 21, 22 to understand, Yo, you trying to get to the league too? All right, let's work,'" he told the *NFL Players: Second Acts* podcast in 2024. "And I knew it would be easier to convince that body of people to commit to something rather than a team that only had four seniors returning."

Meanwhile, Auburn was trying to find its footing in the post-Tuberville era. A 5–19 record as a head coach—including a 10-game losing streak—generally doesn't open many doors. So it was no small shock when Auburn decided to fill the empty space Tuberville left behind with a coach by the name of Gene Chizik, who had managed only a 5–19 record at Iowa State.

But Chizik was more than just a number that college football sickos briefly used as a gag, calling May 19 "Gene Chizik Day." For one thing, he looked the part, still sporting the stone jaw that had helped him develop a fearsome rep as a high school linebacker in Seminole, Florida, before playing (briefly) for the Gators. For another, he'd coached some of Auburn's most brutal defenses in recent history, as defensive coordinator from 2002 to 2004 under Tuberville—a run that included three wins over Alabama.

Chizik prized defense, and he built his team from the defense outward. He hired Gus Malzahn to serve as offensive coordinator. And then Chizik and Malzahn received the finest gift a coach could get—the greatest offensive college football player to hit Auburn since Bo.

In the second game of the season, Newton's Tigers beat Dan Mullen and Mississippi State 17–14 on a Thursday night. Newton sought out Mullen to shake his hand after the game, but found him standoffish—exhibiting what Newton would later call "iffy" body language. Two weeks later, Newton was informed about an investigation prompted by two sources who claimed that he and his family took money to play football for Auburn.

Chizik called Newton and his parents into his office. As Newton recalled, Chizik said, "You're about to go into an investigation. The NCAA feels that somebody benefited from money." The Newtons asked Chizik how much money was involved. "Two hundred thousand," he replied, and they laughed. Chizik wasn't laughing.

"Bro, $200,000 in my culture, you're going to see that shit some way," Newton told *NFL Players: Second Acts* in 2024. "A car, some enhancements to the house. My father is still a preacher to this day and was then, too. You would have seen some enhancements to the church. Or some type of lifestyle upgrade. Man, motherfuckers looked at years and years of bank statements. It was almost embarrassing to provide. 'Motherfucker, we broke.' Pressing the shift button, holding the shift button: B-R-O-K-E, exclamation point. We *broke*."

Newton would be declared ineligible on two separate occasions—November 10 and November 30—but reinstated in time for Auburn's next game in both cases. The NCAA found that Newton's father Cecil and former Mississippi State player Kenny Rogers solicited money in return for Cam's services, but that Cam had no knowledge of the pay-for-play scheme. Cecil Newton would later say he "willfully fell on the sword" to maintain his son's eligibility and keep Auburn's national championship hopes alive.

"There was one individual who tried to navigate the services for Cam," Cecil Newton said. "Were we promised stuff? Were we gifted with stuff of this sort? No. Never."

After a 13-month investigation, the NCAA released a statement in October 2011 indicating that Cecil Newton and Rogers sought anywhere from $120,000 to $180,000 for Cam to sign with Mississippi State. Instead, he agreed in February 2010 to go to Auburn. Mississippi State was cleared of any wrongdoing in the case.

"I don't know that there's any top programs in America that are lily white," Pat Dye said many years later. "The only thing I do know is that if (Auburn athletic director) Jay Jacobs or Gene Chizik had any questions about his eligibility, he wouldn't have played."

In the heart of the controversy, *Sports Illustrated* estimated that if Newton could have been paid fair-market value, he would have commanded $3.5 million of Auburn's $60 million in TV revenue, ticket sales, sponsorships, and jersey sales for the 2010 season ... making a hypothetical $180,000 payment a steal of a deal.

Even as Newton struggled with swirling crises off the field, he was spectacular on it. He finished his one year at Auburn with 4,327 yards of total offense, throwing for 30 touchdowns and rushing for another 20. In a game against Louisiana-Monroe at Jordan-Hare, he hurled a 94-yard touchdown pass to Emory Blake, a pass that still stands as an Auburn record for longest pass completion. Against LSU, he unleashed the signature run of his college career, a 49-yard touchdown scramble during which he broke at least six tackles and outran the entire LSU defense.

Nothing could stop Newton and the Tigers ... right up to the moment they met the national champions.

IRON BOWL 2010: THE CAMBACK

Sometimes revenge is served cold, and sometimes it's thrown, still boiling, right into the faces of your enemies. The Iron Bowl had never seen a player quite like Cam Newton—hell, outside of superhero movies, no one had—and so when Newton turned even mighty Alabama into bit players in his ongoing bravura tour de force of a season, nobody could really say they were surprised.

November 26, 2010, dawned cold and overcast, but that didn't much matter to the Alabama faithful. Yes, the Tide had already lost two games that year, so a national title was pretty much out of the question... but vengeance wasn't. If you can't have a trophy of your own, there's nothing better than making sure your rival can't, either.

Auburn came into Tuscaloosa with a gaudy 11–0 record and a No. 2 national ranking. Newton had spent the last few weeks in silence over the scandals that swirled around him. Outside Bryant-Denny prior to kickoff, T-shirt hustlers sold shirts printed with $CAM NEWTON. The stadium PA system played "Take the Money and Run" and "Son of a Preacher Man," a move that got someone in the athletic department fired. But sometimes you've got to fall on the grenade for your team.

With an offensive attack that included 2009 Heisman Trophy winner Mark Ingram and future NFL icon Julio Jones, Alabama leaped out to a 24–0 advantage. It seemed like the bumpy, remarkable story of Cam Newton would come to a sudden end on the Bryant-Denny turf.

Not quite. Newton hurled a 36-yard touchdown pass to Emory Blake right before the half. On the second play of the third quarter, he fired a pass to the center of the field. While Alabama's Mark Barron appeared to have the toss lined up for a backbreaking interception, Auburn's Terrell Zachery edged past him, caught the ball, and took it to the house for a 70-yard touchdown. Just like that, the score was 24–14, and things didn't seem quite so comfortable for the Tide anymore.

Newton ascended to an even higher level then, leading Auburn to two more touchdowns on its next three possessions, and the final score stood at a shocking Auburn 28, Alabama 27. It was one of the great individual performances in Iron Bowl history, and the fact that it had been delivered on Alabama's turf was all the more humiliating. Newton ran around the field with his hand over his mouth, perhaps mocking the crowd's silence, perhaps pretending not to crow in victory.

In the SEC Championship, Auburn flung South Carolina right out of the Georgia Dome, winning 56–17 to claim the No. 1 ranking and set up a national championship showdown against Oregon. But before that could happen, there was the matter of the Heisman Trophy ceremony.

The candidates that year included Newton, Stanford's Andrew Luck, and Oregon's LaMichael James. Newton was the overwhelming favorite despite the controversies that dogged him throughout his year at Auburn. Because of those controversies, the NCAA informed Cecil Newton that he would not be welcome at the ceremony, so he stayed in his hotel room.

Newton won the award in a landslide, taking 729 first-place votes and more than doubling runner-up Luck's total. As he held the Heisman, he looked at his mother, and the two headed back to Cecil Newton's hotel room to show him the trophy. Newton hasn't been to a Heisman Trophy ceremony since then, and even now remains incensed at the NCAA for its treatment of his father.

"My dad ain't no different than [LaVar] Ball. No different than Archie Manning. No different than King Richard [Williams, father of Serena and Venus]. No different than Ja Morant's father. No different than any hands-on father. Deion Sanders," he said in 2024. "And it's like, I still have a hard time looking at that award as something I just take pride in."

Auburn won the national championship by a knee... or, more properly, by the lack of a knee. The Tigers and Ducks battled to a 19–19 tie late in the fourth quarter. With just over two minutes remaining and 73 yards from glory, Auburn began driving. On one of the drive's early plays, the Tigers lined up on their own 40. Newton called for the snap, handed off to freshman Michael Dyer, and then watched as Dyer was tackled after a 6-yard run.

Dyer stood up, looked around... and began sprinting down the right sideline. He realized what the Oregon defense hadn't: his knee never touched the ground on the tackle. He'd simply rolled over the top of his tackler and popped back up. He was pushed out of bounds at the Oregon 23-yard line, a monstrous 37-yard gain that put the Tigers in game-winning field goal range.

A few plays later, with just two seconds remaining on the clock, Auburn's Wes Byrum drilled the go-ahead field goal, giving the Tigers a 22–19 victory and their first national championship since 1957. Delirious Auburn students cast a blizzard of toilet paper onto Toomer's Corner, and for a moment, all was perfect on The Plains.

It wouldn't last. Without Newton—who relinquished his final year of eligibility, turned pro, and became the NFL's No. 1 pick—or Malzahn—who left after the 2011 season to coach at Arkansas State—Chizik floundered, going 8–5 in 2011 and 3–9 in 2012. Off-field problems mounted as well; in addition to the chaos swirling around Newton, four members of the 2010 national championship team were arrested in March 2011 on robbery charges, and other players had less severe run-ins with the law.

Dismayed at his downfall and unwilling to wait out a rebound, Auburn bought out Chizik's contract. Just like at Iowa State, he lost 19 times at Auburn... but he won 33, including 11 during that magical, untouchable national championship season.

Auburn lost its final three SEC games of the 2012 season by a combined score of 150–21. The killing blow: a 49–0 loss to Alabama. The decline was the most dramatic fall of any national championship team since the AP began taking polls in 1936, and it was Auburn's worst performance since the 0–10 season of 1950.

"Would we have loved to see him get another year, another opportunity? Yes," Auburn tight end Philip Lutzenkirchen said at the time, "but at the same time... three wins isn't going to cut it in our league."

After the devastating 2010 Iron Bowl loss, Alabama—out of the national championship conversation, out of the top 10 entirely—found its footing and beat the mess out of Saban's former Michigan State squad, 49–7, in the Capital One Bowl. Nobody much cared, given that Auburn was in the process of winning a national championship.

"At the end of the day, all they want to be is us," Saban told his team after the Iron Bowl loss. "They will always want what we have. But they will never be us."

Maybe so; maybe not. But as Cam Newton proved, while Auburn may not *be* Alabama, there's always a good chance Auburn can *beat* Alabama.

"You look at Alabama and how many great runs they've had, and the dynasties they've built in several different decades," says Justin Ferguson, who writes the *Auburn Observer* Substack. "A lot of Auburn's history is tied to, 'Here's the time where we messed it all up for them,' or 'Here's the time we jumped them and got to have our time in the sun.'"

After the highs of 2009 and 2010, some around the Iron Bowl were in a contemplative mood. "Fans on both sides of this rivalry need to put down their weapons, put down their arms, put down their attitudes," legendary Tiger quarterback Pat Sullivan told Auburn stalwart David Housel. "They need to look at what this state has accomplished in the last two years."

It was a nice idea, in theory.

2010 IRON BOWL

Final Score: Auburn 28, Alabama 27

Chapter 32

THE MAN WITH TOO MUCH BAMA IN HIM

Harvey Updyke spent a good portion of his life trying to convince people he wasn't crazy.

Al from Dadeville, on the other hand, didn't give a good goddamn what you thought of him.

The trouble for Harvey was both men occupied the same body. And both men had a love of Alabama football that transcended all reason.

Harvey Updyke was a loving grandfather, a man of neatly combed white hair and a high-pitched, gentle accent. His alter ego, Al from Dadeville, had a cold, grating, evil voice with the kind of kiss-my-ass-on-Sunday edge that has defined a certain kind of Southern man for more than a century.

Harveys and Als dot the South. They hang out at barbecue joints on Saturday afternoons and in high school bleachers on Friday nights; they work a certain kind of blue-collar job that keeps them from getting too refined and too far from the dirt where they were raised. They subsist on a steady diet of propaganda, diving deep into social media and message boards and listening to sports talk radio, their rage always on a hair trigger. They love Alabama, yes they do, but it's just as important that you realize just how much they love the Crimson Tide.

Enough to build their lives around the Tide.

Enough to build their legacies around the Tide.

Enough to kill for the Tide.

For all the twists and turns in the Alabama–Auburn rivalry, there was never a moment quite like the swerve into insanity in 2011, never a fan quite like Al from Dadeville, never a crime quite like the killing of Toomer's Oaks. Fandom is a mysterious, maniacal force in Alabama, and in 2011, the nation saw the worst of that fandom . . . and also the best of what it could inspire.

Young Harvey's family didn't have much, but they did have a television, and that meant Harvey could tune in to *The Bear Bryant Show*, sponsored by Golden Flake Snack Foods and Coca-Cola. ("Great Pair, says 'the Bear.'") He'd watch every installment of the show, listening with religious devotion as the Alabama legend intoned, in his unmistakable bass, about how the boys needed to step up against Tennessee or find a little something extra in themselves against Mississippi State.

Originating from a Birmingham TV station every Sunday afternoon precisely at 4:00 p.m., *The Bear Bryant Show* was part of a long-standing ritual for Tide fans: church, Sunday dinner, Bear . . . and that order didn't necessarily reflect their importance. The routine was always the same: the cohost—usually Alabama athletics official Charley Thornton—would set up Bryant with a bit of game film, and then Bryant, his thundering rumble deep enough to crack the Earth's crust, would grind through the past week's highlights with a cadence as familiar as a 12-bar blues progression.

"Now that's Pat Trammell rolling out with the ball," he might say. "He's a fine runner. Came to us from Scottsboro. Scottsboro's a fine town. I have a load of friends in Scottsboro. Pat's got a fine mamma and daddy. Fine folks, like all of them in Scottsboro."

If that doesn't exactly seem like scintillating insight from one of the most brilliant football minds of his day, well, you're not wrong. Bryant didn't offer up any kind of glimpse into his strategic thought processes; instead, he gave the Tide faithful a warm, soothing bath of the familiar, a gentle, comforting reassurance that everything was going to be all right, because ol' Bear was in charge. Bryant was a father figure for hundreds of thousands of Alabama fans, maybe more. And wouldn't you do anything for your daddy?

After Harvey retired, he moved to a small town in Tallapoosa County, just northwest of Auburn, a town called Dadeville. He happened to arrive at a most fortuitous moment in Alabama history, settling in Dadeville just in time for the 2009 season. He managed to wrangle a ticket to the Rose Bowl and watched ecstatically as Nick Saban led the Tide to its 13th national title.

As glorious as 2009 had been for Harvey, 2010 would play out as its dark mirror image. After watching Cam Newton mount that Iron Bowl comeback, Harvey seethed in the stands at Bryant-Denny. He'd spent $275 for a ticket, $275 he really couldn't afford to just piss away. He and a friend had a hotel room in Tuscaloosa—at a cost of another several hundred dollars for a game night—but didn't even bother staying. They just drove back home, back toward Dadeville.

Harvey spent days listening to sports talk radio. Specifically, *The Paul Finebaum Show*, the ESPN radio program that's the pulse of the Southeastern Conference. Day after day, he'd hear the Auburn fans gloating and the Bama fans crying conspiracy. He became radicalized, convinced that Auburn had stolen what was rightfully Alabama's.

And that was when he decided to take action.

At the corner of College and Magnolia, on the edge of Auburn's campus, you can walk into Toomer's Drugs and buy a 64-ounce ice-filled Styrofoam cup of the best damn lemonade in the South. You can read about the legend of the War Eagle that gives Auburn its rallying cry. You can stand out front and take in the view of Auburn's majestic red bricks and soaring Gothic architecture.

It's a magnificent corner, a bucket-list stop for every college football fan. And it was even finer back when the original Toomer's Oaks loomed over it all.

The original oaks were roughly 80 years old, their branches reaching high into the Alabama sky like hands lifted in song. Most days, they'd stand as guardians and icons, but every so often, they'd host one of sports' great traditions: the rolling of the trees.

Auburn students took every chance they could get to throw rolls of toilet paper high into the trees. Graduation? Roll the trees. Wedding? Roll the trees. End of classes? Start of classes? Canceled classes? Roll, roll, roll the trees.

The tradition began in the early 1960s, a marked improvement over the days when cars and buildings around Toomer's Corner were doused in (washable) blue and orange paint and bonfires were set in the middle of the intersection. From a silly prank rose a tradition that has a strange kind of beauty, thousands of long streams of delicate paper waving in the wind like a rare snowstorm in the Deep South. It's one of college football's finest traditions, and when it comes at the expense of Alabama, the prevailing mood is as euphoric as the high of a national championship win.

The Auburn faithful roll the trees as students, roll them again when they get married, and then watch as their children and grandchildren roll the trees too. It's not too much to say the oaks were the true heart of Auburn University.

The dark figure slid like oil through the small town, four milk jugs filled with poison in his hands.

Four hours from now, these streets would be full of students on their way to class. At this moment, though, all was silent at the corner of College and Magnolia. Toomer's Drugs, home to that beloved lemonade, sat dark. The odor from a distant overnight smoker carried the scent of barbecue through the air. The hum of the traffic lights overhead was the night's only sound.

Outlined against the night sky, Toomer's Oaks loomed, watching the figure in silence.

The man had dreamed of this moment his entire life, and he'd planned it in detail over the last few weeks. He'd spent months—long, sleepless nights—watching the trees on webcams, plotting exactly when they'd be most alone, most vulnerable. He'd chosen this particular time—four o'clock on a Monday morning—as the perfect moment to exact his revenge. He'd gamed out his plan like a bank robber scheming for the score of a lifetime.

He worked quickly. He'd brought those four milk jugs, two for each tree, filled with a mixture of water and an industrial herbicide called Spike 80DF. He doused the roots of the first tree, then ran 80 feet to the trunk of the other and repeated the process. It took less than a minute to empty all four jugs and soak the soil with 500 times the amount of herbicide needed to kill the legendary trees.

"I wanted Auburn people to hate me as much as I hate them," Al from Dadeville later said, in Harvey's voice.

And he would have gotten away with it too, if he hadn't sabotaged himself.

On January 27, 2011, with Auburn still basking in the warm glow of a championship won in part at its rival's expense, Harvey dialed

THE MAN WITH TOO MUCH BAMA IN HIM

855-242-PAUL—the number for Finebaum's show. The screen in the studio read "Al From Dadeville... Bear Bryant's death," so Paul took the call.

Right out of the gate, Al from Dadeville was fired up. He led off by repeating an old Bama conspiracy theory that Auburn students had rolled Toomer's Oaks on the night of Bear Bryant's death in 1983.

"Now stop, stop, stop, stop, stop, stop," Finebaum replied. "I just have the most difficult time believing that Auburn students rolled Toomer's Corner when the news broke that Coach Bryant died. Does anyone else remember that? I don't."

Al claimed to have newspaper proof of the desecration, but Finebaum dismissed that. Al pressed on, clearly laying the groundwork for... something.

"This year," Al growled, "I was at the Iron Bowl and I saw where they put a Scam Newton jersey on Bear Bryant's statue," referring to the 10-foot-tall bronze statue of Bryant outside the stadium that bears his name. (This, at least, was the truth; a photograph captured the moment, but the jersey didn't stay up there long.)

Finebaum's studio, like all radio nerve centers, had a kill button—a large red X that, when pushed, dumped the caller into the abyss. Finebaum, weary of rehashing old Bama grievances yet again, remarked that Bryant had been dead at that point for 28 years. His finger hovered over the kill button, giving Al from Dadeville one last line to get back on track.

With that line, Al from Dadeville turned college football sideways.

"The weekend after the Iron Bowl, I went to Auburn, Alabama, because I lived 30 miles away" —again, "Al" wasn't exactly disguising his identity—"and I poisoned the two Toomer's trees."

"OK, well, that's fair," Finebaum laughed, understandably not quite getting the gravity of Updyke's words.

"I put Spike 80DF in them," Al growled.

"Did they die?" Finebaum replied, not quite sure whether to take this seriously.

"Do what?" Al said.

"Did. They. Die?"

"They're not dead yet," Al said, then added, with the chilling finality of an undertaker, "but they definitely will die."

"Is it against the law to poison a tree?" wondered Finebaum, who was still thinking this might just be a radio bit.

"Do you think I care?" Al asked, and the cold tone of his voice obliterated any trace of empathy. After a bit more banter, he signed off with an icy "Roll Tide."

And just like that, Harvey Updyke destroyed his entire life in one minute, 59 seconds.

Auburn fans, upon hearing the exchange, quite justifiably lost their minds. They demanded an investigation; they demanded "Al" from Dadeville's head. Botanists from Mississippi State investigated the soil and quickly found that, yes, enough poison to bring down the oaks had been introduced into their root system. That got the Department of Homeland Security involved, since the amount of poison that had been dumped onto the trees could have been enough to contaminate the water table that runs beneath the entire region. This wasn't just vandalism or even desecration—it was bordering on full-scale terrorism.

Auburn agronomy professor Scott McElroy, asked to assess the damage, took an unscientific but utterly appropriate view. "It's evil," McElroy told Finebaum in 2011. "It's malicious. I don't know what else to say other than that."

"You have to understand," Finebaum later wrote, "the Toomer's Corner trees were sacred at Auburn. In Mafia terms, they were made men. To damage, desecrate or poison those trees was to wage holy war on all those who held Auburn dear to their hearts."

Harvey didn't realize the hellstorm he'd unleashed. He glibly told his friends that he wanted to get caught, just so he could boast about being the one who killed those dang trees. He expected he'd be slapped with a fine of a few hundred dollars. Instead, he became the most hated man in Alabama. In *all* of Alabama.

"There's always somebody in every crowd who takes the joke too far," says journalist Tommy Tomlinson, who delved deep into the Toomer's Oaks story for *Sports Illustrated* in 2011. "If you're sitting around a room and telling jokes and stories and maybe roasting each other a little bit, there's always somebody who doesn't know where to stop. Harvey was that guy."

In what must have felt like the ultimate betrayal to Harvey, the University of Alabama condemned the attack and distanced itself from him. Not only that, but scientists from Alabama traveled to Auburn to try to salvage the trees.

For a time, Harvey attempted to claim innocence. To hear him tell it—or maybe this was Al talking—Auburn was trying to put up a smoke screen to distract from its alleged pay-for-play scheme involving Newton. When four Auburn players were arrested for armed robbery not long after the poisoning, Harvey began obsessing over them and what he perceived as his unfair treatment compared to the way Lee County law enforcement handled the players' fates.

As time went on, Harvey—or, again, maybe Al—began inventing more and more justifications, trying to rationalize what he'd done. Other teams' fans committed pranks all the time, stealing mascots and painting their colors on goalposts! Where was all this outrage then? (Not mentioned: the pranksters generally didn't murder the mascots.) In Harvey's mind, Auburn fans had defecated on Bear Bryant's grave and vandalized Nick Saban's lake house . . . probably, right? It didn't matter if the accusations were true; it mattered that Harvey believed they *could* be true.

All the while, his beloved Alabama turned its back on him. Former

Tide players lit him up on social media. A Facebook group, Tide for Toomer's, raised more than $50,000 toward the trees' potential rehabilitation. Nick Saban himself wrote a check to help try to save the trees. Upon hearing that news, Harvey sounded like a child stunned that he'd been punished so badly. "It hurt my feelings," he said.

Alabama grads, with more than a little condescension, call people like Harvey—folks who don't have a diploma from the school, but do have a bumper full of stickers and a closet full of Tide gear—"Dirt Road Alumni" or "Pickup Truck Alumni." The vast majority of actual Alabama grads wanted nothing whatsoever to do with him.

Meanwhile, Lee County law enforcement was out to get Harvey, and he was looking at serious jail time. At 62, in ill health, frail, and scared, he wasn't sure how or why he'd come to this point. He thought he deserved probation, maybe a bit of community service or a fine. But jail? For a couple trees? Really?

What Harvey didn't realize was that in a single stroke, he managed to carve a scar into the hearts of two universities. Auburn lost a symbol of pride and resilience. Alabama lost the moral high ground it eternally craved. The rivalry always had heat, but now it had drawn blood.

Harvey made a return appearance on *The Paul Finebaum Show* in April 2011. While his first call had lasted just two minutes, this one ran 45. He cycled through a list of apologies—to "my children, the University of Alabama and my high school coach"—but notably not to Auburn or its fans.

His regret wasn't that he got caught. It was that he phoned in to the radio show and gloated. He called it "one of the biggest mistakes I ever made in my life. All my adult life my wives kind of said I'm a crap-stirrer. I like to stir crap. I was just trying to upset the Auburn Nation. Paul, I never thought it'd come to this."

Harvey tried to make sense of his place in the world, his crimes, and his punishment, and—true to form—he could only do it in terms of Alabama football. He referenced Tommy Lewis, the Alabama football player who leaped off the bench at the 1954 Cotton Bowl and tackled a Rice player who was headed for the end zone. He paraphrased Lewis's explanation for his behavior: "I just have too much Bama in me." It was a condition Harvey understood.

But Al from Dadeville wasn't yet done. As Harvey prepared to sign off, Al forced his way into the conversation. "This is gonna make people mad, but I gotta do it," he said. "Roll Damn Tide."

Harvey Updyke was charged with criminal damage to an agricultural facility, a felony. He would go on to serve 76 days in jail and supervised probation until the end of his life. He was ordered to pay $800,000 in restitution.

The light sentence incensed Auburn fans, as well as a few in positions of power. "I think it was garbage," Lee County District Attorney Brandon Hughes later said. "I think to call it a slap on the wrist is overstating it. I think it was a kiss on the cheek."

Updyke spent his two-plus months in the Lee County Detention Center, about 6 miles east of where the oaks stood. He lost more than 50 pounds in jail. His hair and mustache grew out. He scrawled "ROLL DAMN TIDE" over the chest pocket on his Auburn-orange jumpsuit, and he claimed other inmates beat him up regularly and spit in his food.

Meanwhile, the oaks fought for their lives, but there would be no miracle comeback; the Spike 80DF had done its job all too well. Agricultural experts from all over the South descended on Auburn and attempted what amounted to emergency surgery on the trees—everything from injecting sugar into the roots to laying activated carbon over the soil.

Nothing worked. After two years of battle, two years of work by the South's premier agricultural scientists, the truth was clear: the oaks would have to go. With chain saws and ceremony, the poisoned icons were brought down.

The new oaks stood 35 feet tall when they were planted in February

2015, with a third tree tucked away elsewhere on campus in the event of another Updyking or similar sabotage. The trees would take several years to establish roots, which meant that the long-standing tradition of rolling the trees in toilet paper after a victory went on pause for a few years.

After his release, Updyke began serving what was slated to be five years of supervised probation, which included a 7:00 p.m. curfew, a ban on attending any collegiate event, and a ban on stepping onto Auburn University property, which likely didn't cause him significant hardship.

Oh, and then there was the matter of that $800,000 he owed Auburn. It didn't take long for him to run significantly behind on his payments. In the 2017 calendar year, for instance, he made all of two payments, for less than $200 in total.

Even then, he might have gotten away with skimping on his debt if he hadn't sabotaged himself yet again. He left Dadeville and moved to Louisiana, and Lee County officials lost track of him. But then he posted a Facebook update with a crude shot at Auburn, and Lee County decided to take action.

Updyke claimed in a Facebook video that his monthly rent was increasing $200 a month, to $500, with a $500 deposit, apparently explaining his inability to make his restitution payments. But he also added a defiant "Roll Tide." A judge threatened to jail him, and he was cited for contempt of court for failing to appear at a hearing about the unpaid fines.

In November 2019, as Finebaum broadcast from the University of Alabama prior to a mammoth showdown against LSU, Harvey once again called in, this time trying a new angle: it was all an accident.

"I didn't mean it," he said, his voice tentative. Harvey—or Al—only sounded convincing when he was spitting hate at Auburn.

"You didn't mean it?" Finebaum said, not letting Harvey off the hook. "You went to a store and bought poison, you poisoned trees, and you didn't mean it?"

Long pause, and then Al stepped up. "Paul, they're only trees. It's not like I tried to kill that crow [actually, the eagle] that flies around. I didn't try to kill LSU's tiger."

"You still don't get it, do you?" Finebaum seethed, clearly disgusted. "You destroyed something near and dear to an entire university and its fan base, and you're coming on the show laughing about it and joking about it and casting aspersions to this school. You broke a lot of people's hearts when you poisoned those trees." Then he added the kicker: "I don't know any Alabama fans who thought it was a good idea, either."

Less than nine months later, Harvey Updyke, age 71, was dead. He never apologized, never paid up, never repented.

"He was misunderstood at times," his daughter-in-law Marsha Updyke wrote on Facebook, "but anyone close to him understood him, knew his heart, forgave his flaws, and loved him. He made us all laugh. He genuinely cared."

"I'm a good father, a good stepfather, and a very good Alabama fan," Updyke said a few months before his death. "I admit I like 'em too much."

At the time of his death, Harvey had paid only about $6,900 of the $800,000 he owed. Among his last wishes: that his family would spread his ashes around Bryant-Denny Stadium . . . but also around the new Toomer's Oaks, just to get at Auburn fans one last time.

Chapter 33

TRAGEDY AND HEALING

Prior to the spring A-Day game in mid-April 2011, Alabama unveiled a massive Nick Saban statue. Saban thus joined Wallace Wade, Frank Thomas, Paul Bryant, and Gene Stallings as national championship–winning coaches immortalized in bronze near the Walk of Champions. Miss Terry, as she was now known to Alabama fans, was actively involved in the statue's creation, tweaking the tip of the nose and the shape of the earlobes.

There was some question about whether it was too soon to be honoring Saban this way, with a full 9-foot-tall statue. After all, he'd only been at Alabama for four seasons. But that in itself was enough to justify the statue for Alabama boosters, who were all too aware that Saban was in Year Five—right about the time he got itchy feet at LSU and Michigan State. Was it a way to persuade him to stay in town? Perhaps.

Eleven days after it was dedicated, the statue—and Saban's employment—became an irrelevant issue.

———

April afternoons in Tuscaloosa are magical. The heat of the summer hasn't rolled in yet, and the chill of winter is a distant memory. Birds chirp, dogs bark, and—most important—school is almost over for the semester. It's a grim, deadly irony that the same benign conditions that lull people into feeling safe and calm are the perfect conditions for a tornado.

Tornadoes can be the most terrifying storms of all, because they move without pattern and without predictability. The most hospitable place on the planet for tornado formation is so-called Tornado Alley, and the ideal time of year for twisters to appear is spring and summer. Tornado Alley runs from the Rockies to the Mississippi Valley, including the states of Texas, Oklahoma, Kansas, Nebraska, and Missouri. An offshoot of Tornado Alley, known as Dixie Alley, runs from Texas to South Carolina. Tornados in Dixie Alley can be stronger and last longer than those in other parts of the country, and the hilly topography of the area often means they aren't spotted on the ground until they're too close to escape.

April 27, 2011, had been a bright, warm day in Tuscaloosa, and as the afternoon wore on, the heat had increased significantly, well into the mid-80s. Wind gusts of 10 to 15 miles per hour picked up and flung loose papers about, but high above, crosswinds reached triple digits. The conditions were terrifyingly perfect for a monstrous tornado, and the entire state was now on alert.

The skies turned gray. The birds stopped chirping. The air became deathly still.

Players were at their apartments, relaxing and unwinding after a day of practice. Saban, meanwhile, was deep in thought, analyzing practice yet again, trying to divine the tiniest nuances of advantage. He finally packed up and left his office at the Mal Moore Athletic Facility around 4:30, driving across the Black Warrior River to his home outside Northport as the skies blackened.

Shortly after 5:00, Tuscaloosa mayor Walt Maddox consulted traffic cams, and what he saw horrified him. A monstrous tornado, winds whipping at 190 miles per hour, was carving its way across the western edge of Tuscaloosa, straight toward the University of Alabama campus and Bryant-Denny Stadium.

The retail center of Tuscaloosa stands at the intersection of 15th Street and McFarland Boulevard. There's a Full Moon Bar-B-Que there, and a Krispy Kreme. Not far away are the requisite Target, Home Depot, and Barnes & Noble stores. It's the heart of commerce in the city, and it was also Ground Zero for the tornado's path.

Tuscaloosa's eyes turned to James Spann, the chief meteorologist for Birmingham's ABC affiliate, who had been issuing warnings all day. He advised parents to put bicycle helmets on their children to protect them from flying debris, or worse. Frantic, shaky cell phone video captured terrifying images of the massive, 30,000-foot-high, mile-wide tornado, so big it dwarfed Bryant-Denny Stadium. And then, not long after 5:00, everything went black.

There's always a cruel silence that comes in the wake of a tornado. It's like some cosmic joke—after the numbing terror, the empty calm settles in. Everything in the tornado's path was gone, just gone. Buildings were pummeled into kindling, smashed as if hit by a massive hammer. Homes were reduced to splinters. Businesses were blown off their foundations. Everywhere, townspeople and students stumbled back into the sunlight, trying to comprehend the life-altering horror that had just devastated Tuscaloosa.

Fifty-three people in Tuscaloosa, including six students, lost their lives in the storm. The tornado destroyed or damaged close to 6,000 homes, leaving a huge scar across the heart of the city. In a cruel irony, the tornado destroyed much of the city's emergency management response capability, including debris-removal equipment, leaving Tuscaloosa beaten down and wounded. Concerns about Alabama football seemed trivial indeed.

The next day, Saban and his associate Thad Turnipseed loaded a pickup truck with 20 cases of Gatorade and bottled water left over from the spring game. They headed toward town and stopped first at what was then known as Ferguson Student Center. More than 300 students were gathered there, scared and uncertain. Saban stepped out of the truck and stepped up onto a small brick wall, and delivered the kind of speech that had inspired his players to win national championships.

"Your time will come," he said, "when you will be able to help and volunteer. We're going to need everybody's effort for a long time to get our city back on its feet. Life is all about challenges, and now we're facing a really big one. But working together, we will get through this. Remember, we have to do this together as one team."

Saban spoke for eight crucial, inspiring minutes, and when he was done, the students cheered, filled with resolve and determination. He and Turnipseed then headed to Tuscaloosa's Ground Zero, and what they saw was terrible indeed—a city torn to pieces and crushed as if beneath a giant boot heel.

Saban leaped out of the truck and began handing out water bottles to first responders. He shook hands and offered words of support, knowing he needed to remain strong, to present an image of stability to the battered, broken community.

He and Turnipseed later went to a nearby church, where 1,500 volunteers had showed up, looking to help. Saban asked where he could help most, and a church official directed him to the city's Belk Activity Center. There, hundreds of people abruptly left homeless were waiting, adrift and unmoored.

Saban, later with Terry alongside him, spent the rest of the day listening to the pain and anguish and despair of those who had lost everything, who had seen their lives uprooted and annihilated.

Soon after the storm, President Barack Obama toured Tuscaloosa alongside Maddox. "I've never seen devastation like this," Obama said during his visit. "We were just talking to some residents here who were lucky enough to escape alive but have lost everything. They mentioned that their neighbors had lost two of their grandchildren in the process."

He continued: "The mayor said something very profound as we were driving over here. He said, 'What's amazing is when something like this happens, folks forget all their petty differences. Politics, differences of religions or race, all that fades away when we are confronted with the awesome power of nature. And we're reminded that all we have is each other.'"

By the time college football season began in the fall, roughly 85% of the debris had been removed. As Maddox noted, that was enough to fill Bryant-Denny from the field to the top of the lights three times. Still, the mayor welcomed the return of Crimson Tide football.

"It will let us know that it's OK for us to live our lives again," he said. "For a few hours we can have some fun and enjoy ourselves."

Did the tornado change Saban? Perhaps. For the first time in his adult life, he wasn't actively thinking about football. He was reckoning with ways to help his community, and also pondering the size of his persona and his ability to make a difference. He remembered his Kent State days, and the way the football team had unified the college in the wake of unimaginable horror.

He spoke to his scarred and scared team less than two days after the tornado hit. Many of his players had helped pull the dead and dying from the rubble, and all were dealing with the trauma of knowing how close they had come to death that day. They grieved for their teammate Carson Tinker, whose girlfriend, Ashley Harrison, had been torn from his arms and died in the storm.

Saban stared at his players. They had the option to go home if they wanted; classes were canceled for the semester. But when they returned to campus, they would have a mission.

"Once we all get back here and really start preparing for the season, we're going to have a chance to do something very special for our community," he said. "These people are hurting, and we're going to be able to show them that we've got their backs. We're going to win for Tuscaloosa."

Alabama was coming off that disappointing three-loss 2010 season, which, to the Tide faithful, was the equivalent of a 30-loss season. Saban had warned his players about getting complacent, getting soft, getting too fat and happy and satisfied with their lot as national champions, and by God, they hadn't heeded his warning and had fallen prey to exactly that. They'd been beaten down by South Carolina, LSU, and—in that horrendous Camback game—Auburn. This would not do.

The 2011 season began with wreckage from the tornado still strewn across Tuscaloosa. Abandoned homes bore the spray-painted X's identifying who—or what—might be inside. Empty lots sat where buildings and homes once stood. The Tide opened with a win against Kent State and then defeated Penn State in Saban's last meeting with Joe Paterno. Saban had a 4–3 overall record against the Happy Valley legend, who was fired later that season as part of the school's rampant child sexual abuse scandal.

As it turned out, the 2011 Alabama team had one of the most vicious defensive units in college football history. Saban and defensive coordinator Kirby Smart devised a defense that allowed an average of just eight points a game. The team that scored the most against the Tide that year was Georgia Southern, which dropped 21 on Alabama thanks in part to its freaky triple-option offense, which is difficult to defend against and—frustrating to Saban—difficult to prepare for since few teams run it.

The kicking game had dogged Saban for many years, and its deficiencies became especially pronounced in 2011. Toward the end of the season, Alabama played LSU in the latest version of the Saban Bowl, a matchup billed as "The Game of the Century." It turned out to be anything but, a 9–6 kickfest that Alabama lost in overtime.

Auburn fans felt bad for Tuscaloosa, yes, but they still wanted to win that year's Iron Bowl. That didn't matter. This Alabama team was on a mission, true, but they were also simply one of the finest teams Bama had ever assembled. One of the motivating slogans for the year—much like the tornado—was "NEVER AGAIN," a mantra forbidding complacency or anything like what had happened the year before.

Alabama dominated Auburn 42–14, and the game probably wasn't even that close. Trent Richardson rushed for 203 yards and thoroughly dissected the Auburn defense. Quarterback A. J. McCarron threw for 18 of 23 completions, 184 yards, and three touchdowns. As Alabama fans shouted "LSU! LSU!", demanding a rematch, Saban jabbed his right index finger toward the sky, an uncharacteristic display of attitude over business.

Fortunately, the chips fell in Alabama's favor once again. Oklahoma State and Stanford both dropped games late in the season. The final regular-season BCS standings gave Alabama its rematch against LSU in the title game on January 9, 2012. It would prove to be one of the most talent-laden matchups in college football history: 31 players from the game were selected in the next two NFL drafts.

Saban stalked the logo at midfield of the Sugar Bowl. He took "field notes" before every game, scrawled on a small piece of paper and tucked into the back pocket of his khaki pants. Bear Bryant used to lean against a goalpost prior to each game, confident of his preparation. Saban, by contrast, was always in motion, always tinkering, always looking for that last little edge, even though he likely out-prepared the Bear by a factor of 10.

Saban presented an almost humorous image when he was among his players, a tiny elfin figure amid behemoths. But there was never any doubt about who was in charge—just study the way the players reacted to Saban's presence, the way he made them lock in and focus on their task with renewed efficiency and determination.

The LSU game was a testament to the power of misdirection and assumption. Alabama's Smart had planned a blitzing attack that would force quarterback Jordan Jefferson to go to his left, where he was less accurate. Wherever he went, the Alabama defense would be waiting for him.

The gambit worked. LSU gained a total of five first downs in the entire game. McCarron, meanwhile, was in control. Alabama kicked five straight field goals to take a 15–0 lead, and then, finally, with less than five minutes remaining, Richardson found daylight and raced for the first touchdown either team had scored against the other in almost eight quarters of football. (The two unremarkable Alabama–LSU games that season would be the impetus for college football's power brokers to ditch the BCS once and for all and institute a playoff that invited first four, and later 12, teams to the postseason party.)

The glorious, magical 2011 championship title was Alabama's reward for months of straining against the unimaginable, months of carrying the burden of an entire city on their shoulders. In the locker room after the game, Saban lifted his right hand, and the delirious gathering grew silent. He looked from man to man, and finally said, "We buried the pain tonight."

There's no such thing as a "routine" national championship, but Alabama's march to the 2012 season title came very close. Aside from one player and one near-miss play, Alabama carved through the entirety of college football like they were spooning up banana pudding at Tuscaloosa's beloved Dreamland Bar-B-Cue.

Perhaps no football player outside of Cam Newton vexed Saban quite like Johnny Manziel did. In 2012, Manziel effectively locked up the Heisman and locked down Alabama, throwing for 253 yards and two touchdowns, running for another 92 yards, and generally looking unstoppable at Bryant-Denny. A&M handled Alabama in a 29–24 contest that wasn't anywhere near as close as the score would indicate.

But the Tide regrouped and decimated Auburn 49–0; Gene Chizik was fired shortly thereafter, one of so many coaches to lose his job because of Saban. Alabama knocked off Georgia, 32–28, in a down-to-the-wire SEC championship game that ended on a broken play, when Georgia tight end Chris Conley instinctively caught a tipped ball just short of the end zone, with no timeouts to stop the final seconds from ticking away.

When Saban returned to Miami to play in the BCS national championship game against Notre Dame, he was targeted by the Miami media, still miffed over his ugly departure six years earlier. "We all learn things about ourselves as we go," he said. "Some things we all would like to do differently. I just think we all make mistakes and would like to do things differently. You know, you don't get the opportunity to get it back."

He conceded that he'd made mistakes in bailing on Miami. But he also knew that he had to move forward too.

On one hand, it seemed like fate—two of college football's blue-blood programs back at the pinnacle, ready to do battle just as they had in the days of Bear Bryant and Ara Parseghian. Bryant, however, had never beaten Notre Dame in all his years at Alabama.

On the other hand, this was Nick Saban's Alabama, and Notre Dame didn't stand a chance. Alabama leaped out to a 28–0 lead, and won 42–14. There was no doubt whatsoever; the game's only real highlight was ABC broadcaster Brent Musburger fawning over Katherine Webb, the girlfriend of Alabama quarterback A. J. McCarron. The Tide annihilated Notre Dame that night, not allowing the Irish even a glimmer of hope. Bear Bryant would have been proud.

Back in Tuscaloosa, the crowd spilled out onto the streets. One sign summed up the entire Saban era to that point: "Cam Lied/Trees Died/Tebow Cried/Roll Tide."

Surely nothing could stop Alabama from achieving a three-peat . . . right?

IRON BOWL 2013: KICK SIX

There's no other way to put it: the 2013 Iron Bowl is the greatest game Auburn and Alabama ever played, and it's in the running for the greatest games in sports history too. The stakes, the weight, the implication, the finish... everything combines to make this game one of the most memorable ever played in America.

Consider: Auburn at last won the ultimate reward for its century-plus of suffering relentless jabs, insults, condescension, and dismissal at the hands of its cross-state rival. Alabama finally discovered the price it had to pay for all those decades of success. No matter how many more rings Alabama gets than Auburn, no matter how many dynasties the Tide stack on top of each other, Auburn fans will always be able to pierce their armor with two. Little. Words.

The Gene Chizik era at Auburn had ended quickly and unceremoniously. The Tigers went a combined 3–17 in SEC play in Chizik's final two years, and that was enough to convince the power merchants in Auburn that a change was necessary. So Auburn reached out to Gus Malzahn—whom many not-so-privately suggested had been the true driving force behind Auburn's national championship—and the former offensive coordinator came back to The Plains to start the 2013 season. A bespectacled onetime high school coach, Malzahn set about installing an aggressive, wide-open offense that specialized in piling up points in a hurry. It was exactly the injection of spirit the program needed, and it was about to pay off faster than even the most fervent Auburn acolytes could have imagined.

Malzahn immediately led the Tigers to a 9–1 record heading into the season's final games, a run that had included last-second wins over both Mississippi State and Texas A&M. But that was merely the tiniest appetizer before the feast that was to come.

First, there was the latest installment in the South's Oldest Rivalry. Auburn was down 38–37 to Georgia, facing fourth and 18 with 36 seconds remaining in the game. Quarterback Nick Marshall heaved the ball downfield, where it tipped off the hands of two Georgia defenders and right into the arms of Ricardo Louis, who scooted away for a miraculous 73-yard touchdown that kept Auburn's national championship hopes alive.

That was the Prayer at Jordan-Hare. For any other program, it would have been the most famous play in the school's history. For Auburn, it wouldn't even be the most famous play of the month.

Perhaps the strangest element of Nick Saban's Alabama tenure was that many of the most memorable games of his time in Tuscaloosa are the ones he lost, because they came so rarely and required such a confluence of skill, luck, and random weirdness. Any victory over Nick Saban deserved a celebration, but a victory with national championship implications deserved its own holiday.

Alabama arrived in Auburn on the afternoon of November 30, 2013, as a colossus, the two-time defending national champion and No. 1–ranked team in the country, winner of all 11 games so far that season. Auburn, meanwhile, lurked at No. 4. The Tide was the 10-point favorite, but the Tigers were still carrying fresh memories of the Prayer at Jordan-Hare and a belief that no game was over until the clock read 0:00. Advantage: neither.

"I've been to a number of Iron Bowls, and you can feel it in the air, that tension," says journalist Dan Wetzel. "Even when you're good, you're worried about losing. Especially when the game's in Auburn. You've got to have that healthy respect of, 'We could lose, and this could be horrible.' So before the game, it's not festive. It's tense. There's a palpable fear of what could go wrong."

This game marked only the second time that both teams came into the Iron Bowl ranked in the top 5, and this particular combination was the highest-ranked pair ever. The winner would head to the SEC championship game and have a clear path to the national championship game.

So there was no need to hype this game, but everyone involved did it anyway. Auburn had begun the season unranked and had won its way into contention thanks to those exceptionally lucky and timely victories. As a result, few gave the Tigers and Malzahn much of a chance against Saban. *College GameDay* posted up on campus at Auburn, and every single one of the regular panelists picked Alabama to win. The only dissenter? Guest picker Charles Barkley, who went with his beloved alma mater.

With tension at a fever pitch, the game began, and Alabama got off to its customary slow start. The Tide under Saban tended to spend the first quarter sizing up its adversaries, testing their strengths and searching out weaknesses. That could lead to opponents getting early scores, and even leads, against Alabama—which all too often proved to be false hope.

In this case, Auburn's Marshall put the Tigers up 7–0 with a 45-yard touchdown run midway through the first quarter. And then the Tide began to rise. A. J. McCarron fired off two quick touchdown passes and led a third scoring drive to put Alabama up 21–7. A late Auburn touchdown by Tre Mason pulled the Tigers back to within seven at halftime.

Normally, the game would be over. Alabama to that point had a 73–3 record under Saban when leading at the half. But the Iron Bowl has a way of obliterating statistics and upending narratives.

One element forgotten in all the chaos that was to come: McCarron put the Tide ahead 28–21 with a 99-yard touchdown pass, the longest in Alabama history. Had things worked out differently, that would've been the story of the 2013 Iron Bowl. Instead, it's barely a footnote.

One element very much not forgotten: Alabama kicker Cade Foster missed three field goals over the course of the game. Kickers and Nick Saban had an uncomfortable, even hostile, relationship, and on this night, the relationship turned toxic.

Late in the game, facing fourth and one on the Auburn 13, Saban elected to go for the first down rather than attempt a short field goal. Up 28–21, a touchdown would have salted away the game for Alabama, but T. J. Yeldon was stopped at the line by Carl Lawson, a freshman defensive end. A few minutes later, faced with the same situation at the Auburn 25, Saban opted to go for the field goal—which was promptly blocked for Foster's third miss of the game. Up until that point, he had missed only one field goal all season.

Then came 32 seconds that will live in Auburn memory as long as that little school on The Plains exists. Marshall spotted Sammie Coates open, hitting him for a 39-yard touchdown to tie the game at 28. Alabama pounded its way down to Auburn's 38-yard line, but defensive back Chris Davis knocked Yeldon out of bounds as time expired. Overtime awaited.

Or did it? Saban argued that one second remained when Yeldon went out of bounds, and appealed to the officials. A replay upheld Saban's challenge, putting a second back on the clock.

On the sideline, McCarron loosened up, apparently thinking there would be a Hail Mary. On the CBS broadcast, Verne Lundquist and Gary Danielson thought the same thing.

But Saban opted to go with freshman kicker Adam Griffith instead of Foster. Auburn called a timeout to give Griffith time to think about the most important kick of his life. Auburn defensive coordinator Ellis Johnson, observing the Alabama formation, suggested putting Davis, a quicksilver punt returner, in the back of the end zone, just in case. Malzahn switched out safety Ryan Smith for Davis, Auburn's regular punt returner.

The field goal attempt sailed into the night, and fell right into Davis's hands. Standing above the *E* in TIGERS, his heels almost out of bounds, Davis caught the ball and raced up the left sideline, outrunning every single one of Alabama's beefy linemen. A long kick requires a low trajectory, and a low trajectory means that more linemen have to hold off a charging defensive line, and more linemen means fewer speedy players on the field to catch a phenomenally unlikely—but still possible—return.

Auburn radio commentator Rod Bramblett's call of the final play is so perfect, it's worth recalling in full:

"Chris Davis is going to drop back into the end zone in single safety. Well, I guess if this thing comes up short, he can field it and run it out. All right, here we go. 56-yarder, it's got—no, it does not have the legs. And Chris Davis takes it in the back of the end zone. He'll run it out to the 10, 15, 20, 25, 30, 35, 40, 45, 50, 45—there goes Davis!"

"Oh my God! Oh my God!" shouts booth partner Stan White.

"Davis is going to run it all the way back! Auburn's gonna win the football game! AUBURN'S GONNA WIN THE FOOTBALL GAME! He ran the missed field goal back! He ran it back 109 yards!"

The fans began streaming onto the field, and Bramblett exulted.

"They're not gonna keep them off the field tonight! Holy cow! Oh, my God! Auburn wins! Auburn has won the Iron Bowl! Auburn has won the Iron Bowl in the most unbelievable fashion you will ever see! I cannot believe it! 34–28! And we thought 'A Miracle in Jordan–Hare' was amazing! Oh, my Lord in Heaven! Chris Davis just ran it 109 yards and Auburn is going to the [SEC] championship game!"

Fans leaped from the stands into the bushes that ring the sidelines. They stayed on the field for an hour, running Davis's route, cutting pieces of the field or twigs from the bushes for souvenirs. Elsewhere on campus, students threw toilet paper rolls over wires installed for just that purpose as the new oaks awaited transplant on Toomer's Corner.

Kick Six was literally a play without precedent. In the history of FBS-level college football, a missed field goal had been returned for a touchdown only four times, and never in a walk-off.

"Auburn picked up a lot of accidental War Eagle fans during the Saban era, because Auburn was the last line of defense," ESPN's Ryan McGee notes. "If you're going to keep Alabama out of Atlanta [for the SEC championship] or out of the college football playoff, you felt a nation pulling for Auburn because everyone wanted someone different to be playing for a national championship. Everybody just got sick of hearing about Alabama, and sick of hearing about Saban."

The stunning Kick Six facts abounded. According to ESPN, Auburn had now won three games in which its win probability was less than 10%. At the end of the game, 82% of the televisions in Birmingham were tuned in to the Iron Bowl. And Davis got a standing ovation from his classmates when he walked into his Monday morning geology class.

"This is going down in history," Davis said after the game. "This is one of the moments I'll tell my son about."

"That was not," Saban allowed afterward, "a great way to lose the game."

Barkley, still in town after his *GameDay* stint, threw down $1,000 to buy a round of drinks at nearby Hamilton's. "It was a payback moment for poisoning our damn trees," he said, "and man, it was sweet. One of the great moments in my life."

"War Eagle," Cam Newton crowed as he opened his postgame press conference after the Panthers beat the Buccaneers the next day. "War Eagle. War Damn Eagle!"

A seismometer in Huntsville measuring the movement of the Earth in the state of Alabama registered an intriguing seismic signature beginning at 6:25 p.m.—the exact moment of Kick Six.

The Tigers would go on to knock off Missouri in the SEC

championship, and when No. 2 Ohio State lost to Michigan State in the Big Ten championship, Auburn was suddenly back in its second national championship game in four years. That title game didn't work out quite so well; Florida State and Jameis Winston outran Auburn 34–31 to at last defeat the Cardiac Tigers of 2013 in the final minute.

Still, Auburn will always have Kick Six. It's in the conversation for the greatest sports play of all time, in any sport. If nothing else, it will endure as long as the Auburn–Alabama rivalry does, a symbol that no game is ever lost—or won—if time remains on the clock.

2013 IRON BOWL

Final Score: Auburn 34, Alabama 28

Chapter 34

JOYLESS MURDERBALL

If—depending on your loyalties—The Kick or Kick Six sums up the Iron Bowl, then one play on a warm January night in Arizona encapsulates the entirety of the Nick Saban dynasty at Alabama.

The scene: University of Phoenix Stadium, January 11, 2016. The event: the College Football Playoff National Championship. The teams: Alabama and Clemson, far and away the two best teams in the country, deep in a heavyweight fight. The teams had been trading touchdowns and field goals and, with just over 10 minutes remaining in the game and the season, stood tied at 24 apiece.

Saban and his assistants had been watching Clemson, and noticed a tiny flaw in the Tigers' game plan, something so small that no other coaching staff might have caught it, much less been able to capitalize on it. They'd noticed that on kickoffs, the front line of Clemson's return team stacked up heavily in the direction of the kicker. The Tigers bunched up in order to provide as much defense as possible for their return man. But in so doing, they'd left a vast gulf of green space available. And Saban had spotted that gulf, and knew exactly what to do next.

Four times, Alabama kicked off to the Tigers. Four times, Saban and his coaches observed that enormous hole in the Clemson receiving formation. And finally, in the most crucial quarter of the most crucial game of the season, Saban made his move.

He called for an onside kick. Alabama lined up exactly as normal, hoping not to tip its hand. Kicker Adam Griffith ran toward the ball—slightly slower than before, but no one noticed that in the moment—and punched it upward on a high arc, like a chip shot onto an elevated green. Coverage man Marlon Humphrey, streaking from the right side of the Tide line, zipped straight into that empty space on the field, and snared the falling ball as it dropped straight out of the Arizona night. Ball, Alabama. Clemson never had a chance, and two plays later, Alabama was in the end zone again.

The play was both poetry and genius. Humphrey, the son of legendary Alabama running back Bobby Humphrey, etched his own name into Tide lore alongside his father's that night. Until that moment, Griffith had been best known as the redshirt freshman whose would-be game-winning field goal kick hadn't quite reached the end zone in the 2013 Iron Bowl. This was redemption and then some.

The truly fascinating part about that onside kick: Alabama had practiced it *all season long* for exactly a situation like this. Preparation for every possibility, no matter how remote, was a Saban trademark. That was how he won championships throughout the 2010s and beyond, and how he bent the entire game of college football to his will.

And so after Griffith, Humphrey, and the Tide snared that ball, while Clemson head coach Dabo Swinney frothed and fumed to the referees, Saban strode along the sideline, looked out at the field... and *smiled*.

If there's a more terrifying sight to see from the other sideline in college football than Nick Saban smiling, no one who's seen it has lived to tell the tale.

As for the game's outcome... come on, do you even have to ask?

"Joyless Murderball," they called it—an Alabama-born, Saban-honed style of football that prized brutal, unrelenting punishment for 60 long minutes. It wasn't fun, but it produced some very fun results for Alabama fans . . . even if Saban himself never seemed quite satisfied with how his team was doing, or how the fans around him were reacting.

Even before Kick Six, Saban was feeling an old familiar itch, not to mention a familiar dose of frustration at Alabama's players, fans, and boosters. After three titles in four years, he felt his players had grown too content and his fans had grown too accustomed to success. It was the supreme irony: the more satisfied the fans were, the less satisfied Saban was.

Miss Terry hinted at that in a November 2013 interview with the *Wall Street Journal*, when she offered up a chilling not-quite-threat. "You come to a crossroads and the expectations get so great, people get spoiled by success, and there gets to be a lack of appreciation," she said. "We're kind of there now."

Terry's influence on Saban can't be overstated, nor can her power. One of the best-known—and also best—stories about her: When she and Nick visited Big Nick's old gas station in Monongah in 2009, they spotted one of Terry's former boyfriends.

"See, if you would have married him," Nick said, "you would be over there helping him run the gas station."

"If I married him," Terry replied, "he'd be the head coach at Alabama."

When word leaked out that Saban's agent, Jimmy Sexton, had been in contact with the University of Texas, Alabama fans realized the tidal wave that had swamped other towns was headed their way too. Saban had been at one spot too long, had grown weary, had started looking around, had issued denials of interest in anywhere else. This had happened before—at Kent State, at Michigan State, at Miami, at LSU—could it possibly be happening in Tuscaloosa too?

So Alabama did what LSU and the others couldn't, showering Saban with money, prestige, and a too-good-to-refuse offer. First, the Crimson

Tide Foundation bought Saban's house from him for $3.1 million, a $200,000 profit over the purchase price a few years prior. Saban continued to live there, of course; the arrangement was similar to one the university had with Bear Bryant decades before. On top of that, Alabama offered Saban another meaty raise, boosting his annual salary to around $7 million, and an extension that would keep him in Tuscaloosa through at least 2021.

Although rumors flew that Texas had offered him a contract—and, worse, that he had accepted it—there was never an official conversation between the Longhorns and Saban. Saint Nick would stay in Tuscaloosa for at least the rest of the 2010s, and he would be worth every nickel of the millions he would be paid.

In a state like Alabama, where so many residents live at or below the poverty line, it seems inappropriate, if not downright immoral, to pay a football coach that much money. But the impact Saban has had on Alabama as a whole is immeasurable. Consider not just the upgraded football facilities, but the growth in size and prestige for the university. Alabama's enrollment increased by 51 percent in the wake of Saban's arrival, from 25,580 to 38,645 students. Over that same period, the school tripled its endowment, passing $1 billion in 2022, and doubled its footprint in Tuscaloosa. Out-of-state students made up 79 percent of Alabama's applicants in Saban's last season on the sidelines. The growth isn't entirely due to Saban, but like George Denny understood nearly a century before, having the most successful football program in the country is a fine recruiting tool.

"I'm torn because, number one, I think it's stupid for anybody to make that much money for [coaching football]," says John Archibald, a Pulitzer Prize–winning Birmingham journalist. "Especially because basically enough people have come through there that we know that the quality of what your job is doesn't necessarily dictate the amount of money you're worth. But at the same time, [Saban] is one of the very, very rare cases where he became an institution that created a lot of other economic opportunities for a lot of people."

In 2014, Saban began what was informally known as the Nick Saban Home for Wayward Coaches with the arrival on campus of Lane Kiffin, last seen getting fired by USC on the tarmac at an airport. Saban knew that talent and public image didn't necessarily work in tandem, so he would target coaches who had suffered a personal or professional setback, give them a few years to do their thing in relative anonymity and silence, and send them back into the head coaching world with a scrubbed-clean reputation. Thanks to the massive contract buyouts that universities pay disgraced coaches to go away, Saban could get many of these scratch-and-dent models on the cheap, benefiting Alabama while someone else footed most of the bill.

Kiffin, Bill O'Brien, Mario Cristobal, Billy Napier, Butch Jones, Steve Sarkisian, and other once-and-future head coaches all spent some time in Tuscaloosa observing the Saban magic, and all found a path back to big-ticket jobs. Along the way, they helped Saban revolutionize his own offensive attack, realigning Alabama from a run-first juggernaut to a pass-first fighter jet. Like Bear Bryant before him, Saban made a mid-career pivot to keep up with the changing game, and like Bryant, he won three more titles with his new-look team.

He also hewed to his long-standing quirks. He would awaken at 6:00 a.m., watch the Weather Channel to determine how the day's practice was going to proceed, and then breakfast on coffee and, famously, two Little Debbie Oatmeal Crème Pies. His lunch was the same every day, too: iceberg lettuce and cherry tomatoes topped with turkey slices and fat-free honey Dijon dressing in a Styrofoam container. It may have seemed absurd to anyone on the outside, but you couldn't argue with the results.

By 2014, Alabama was as much an institution as a football program, one of the most valuable and well-known brands in the country, in any sport. He helped literally remake the entire sport; thanks to his success, and the comparable success of the SEC as a whole, college football instituted a playoff system starting in the 2014 season that would, in theory, give other schools a chance at a title. A slim one, but a chance nonetheless.

"In college football, [playoffs] were going to happen anyway, but Saban accelerated it," ESPN's Ryan McGee says. "When there's just one person guarding the door... college football had to be creative to widen the door a little bit so that anyone else could get in. You know [Saban]'s going to do it. But all you try to do is maybe make the room more crowded."

Not that Alabama worried. "Alabama won when there were no polls, they won championships in the poll era, they won championships in the College Football Playoff," sports historian Kirk McNair says. "So it's been a 'Whatever you want to throw at us' kind of attitude."

SEC teams had won seven of the last eight national championships, and the 2013-season Auburn Tigers had narrowly missed making that a perfect eight. The evolution of the Bowl Championship Series, which pitted No. 1 against No. 2, into the four-team College Football Playoff was a direct result of the SEC's dominance, and the SEC's dominance was a direct result of the arms race inspired by Saban and Alabama.

Naturally, the Tide not only made the first CFP, but were the No. 1 overall seed. But they ran into a determined and hungry fourth-seeded Ohio State team in the Sugar Bowl, and despite jumping out to a 21–6 lead, they couldn't keep the Buckeyes in check. Ohio State would go on to win the game 42–35 and, later, the national championship.

Alabama rebounded just fine, reaching the title game after the 2015 season, producing the school's second Heisman Trophy winner—bruising running back Derrick Henry—and knocking off Clemson thanks in part to that infamous onside kick. The Tide had fought through the first wave of "The dynasty is dead!" proclamations earlier in the season after losing to Ole Miss. But the win over Clemson and Deshaun Watson, the kind of unpredictable quarterback who always gave Saban fits, proved that Alabama had no intention of striking the tents on the dynasty. Saban's Alabama title count: four and rising.

Watson and Clemson would get their revenge the very next year, as—once again—Alabama surrendered a go-ahead score, and with it the national championship, with one second remaining. Once again, no one outside Tuscaloosa felt particularly bad for Alabama. And once again, Alabama would have its revenge on the world.

If the Clemson onside kick typified Saban's maniacal preparation, the game-winning play after the 2017 season exemplified the astounding good fortune that comes from preparation, planning, and execution.

One phrase sums up the lucky-as-hell side of the Tide: Second-and-26. The final play of the 2017 season, in the 2018 national championship game, Second-and-26 was the culmination of a whole season's worth of narrow escapes, lucky breaks, and an ocean-deep roster.

Alabama lost the Iron Bowl that year, and Auburn was in position to win the SEC championship and claim its first College Football Playoff berth. But the Tigers couldn't get the job done in Atlanta against Georgia, so Alabama slid into the playoff as the fourth seed. After pasting top seed Clemson, Alabama took Georgia—coached by Kirby Smart, a Saban disciple—all the way to overtime, where the Tide trailed 23–20.

At halftime Saban had made the remarkable move of swapping out starting quarterback Jalen Hurts—who had guided the Tide all season—for freshman Tua Tagovailoa. On Alabama's first snap in overtime, Tagovailoa was sacked for a 16-yard loss. But on the very next play, offensive coordinator Brian Daboll called "Seattle"—a four-verts, everybody-go-long play—and Tagovailoa spotted fellow freshman DeVonta Smith streaking wide open down the left sideline. He sailed the ball straight into Smith's waiting hands, hitting him in stride for a 41-yard touchdown and yet another national championship.

"I thought Tua would give us a better chance and a spark," Saban said after the game, "which he certainly did."

Second-and-26 made it clear: you might land a glove on Alabama, but you couldn't ever bring them down, not for long. Surely at some point the Tide would stop winning, but that day wouldn't come for a long, long time.

Meanwhile, over in Auburn, chaos reigned.

Chapter 35

CHAOS ON THE PLAINS

If a genie had appeared to an Auburn fan in November 2013 and offered a deal—*Alabama will suffer the most humiliating loss in college football history, but Auburn will have to wander the desert for more than a decade*—the Tigers fan would've taken that deal in a heartbeat. But as the 2010s neared their midpoint, and Alabama piled up even more titles, that fan would've realized just how long a decade can be.

In the days immediately after the loss to Florida State in the 2014 BCS National Championship Game, optimism ran high on The Plains. Auburn had come within 13 seconds of winning its second national title in four years, and the Tigers still had possession of Alabama's soul thanks to Kick Six. Auburn Jesus—the mysterious force that too-online Tigers fans believe tips passes and curves field goal attempts into Tiger hands—was at the height of His powers.

The Tigers began the 2014 season as the AP's sixth-ranked team in the country. A massive 41–7 annihilation of LSU lifted the Tigers all the way to No. 2 . . . whereupon they promptly lost to Mississippi State. As of 2025, Auburn hasn't climbed that high in the polls again.

From there, the slide was slow but steady. After that season-high

No. 2 ranking, the Tigers fell to 8–5 in 2014. The 2015 season ended with Auburn's return to Legion Field in Birmingham for the Birmingham Bowl—the kind of nostalgia that nobody particularly cared to relive.

Hope flickered briefly in 2016 with a trip to the Sugar Bowl. The next year brimmed with possibility after Auburn knocked off two No. 1 teams—Georgia and Alabama—only to get hammered by the Bulldogs in a rematch in the SEC Championship. (That was the game that allowed Alabama to backdoor its way into the College Football Playoff and later defeat Georgia on Second-and-26.)

Three more solid-but-unspectacular seasons followed, and in December 2020, Auburn fired Malzahn despite the fact that he'd never posted a losing season. Hampered by pandemic-enforced rules governing the 2020 football season, Malzahn's Tigers got blown off the field by Georgia, Texas A&M, and—worst of all—Alabama, ending the year with a seventh straight season of four or more losses.

While that Alabama team would go on to win a national title and establish itself as one of the great college football teams of all time, the fact remained that Auburn had now lost five straight in Tuscaloosa. Moreover, Malzahn was 8–17 against the big dogs in the SEC—Alabama, Georgia, and LSU. That simply would not do.

Malzahn made the crucial mistake of appearing to blame his woes on the pandemic-enforced all-SEC schedule, saying, "If you had a normal nonconference schedule, it'd be a solid year." It didn't need mentioning that other teams—starting with that one across the state wearing crimson—also played nothing but SEC teams in 2020 and seemed to handle themselves just fine.

Even with his mediocre results, Malzahn remains the fifth-winningest coach in Auburn history, after Jordan, Dye, Donahue, and Tuberville. He took a $21.45 million buyout—at the time, the largest in college football history—and relocated to Orlando to begin coaching the University of Central Florida.

So that left Auburn flailing for a new coach and a new identity. Names like Kiffin, Sarkisian, and Cristobal were mentioned in connection with the job, but less than 10 days after firing Malzahn, Auburn announced that Boise State's Bryan Harsin would become the Tigers' new head coach, starting with the 2021 season.

Calling the Harsin experiment a disaster would be generous. In 2021, despite taking Alabama all the way to four overtimes before losing, the Tigers went 6–7, the program's first losing record since 2012. A mass exodus of players and coaches, led by quarterback Bo Nix, added to the chaos around Harsin's rule.

"I want this thing to work, and I've told our players and told everybody else there is no Plan B," a frustrated Harsin said in a defensive interview with ESPN in February 2022. "I'm not planning on going anywhere. This was and is the job. That's why I left the one I was in, to come here and make this place a championship program and leave it better than I found it."

He didn't. Much like Terry Bowden two and a half decades before him, Harsin ran afoul of Auburn's trustees—in Harsin's case, Jimmy Rane, the wealthy Tigers fan who'd replaced Bobby Lowder as the power behind the Auburn throne. As rumors about everything from Harsin's treatment of redshirt players to his personal life swirled around The Plains, the Tigers continued to tumble. Eight games into the 2022 season, Auburn had seen enough, and Harsin was fired after going 3–5.

Given another chance to make a strong hire, Auburn again steered into controversy. Two days after suffering yet another Iron Bowl blowout in Tuscaloosa—this one a 49–27 shellacking—Auburn announced that it had hired former Ole Miss and Liberty head coach Hugh Freeze. It was, to say the least, a debatable hire.

Freeze arrived in Auburn carrying an entire plane's worth of baggage from his earlier coaching stops. He had resigned from Ole Miss in 2017 under a cloud of personal and professional controversy, as an internal investigation revealed what chancellor Jeffrey Vitter called "a pattern of personal misconduct inconsistent with the standards we expect from the leader of our football team."

A 2017 ESPN review of Freeze's phone records indicated his phone had dialed "at least 12 numbers . . . associated with online advertisements for female escorts" over a 33-month period. Ole Miss officials began investigating the records after being tipped off by an attorney for another former Ole Miss coach, Houston Nutt, who was in the midst of a civil lawsuit against the school . . . in part because Freeze and other Ole Miss officials attempted to blame recruiting violations on him. (In the SEC, no scandal is routine.)

Also in 2017, the NCAA hammered Ole Miss for those recruiting violations, which it deemed "an unconstrained culture of booster involvement in football recruiting." The Rebels vacated 33 wins, most of which occurred during Freeze's tenure.

Critics of the Freeze hire—and there were many, even inside the Auburn family—pointed to other allegations of inappropriate behavior, both at Liberty and at a Christian school in Memphis in the late 1990s. But university officials pressed on, signing Freeze to a six-year deal paying him an average of $6.5 million annually. In the SEC, off-field controversy and past misconduct are easy to wave away if there's a good chance that you can post up some wins against your rival. Worth noting: Freeze beat Saban straight up two times in 2014 and 2015, and that carries serious weight at Auburn.

"Being a coach now at college is 100% different than it was just five years ago," says Stan White, the former Auburn quarterback. "You have to re-recruit your own team every year. You've got to deal with these players getting paid. It's not changing by the month, it's changing by the day. The person that can adapt and adjust to that is going to have the success, and I think Hugh has a feel for that."

In a way, Freeze bears some small responsibility for Alabama's continued dominance. In 2012, while he was coaching Ole Miss, the Rebels ran a hurry-up offense that confounded and exhausted defenses. Well, except for Alabama's—the Tide won their matchup 33–14 that year. But the philosophy was enough to make Saban wonder about the direction the game of football was headed.

Saban often disguised his strategic questions as high-minded concerns. "I think that the way people are going no-huddle right now," he said at the time, "that at some point in time we should look at how fast we allow the game to go in terms of player safety."

All the while, he was cherry-picking the most significant elements of every new system and using them against their own practitioners. It was the 21st-century equivalent of Bum Phillips's observation that Bear Bryant could beat yours with his, and his with yours—Saban would beat you with his system, and then turn around and beat you with yours.

In this particular case, Saban adjusted from a grind-it-out offense to an air-it-out one. He met Freeze's challenge by bringing in Kiffin, who in turn brought in playmakers like Jalen Hurts to run a more wide-open style of offense. The results were obvious: Saban won three national titles after revamping his offense, and four of his quarterbacks—and counting—would end up starting in the NFL.

That wasn't exactly the history Auburn was looking to draw on when it hired Freeze, but then Auburn tends to be college football's epitome of the law of unintended consequences. As it turned out, Freeze's first Iron Bowl would be a memorable one indeed.

It's worth asking why Auburn always seems to be pinballing from scandal to chaos to glory, sometimes all within the space of a calendar year. Longtime Auburn observers have spent years trying to untangle that riddle, and it generally comes down to this: Alabama, consciously or not, tends to break Auburn's brain.

"[The Tigers] don't quite have as big a budget or as many resources [as Alabama], so the floor is going to be a lot closer," says journalist Spencer

Hall. "Auburn can't achieve the kind of altitude consistently that Alabama can, so sometimes they hit the ground, and they do it with a little more frequency than Alabama does."

"You have a little brother syndrome to the bigger brand, your rival, that's in your state," says Ross Dellenger, a former Auburn-based journalist and now a national columnist for Yahoo Sports. "Because of that, you have at Auburn an involvement with so many people, boosters and alumni, that want to win so badly and get out of that shadow from the big brother that they do whatever they can, by any means possible, to win."

"They are driven to caring as much as Bama does, without the same level of resources," adds journalist Jason Kirk. "When you try that hard, something's going to go either really really right, or really really wrong. It's a level of caring that leads to deeply abnormal results."

Chapter 36

MAKE BAMA GREAT AGAIN

It's not often that Nick Saban is the second-most-powerful man in the building, but then, it's not often that the president of the United States comes to Bryant-Denny Stadium either.

The date: November 9, 2019. The scene: the most anxiously awaited college football game of the season. LSU–Alabama was a rivalry born of excellence more than proximity; the two schools didn't cross over much, except at the top of the SEC West standings. Saban, of course, had jilted LSU for the NFL, only to return to the college ranks two years later to join Alabama. That rankled the purple-and-yellow-clad LSU faithful, who could go toe-to-toe with Bama fans for the chaotic distinction of most unhinged fan base in the SEC.

Saban had brought LSU a national title in 2003, and then Les Miles, using many of the same players and techniques as Saban, brought another one to Baton Rouge in 2007. It had been a long, fallow, title-free decade-plus since then, but now Ed Orgeron, a man built like a bowling ball with a voice like a mountain troll, had managed to create a weapon so impressive even Nick Saban had to take notice. In 2019, LSU's offense, led by Heisman-winning quarterback Joe Burrow and receivers Ja'Marr Chase and Justin Jefferson, absolutely mowed through the SEC like a scythe through soft cotton.

The entire country had been eyeing this game for months, and as LSU grew stronger and stronger, the anticipation only increased. To be the man, you've got to beat the man, the old saying goes, and Alabama is, always and forever, The Man. Expectations ran high. The game would pit No. 2 LSU against No. 3 Alabama, and there wasn't a soul in crimson who didn't think those rankings should be reversed. ESPN sent its *College GameDay* crew to Tuscaloosa, and once again, the entire country turned its eyes to Bryant-Denny Stadium.

Naturally, this made the game an irresistible magnet for President Donald Trump.

By the final year of his first term in office, Trump lived in perpetual campaign mode, careening from rally to rally, basking in the glow of adoring crowds. Within a few months, he'd have to confront one of the most significant crises any president had faced in generations, but in November 2019, with the election still a year away, he was happy to be the world's most powerful sports fan.

He chose selectively, however, picking venues that he knew would be friendly to him. No courtside appearances at NBA games, for instance. He locked in on deeply conservative events—MMA fights, NASCAR's Daytona 500—and a college football game in the heart of blood-red Alabama fit the bill.

Trump and Alabama had a deeply intertwined recent history. His presidential campaign had begun in earnest in 2015 on a stage in Mobile when then-US Senator Jeff Sessions introduced him to a skeptical, if not outright dismissive, national audience. Two years later, with the election won, nobody was indifferent when Trump took the stage at a rally in Huntsville, Alabama, in the fall of 2017. Veering, as he always did, from topic to topic, riffing like a stand-up comedian working the crowd, he settled on the issue of the day—Colin Kaepernick, the former quarterback of the San Francisco 49ers, kneeling during the national anthem—and heaved chunks of red meat to the crowd.

"Get that son of a bitch off the field!" Trump crowed, and with those words he set off a multi-year culture war between his base and the entire National Football League. But through it all, he had the support of (most of) the state of Alabama behind him.

So when he arrived at Bryant-Denny Stadium in 2019 with wife Melania and a coterie of Alabama politicians in tow, Trump expected—and received—a Roman emperor's welcome. There were boos among the cheers—how many of each you heard depended on where you were sitting and how you'd voted in the 2016 election—but for the most part, Trump was in friendly territory.

LSU won that game 46–41, the first time an opponent had won in Bryant-Denny since 2015, a span of 32 games. No one came that close to beating LSU again for the rest of the season.

Trump, for his part, believed he had an ally in Saban . . . at least until the summer of 2020, when everything turned sideways and the country veered in unexpected directions.

Spring practice for Alabama was scheduled to begin at 3:30 p.m. Central time on March 13, 2020, a day when social media boiled with reports and fears about the rapidly spreading coronavirus. Alabama students were on spring break, and the university had just declared that classes would be virtual upon their return, despite there being no active cases yet in the state of Alabama. Most sports leagues had suspended their seasons the day before Alabama would begin practice, so what came next wasn't exactly a surprise.

Thirty minutes before Saban intended to stride down onto the practice field and kick off the Tide's pursuit of an 18th national title, the call came down from SEC headquarters: Commissioner Greg Sankey had suspended all operations for all SEC institutions through at least April 15.

As the first weeks of the pandemic wore on, Saban and his crew had a decision to make for the good of the team. They knew they'd be playing football; the SEC never wavered from its intention to get back on the field even as the Big Ten and the Pac-12 fretted. So Saban's coaches came up with an innovative idea: Apple Watches for every single player, synced to a central information clearinghouse. Every player would have his heart rate, exercise, steps, and sleep time tracked throughout the COVID lockdown period. And if that sounded a little too Big Brother, well, the University of Alabama isn't for everyone.

The Tide was coming together while apart. And then, on May 25, George Floyd was killed during a police action in Minnesota. For a nation pent up and locked down, it was the spark that lit a bonfire, and outrage reached even the confines of Tuscaloosa. A week later, on May 31, Saban released a statement saying he was "shocked and angered" by the deaths of Floyd and Breonna Taylor, who was shot to death in Louisville as she slept.

Several Alabama players, spurred to action, began to devise a statement of their own. Alex Leatherwood created a video titled "All Lives Can't Matter Until Black Lives Matter." The video starred notable Alabama players of the day—Mac Jones, Patrick Surtain II, DeVonta Smith, Jaylen Waddle—speaking with one voice. Even Saban got involved.

"Until I listen with an open heart and mind," Saban says in the video, "I can't understand his experience and his pain." It was a remarkably open statement from a man in a profession hardwired to regard everything that happens outside the playing field as an intolerable "distraction."

On June 2, Alabama players began reporting to the Mal Moore Athletic Facility—and immediately began giving COVID to one another. Alabama declined to disclose its number of COVID-infected players, which enraged other coaches. "For me, transparency is really good," said

Malzahn, at that point still the coach of Auburn. "So I'd be all for [an SEC policy mandating the disclosure of positive tests]."

Auburn, it must be noted, had COVID-related troubles all year long. Linebacker Josh Marsh, struggling with symptoms of COVID, opted out of the season, much like Georgia's projected starting quarterback Jamie Newman, LSU wide receiver Ja'Marr Chase, and many others. Auburn's entire offensive line came down with the virus, which caused problems that cascaded throughout the season.

The state of Alabama mobilized its COVID response unlike most others in the nation. Governor Kay Ivey, an Auburn graduate, took a portion of the $1.9 billion allotted to the state under the CARES Act and mandated testing for everyone who would be attending an Alabama college or university in the fall of 2020. It was the most comprehensive higher-education testing program in the nation, and it created free COVID tests for more than 200,000 students.

On July 7, 2020, the White House held a summit on education during the pandemic. Finis St. John IV, chancellor of the University of Alabama System, was on the task force, and he found himself the target of Trump's intense interest.

"Will Alabama be playing some great football? What's going on with Alabama?" Trump asked.

"Mr. President, that's not the first time we've heard that question, I can promise you," St. John replied to laughter. "We are planning to play the season at the University of Alabama... It's important to a lot of people, but we're doing our best on that one."

Rumors spread of COVID parties, where students put money in a pot and whoever got the virus first won the pot. Those were the kind of urban legends, like kidney-stealing ladies of the evening or drug-laced

Halloween candy, that terrified parents, but no real evidence of such parties ever came to light. Nevertheless, Alabama students were happily gathering together in large groups even as the administration tried to warn them off what was then seen as unaccountably reckless behavior.

Chris Owens, a center on the Alabama team, took a picture of a mass gathering near the Strip in Tuscaloosa and tweeted it out with the words "How about we social distance and have more than a literal handful of people wear a mask? Is that too much to ask Tuscaloosa?"

"Who wants college sports this fall? Obviously not these people!!" athletic director Greg Byrne tweeted in agreement. "We've got to do better than this for each other and our campus community. Please wear your masks."

Saban appeared in PSAs alongside Alabama's elephantine mascot Big Al, pleading for students to use what, at the time, was believed to be common sense. It didn't help. In the first few days of the fall semester, Alabama reported a thousand new cases of COVID, and in response, Tuscaloosa mayor Walt Maddox ordered a two-week shutdown of all bars.

The bad publicity incensed local bar owners, including Jeff Sirkin, the co-owner of Gallettes, the Tuscaloosa establishment famous for its boozy Yellowhammer drinks. "If you think we just threw caution into the wind today because 'we don't want a football season and don't care' you couldn't be further from the truth," he wrote on Facebook on August 16. "Our industry is not the fallguy [sic] for any of this. 25,000-30,000 students showed up this weekend. Did you expect them to sit at home and read?"

Saban set up rigid testing programs after a first round of COVID swept through the Alabama locker room. Every morning at eight o'clock, everyone was tested in the end zones of the practice field. No exceptions.

The Pac-12 canceled its season on August 11. Six days later, the SEC announced its schedule: 10 games, SEC only. The conference planned to implement a testing regimen, hoping to both save jobs and protect public health. (The Alabama High School Athletic Association just went full steam ahead with playing, without testing.)

The Big Ten tried to emulate the SEC's will to play. Ohio State quarterback Justin Fields began an impassioned social media campaign with the hashtag #WeWantToPlay. Trump cannonballed into the debate, trying to motivate Big Ten commissioner Kevin Warren. The ploy was obvious—angle for the electoral votes of crucial Midwestern states by bringing football back—and on September 16, the Big Ten announced the season would start on October 24.

Nick Saban had firsthand experience with protests on college campuses. As a student at Kent State in 1970, he was on campus when the Ohio National Guard opened fire on protesters, killing four students. He had been in a class with one of the students, Allison Krause, and the massacre had stuck with him ever since.

"To have students on your campus shot, killed and—actually, didn't see it happen, but saw the aftermath, right after it happened—it made me have a lot of appreciation for a lot of things," Saban said in 2016. "It was a pretty chilling experience and something that makes you view things a little bit differently, and certainly have a much better appreciation of not taking for granted life itself."

In late August, yet another shooting made news when Jacob Blake was wounded in Kenosha, Wisconsin, during a police response to a domestic violence call. The Tide locker room called a players-only meeting, and a decision was made: something had do to be done, something to show the resolution of this community.

Several players—Najee Harris, Daniel Wright, and Phidarian Mathis—walked into Saban's office with an audacious plan: a march to Foster Auditorium, the site of George Wallace's stand in the schoolhouse door.

Previous marches to Foster had dotted Alabama's history, most recently in 2013 when protests of segregated sororities—yes, in 2013—made national news. But the players understood that the fact that one of the most high-profile football programs in the nation was taking a stand would make it a significant escalation of the players-versus-the-old-order battle. There were plenty of people in the stands at Bryant-Denny—and Jordan-Hare, and Sanford Stadium, and Vaught-Hemingway, and other stadiums all over the South—who were more than happy to cheer for Black players while disregarding literally every single one of their beliefs.

So when the three players went to Saban's magisterial office and made their appeal to him, they were thrilled when he expressed his approval. "I was waiting for you guys to do something like this because if I say it as a coach, it wouldn't be as genuine," Harris later recalled him saying. "I wanted the players to come do it."

The players announced the date of the march on Twitter: Monday, August 31, 2020, at 4:00 p.m. "We want all Alabama athletes to join us," Harris tweeted. "This isn't a fan day ... this isn't a football game ... this is about lasting CHANGE!"

Harris, sporting a "Defend Black Lives" T-shirt, stepped in front of the auditorium door—the same door where Vivian Malone and James Hood once boldly walked past the symbols of Alabama's entrenched white supremacy—and began to speak.

"Black men and women have been undeserving victims of racism," he said. "This is not a problem that will simply come and go in a news cycle. It is not a problem that will eventually dissipate without action."

Harris, perhaps understanding how fragile these moments can be, continued. "I ask you, what's next?" he said. "For certain, we can't let this momentum die. This has to be an ongoing movement until change happens. We must do more as a team and as individuals to keep this movement going."

Chris Owens, who had called out Tuscaloosa students on Twitter a couple weeks earlier, touched on the theme of togetherness. "I just want you to take a moment to look at the people in front of you. What do you see? People of all races and ethnicities coming together to form a team," he said. "Now, look at the status of our country. Unlike the example of our team, our country is not a place of equality and unity at the moment. Because of this, we are unable to accomplish the goals of a just society."

"I'm in awe that the players would do this," Alabama's then-US Senator Doug Jones said, "and that the university would sanction this."

The protests drew the attention of the entire country. Soccer player Megan Rapinoe, the fiery social conscience of the US Women's National Team, praised Alabama on Twitter. So did LeBron James and Dan Rather. For so long, the school—the de facto face of the entire state of Alabama—had carried the stain of an ugly racial legacy. But at last, for a moment, the tide was turning.

"Over the course of a few months," Joe Goodman wrote in *We Want Bama*, "when the country felt more divided than at any time since Vietnam, and everyone else was experimenting with facial hair and hoarding Slim Jims and toilet paper, a college football team in Alabama showed people that the spirit of love, sacrifice and togetherness can accomplish historic things even in hours of darkness and doubt."

Of course, there was still football to be played too. Priorities.

Bonded as one, Alabama fielded perhaps its greatest team ever. Certainly no team in Alabama history—maybe no champion in college football history—played a tougher schedule than the Tide did in 2020, a murderous 10-game SEC-only slate with no cupcake breaks whatsoever. Under the tutelage of offensive coordinator Steve Sarkisian, Mac Jones, Jaylen Waddle, Najee Harris, and the rest of the Tide laid waste to the entire conference.

There were hiccups. After a 63–48 annihilation of Ole Miss, Saban himself tested positive for COVID. It turned out to be a false positive, but the way the matter was handled drew the attention of the *New York Times*, which investigated how he just happened to be able to get back on the sideline in time for the next game. With the benefit of hindsight, it's easy to criticize the cautious atmosphere of the day, but no one quite knew how serious or how long-lasting the pandemic was going to be, regardless of how everyone felt at the time.

Then Saban really *did* get COVID, right before the Iron Bowl, and this time there was no false positive. He spent the next few days in isolation, but isolation, for Saban, was just an unexpected chance to work from home. He was calling recruits the night before Thanksgiving, always keeping the fire burning for the next class.

Saban returned to the sideline for the SEC Championship in Atlanta, and although Florida made a late game of it, the outcome was never really in doubt. Alabama would go on to be seeded first in that season's Bizarro-World version of the College Football Playoff, games where stands were almost empty and everyone besides the players—the only ones actually in close contact with one another—wore masks.

Alabama drew Notre Dame for the Rose Bowl, but unlike most years, the game wasn't played in Pasadena. California's mass-gathering regulations didn't allow for football games. So instead of clashing at Rose Bowl Stadium, the teams met in Arlington, Texas, at the Cowboys' monumental AT&T Stadium. And instead of a sunset reflecting off the beautiful San Gabriel Mountains, the sunset reflected off a Walmart next to the stadium parking lot. The ambience was just a wee bit different.

The outcome was no surprise. Alabama decimated Notre Dame 31–14, moving on to face Ohio State, which had knocked off Clemson in the other playoff semifinal. Alabama was a near-constant playoff participant, but the Buckeyes and Tigers weren't far behind, all of which helped contribute to the 2024 expansion of the playoff bracket.

In the 2020 national championship game, held in a sparsely filled Hard Rock Stadium in Miami, Alabama was seeking to break its own tie in CFP National Championships. To date, the Tide had won two of the title games and lost two.

This time around, Alabama simply eviscerated Justin Fields and Ohio State, 52–24. After Mac Jones hit DeVonta Smith—fresh off his Heisman win—for a touchdown on the first play of the second quarter, the Tide would never trail again. By halftime, the score was 35–17, and Alabama increased that lead to 28 early in the fourth quarter. Jones threw for 464 yards and five touchdowns. Smith, who left the game with an injury in the third quarter, was named the game's MVP thanks to his 215-yard, three-touchdown performance.

It was, quite simply, one of the most thorough season-long beatdowns in the history of college football. The 2020 Alabama team played between the generational greatness of the 2019 LSU Tigers and the 2021 Georgia Bulldogs—also an all-time offense and defense, respectively—and the deep strangeness of the COVID season took a lot of the luster off the Tide's brilliance on a national scale. But the fact remains that this Alabama team did what no other college football team has ever done—powered through an all-SEC schedule—and left no doubt that they were the best team in the country. Even the Bear would have tipped his houndstooth cap to the magnificent 2020 team.

Chapter 37

SENATOR COACH TUBERVILLE

As qualifications for higher office go, "beat Alabama six times in a row" may not rank up there with military service or government experience, but in the state of Alabama, football records carry weight. Tommy Tuberville, who had wandered from Texas to Ohio to ESPN broadcast booths after leaving Auburn, had both the name recognition and the credentials to entice a good swath of Alabama to vote for him.

In most scenarios, the voters of Alabama would vote for almost anyone on the Republican ticket, but it turned out that even Alabamians had their limits. When Roy Moore, a disgraced former judge, attempted in 2017 to run for the Senate seat that Jeff Sessions vacated to serve (briefly) in President Donald Trump's cabinet, voters looked at his record—spotted with a removal from the bench and allegations of sexual misconduct—and said no, thanks. They instead supported Democrat Doug Jones, who had prosecuted the infamous Birmingham church bombers.

Jones's special-election term would run out in 2020, and that meant an opening for Alabama Republicans. They knew the kind of candidate they wanted—a reliable Republican electable by the entire state—so they reasoned, why not a guy who had beaten Bama six straight times? Why not... Senator Tommy Tuberville?

Tuberville, who espoused the usual Republican talking points of strong defense and small government, enthusiastically welcomed the opportunity to run for office. And he leaned hard into Trumpian politics during his campaign.

"God sent us Donald Trump," Tuberville said in one campaign ad, "because God knew we were in trouble." He also happily tore into immigrants: "Folks, they're taking over, and if we don't open our eyes, it's going to be over with."

Over the course of the 2020 campaign, Tuberville sidestepped interviews with all but the most worshipful media outlets, avoided debates, and enjoyed a highly coveted endorsement. Trump backed Tuberville, helping him dust Sessions in the Republican primary . . . even if the president appeared to be a bit confused about some of the nuances of football in the state of Alabama.

"Really successful coach," Trump said of Tuberville, on one phone call with reporters. "Beat Alabama, like, six in a row, but we won't even mention that. As he said . . . because of that, maybe we got 'em Lou Saban . . . And he's great, Lou Saban, what a great job he's done."

Perhaps Trump just mistook Nick Saban for the itinerant (and long dead) college/NFL coach Lou Saban. (No relation.) Or perhaps he was referring to Saban's middle name, which, in fact, is Lou. But Trump could've endorsed Tuberville with a "Roll Eagle" or "War Tide," and it wouldn't have mattered. Tuberville annihilated Jones by more than 20 percentage points, taking more than 60 percent of the vote and cruising easily to a six-year term.

However, Tuberville's benefactor hadn't fared quite so well in the presidential election, winning Alabama but losing both the popular and the electoral vote. So Tuberville spent much of the time immediately after the election repeating Trump's false the-election-was-rigged rhetoric.

"It's impossible, it is impossible what happened," Tuberville told a rally in Georgia in December 2020. "But we're going to get that all corrected." With Tuberville in his pocket, Trump felt his prospects of overturning the election results in January had a much better chance.

On Tuberville's first full day in office, January 6, 2021, the US Capitol was beset by angry Trump supports who believed the election was stolen. Trump attempted to call Tuberville, but reached Senator Mike Lee (R-Utah) by mistake. Lee handed his cell phone to Tuberville as they hunkered down in the Senate chamber. "I know we've got problems," Tuberville later said Trump told him. "Protect yourself."

Tuberville and a dozen other senators gathered in a storage closet to wait out the assault, barricaded in by furniture. Several senators later recalled talking about the mood of the country, and how political division had descended into violence. "I didn't really listen to them," Tuberville later told the *Washington Post*.

The carnage outside the barricaded door did nothing to sway his thoughts on the election. He formally objected to certifying electoral college votes from Arizona and Pennsylvania for president-elect Joe Biden. "I wasn't voting for me, I was voting for the people of Alabama," Tuberville said. "President Trump has an 80% approval there. I told them, 'I'm going to vote how you want me to vote.'"

Once it became clear that Trump would not, in fact, retake the presidency by either force or fiat, it was time for Tuberville to get down to the actual business of governing. He struggled in his first few months on the job, misidentifying the three branches of government ("the House, the Senate, and the executive") and declaring, incorrectly, that Democrats were seeking reparations for descendants of slaves in order to give criminals free government funds.

But he also acted in some decidedly non-Trump-like ways. He hired staff from outside the MAGA universe. He created PSAs urging people to get vaccinated against COVID. He described Trump's inflammatory language in the hours before the Capitol riots as a "mistake."

Tuberville's days stalking the sidelines at Auburn brought him some weight that few freshman senators could match. His fellow lawmakers referred to him as "Coach," and even hardened Washington lifers cozied up to hear tales of the times he beat Bama. In his office, he displayed a painting of his undefeated 2004 Auburn team and a "Coach Tuberville" bobblehead Arby's made for its Alabama restaurants in 2002. He has even attempted on occasion to build bridges with his Democratic colleagues, preferring to use a genial approach rather than a flamethrower.

But Tuberville, a member of the Armed Services Committee, also flexed his muscle in unexpected—and, for some, infuriating—ways in 2023. Using an informal system of "holds" first employed in Congress in the 1950s, he blocked military promotions for 10 months in an attempt to protest the Pentagon's policy on abortion. So stringent, unyielding, and militarily debilitating was his one-man protest that even members of his own party began to grow weary. Several Senate Republicans indicated they would move to sidestep the blockade, so he eventually relented.

Tuberville again ended up in the national spotlight during the 2024 election, when Democratic vice presidential candidate—and former high school defensive coordinator—Tim Walz declared in August that he wanted to be "the anti–Tommy Tuberville, to show that football coaches are not the dumbest people." On X, formerly Twitter, Tuberville called Walz "an embarrassment to the Coaching profession," and hurled back several debatable criticisms of his military and gubernatorial record.

Tuberville will be in office until January 2027, at the very least. It's quite a path, from the Auburn sideline to the Senate, but to Republican-voting citizens of the state of Alabama, it makes perfect sense.

IRON BOWL 2023: GRAVEDIGGER

You never want to get too comfortable slotting Alabama at the top of college football's rankings, given the growth of programs like Oregon, Texas, Georgia, and Ohio State, but you never want to take them for granted, either. By 2023, Saban was the classic never-bet-the-mortgage-against-him competitor. Like prime Tiger Woods or Tom Brady, you could never quite be sure Alabama was dead and buried in a season until around, oh, the next April.

The Tide entered the 2023 regular season in their usual position—preseason top 3—but that was more out of force of habit than anything else. The truth was, no one quite knew what Saban had in this particular Tide team. The heart and soul of both the offense and defense had gone No. 1 and No. 3 in the NFL draft—Heisman Trophy–winning quarterback Bryce Young and linebacker Will Anderson, respectively—and the 2023 squad needed an identity, fast.

They gained that identity the second week of the season: target. Texas, coached by former Saban assistant Steve Sarkisian and always on the verge of being "back," finally made good on their promise by handing Alabama a 10-point defeat in Tuscaloosa that was worse than the scoreboard indicated. As the Longhorns celebrated and the school's most famous alum, Matthew McConaughey, circled the turf at Bryant-Denny giving the two-finger Horns Up salute to the entire stadium, Saban and Tide fans had to wrestle with the fact that this year's team might just be … ordinary.

But losing in September provides true clarity for a championship contender. With a vicious conference schedule—Ole Miss, Tennessee, LSU, and the ever-dangerous Auburn lurked—and an inevitable date with Georgia in the SEC championship game standing in their path to the College Football Playoff, the Tide spent the rest of the season in a do-or-die, must-win sprint.

And *sprint* was indeed the right word: powerful and speedy quarterback Jalen Milroe began to cut loose earlier and earlier in plays, giving his legs a chance to disrupt the defense when his arm couldn't. He threw moon-shot passes that could knock satellites out of orbit, he squirmed loose from defenders' clutches each weekend, he improved seemingly every single week.

Inspired by Milroe, fueled by disrespect and disdain, Alabama embarked on a ramshackle revenge tour, knocking off Tennessee and LSU to avenge losses to both in 2022. And then came the Iron Bowl.

Meanwhile, Auburn in 2023 was trying to find its footing, with Hugh Freeze working hard to establish focus and direction in the wake of the disastrous Bryan Harsin experiment. Auburn had a brutal conference schedule, and proceeded to face-plant as soon as it began. The Tigers lost their first four SEC games—A&M, Georgia, LSU, Ole Miss—and even lost the customary pre–Iron Bowl cupcake game, a 31–10 humiliation at the hands of New Mexico State. In any other era, at any other time, that would have, one, cost Freeze his job and, two, rendered the Iron Bowl a walkover. But the Iron Bowl has a way of flipping expectations, and the 2023 season was no different.

"You can't ever take Auburn lightly," says *Auburn Observer* writer

Justin Ferguson, "because you never know when they're going to just screw up your whole season."

At Jordan-Hare on November 25, Auburn didn't just hang with Alabama—the Tigers held a four-point lead with only 43 seconds remaining in the game. After a wrenching series of failed attempts at the Auburn end zone, Alabama was down to their final play, goal-to-go from 31 yards out. Fourth and 31. Saban and his coaches knew which play to call, and Milroe and wide receiver Isaiah Bond knew exactly how to execute it.

"Gravedigger," they called the play, because, as Bond said simply, it's designed to "put them in the grave." He grinned when he said it, knowing he was revealing a secret from the vault.

Saban always concealed the cold heart of an assassin beneath the detached demeanor of an accountant. He didn't want to give his opponents any kind of leverage at any moment, and that extended to letting them know he cared enough to name a play after their destruction. Nick Saban would happily dance on graves, but only after the mourners had left, and only out of earshot of the media and Alabama fans.

Bond and Milroe had practiced the play all autumn. It required a combination of strength, speed, touch, positioning, and luck, and on this night, they had all five. Milroe took the snap, the Tide sent five receivers into the end zone, and Milroe let the ball fly.

Just as he crossed over the painted *A* on the left side of the end zone, Bond turned, and there it was, a football dropping down from the sky and straight toward his hands. *It's mine*, he thought, and then there was no more time for thinking—it was time to just catch the damn ball. He did, and then Bond—Isaiah Bond—posed with his fingers held in the shape of a pistol, a debonair wide receiver who left Auburn deeply shaken, not stirred. Game saved; championship hopes kept alive.

"If you're in this long enough, sometimes it goes against you in the last play of the game," Saban said. "Sometimes you're fortunate, and it goes for you."

"I think in many ways, Nick Saban destroyed the [Iron Bowl] rivalry," says Paul Finebaum. "And I say that because it used to be literally life or death about who won the game. But after Saban ran off the streak [12–5 in the Iron Bowl], he almost made it more acceptable [for Auburn] to lose." Not only that, Finebaum adds, but Alabama winning a national championship in the 2017 season after losing the Iron Bowl has taken a bit of the importance off the rivalry.

The occasional Kick Six or Camback aside, Alabama maintained its Iron Bowl supremacy . . . and clearly would for as long as Nick Saban reigned.

In the weeks after the 2023 Iron Bowl, Gravedigger didn't quite take hold as a spiritual touchstone the way that, say, Kick Six did—largely because what happened next would overshadow it. After the win against Auburn, Alabama ground Georgia down in the 2023 SEC championship, ending the Dawgs' 29-game win streak and, not incidentally, denying Georgia a chance at three straight national championships. The Tide then managed to make the four-team College Football Playoff even with one loss, which came as quite a shock to undefeated Florida State.

The last four-team playoff before the bracket expanded to 12 carried drama in all its slots. Alabama drew top-seeded Michigan, which had persevered through two separate scandals to go undefeated on the season. In the other bracket, Texas, still riding high on its September Tuscaloosa victory, faced Washington, which would become very important to Alabama's future in just a few weeks.

The Tide's New Year's Day Rose Bowl matchup against Michigan was as maddening as it was anticlimactic. Alabama took a seven-point lead with less than five minutes remaining in the fourth quarter, but then the 2023 team's worst traits—inconsistency and sloppiness—reared their ugly heads. The defense allowed the Wolverines to march down the field and tie the game with a late 75-yard drive.

In overtime, Michigan took the ball first, and running back Blake Corum stomped into the end zone in two plays. There would be no more fourth-down miracles for Alabama. An errant snap forced Milroe into an awkward—and failed—attempt at a touchdown on fourth and goal. Alabama's season was over just short of the goal line, just short of the championship game.

But there was still optimism in Tuscaloosa. They'd conquered Auburn with Gravedigger. Milroe would be back, and so would the young line and secondary. And then there was Saban. You could never count out a team with Saban on the sidelines, after all.

2023 IRON BOWL

Final Score: Alabama 27, Auburn 24

Chapter 38

THE END OF AN ERA

Nick Saban sat in his office in the Mal Moore Athletic Facility, his mind whirling. The Tuscaloosa afternoon was bright and sunny in the first days of 2024. Less than 48 hours earlier, Michigan had defeated Washington to claim the national championship. Saban knew exactly what that felt like, knew what it meant to win a national title, knew just how close he'd been to defeating Michigan barely a week ago.

The offseason at Alabama lasts about as long as it takes to walk from the last game's locker room to the team bus. The rest of college football was exhaling, but Saban had been hard at work. He was on an SEC head coaches' call earlier that morning. He'd interviewed a couple candidates for open coaching positions on his staff. But he could put it off no longer. It was time to face his team.

He had called a mandatory team meeting, and they were gathering right now, All-Americans and walk-ons, future NFL draft picks and former high school stars. They were all waiting, as they always did, to hear from him.

It was 3:55 p.m. on January 10, 2024. And Saban still wasn't sure what he was going to say to his team.

When, at last, he walked into the meeting with his team, he kept his words brief and to the point. He was retiring, he told his players, citing both his age and health issues as the driving forces behind the decision.

The news hit social media like a shock wave, radiating outward from Tuscaloosa across the country at the speed of Twitter. *Saban? Retiring? No way! No freaking way!*

Saban walked out the door of Bryant-Denny Stadium after 17 years helming the Tide, winning six national championships at Alabama—same as the Bear—along with 10 SEC West titles and nine SEC championships. When he left in 2023, his teams had appeared in eight of the 10 College Football Playoff games played to that date, reaching the title game six times and winning three.

But all those years had taken their toll, and Saban understood, like Bryant, that Father Time would always win in the end.

"I actually thought in hiring coaches, recruiting players, that my age started to become a little bit of an issue," Saban would later concede to ESPN's Rece Davis. "People wanted assurances that I would be here for three years, five years, whatever. And that got harder and harder for me to be honest about."

In retrospect, there were tells. Players reported that Saban was more willing to joke around with them in 2023 than ever before. Before the Kentucky game, Saban—not usually a prop comic—set mousetraps around the locker room to warn players against a "trap game." (Alabama won, 49–21.) And after the revenge win against Tennessee at Bryant-Denny, Saban—not a smoker—popped an unlit cigar in his mouth and gnawed on it before jogging around the field to thank fans up close for their support.

Maybe the most obvious tell came before his last SEC championship game. Saban found Kirby Smart, his long-ago defensive coordinator, at midfield of Mercedes-Benz Stadium in Atlanta just before kickoff. "One thing you were right about," he laughed, "I'm too old for this."

"Try to enjoy it, man," Smart replied. "You're a hell of a coach."

It was reminiscent of Bear Bryant meeting his protégé Pat Dye on the field at the Iron Bowl in 1981 on the day he captured his 315th victory. Like Bryant, Saban got the win, and like Dye, Smart would stick around and impart the master's wisdom to the next generation of college football players and coaches.

Outside Bryant-Denny Stadium, in paved semicircles alongside the Walk of Champions, stand five enormous bronze statues, one for each of the coaches who has won a national championship at Alabama. Bear Bryant is there—at 10 feet tall, he's cast at life-size to many Alabama fans—and so is Wallace Wade, and Frank Thomas, and even Gene Stallings, the old Bryant disciple who brought home a title of his own in 1992.

Closest to the stadium stands the statue of Nick Saban, hunched forward, his hands caught in mid-clap and the hands of his massive watch set to 1:00 p.m. It was here, in the hours after Saban announced his retirement, that Alabama fans gathered by the hundreds, to pay homage to a man who had utterly changed the direction of this college, this town, this entire state.

They brought offerings to lay at the statue's enormous sensible bronze sneakers. Boxes of Little Debbie snack cakes, a six-pack of Bud Light, balloons, flowers . . . tributes to Saban on a night when nothing seemed quite real. (A couple of gleeful Auburn students even rolled Toomer's Oaks—much to the disappointment of some Auburn alumni—but most Tigers fans seemed as shell-shocked as the rest of the country.)

Social media outside Tuscaloosa scoffed at the fuss. After all, Saban hadn't died or anything. Indeed, he would be back at the athletic facility the very next day to help with the transition to a new coach—but that wasn't the point. Tide fans were connecting with him for the last time as an Alabama coach, for the last time as the stern, guiding father figure who always eventually brought home the victory. Someone started up a chant—"Anyone but Dabo!"—to let Clemson fans know what Bama fans thought of their coach.

In the days ahead, Saban's retirement would upend half a dozen campuses and put the entire sport on tilt. But on this night, there was only the chill of the unknown, the light on the statue, and Little Debbie snack cakes. So many snack cakes.

No space in the courtyard currently exists for any future coach who carries on the winning tradition at Alabama. But if and when that day comes, they'll make room. Count on it.

There's an old showbiz line that's equally applicable to football coaches: never be the guy to follow The Guy. Replacing a legend is an impossible task; better to let someone else take the fall, and then step in to pick up the pieces. The men that had followed Bear Bryant, for instance, had been a nearly unbroken stream of underachievers and misfits, devoured alive by the Alabama faithful. It was a long, cold 25 years between Bryant's retirement and Saban's arrival, and in all that time, Alabama managed "just" that one Stallings-led national championship.

Before the shock waves had stopped rippling through the college football world, the questions began: Who would replace Saban? Who *could* replace Saban? Who would want to face the challenge of placating a fan base that thinks three losses constitutes unforgivable failure?

Several coaches theatrically removed their names from consideration. Oregon's Dan Lanning and Texas's Steve Sarkisian both appeared in social media hype videos that featured some variant of "I'm not going anywhere!" Names like Clemson's Dabo Swinney, Florida State's Mike Norvell, and Ole Miss's Lane Kiffin swirled across frantic message boards and text chains. (The savvier among them turned rumored interest into lucrative contract extensions.)

Alabama athletic director Greg Byrne pleaded for calm, asking both fans and his own players to give him 72 hours to close a deal. Byrne wasn't just facing the eagerness of impatient fans; he was trying to make the hiring decision in a new era of player empowerment.

After decades of treating players like indentured servants, unable to leave their universities without penalty no matter what their coaches did, the NCAA had seen the light and given players the same freedom of movement as, basically, any other college student. In the case of a coach resigning, his players had a 30-day window to jump into the transfer portal and join another team. Put another way, it was open season on Alabama players, and the poaching started quickly.

Isaiah Bond, the hero of the Iron Bowl only weeks before, bolted to Texas. Caleb Downs, the team's leading tackler, headed for Ohio State. Kadyn Proctor, a budding offensive line stalwart, joined Iowa for about three months before recommitting to Alabama.

All the while, Alabama fans could only watch with growing horror and grim realization. The cold, hard reality of college football had come for the Tide, at long last, and not a single soul outside Tuscaloosa felt even a twinge of sympathy.

But Alabama had advantages that other schools did not, starting with a war chest well into the nine figures. When cost is no object, anyone is fair game... even a coach who, just days before, was leading his team in the national championship game. While fans were throwing around names and checking flight data—one rumor held that Lanning and his family were in Tuscaloosa when in fact they were at home watching *The Bourne Identity*—Greg Byrne was in the Pacific Northwest with another target in mind.

Kalen DeBoer didn't have the outsize profile of most college coaches, in part because he didn't come across as either a raving lunatic or a Marvel-movie supervillain. He simply knew ball, knew it in his bones, and he'd used that knowledge to amass an astounding record of success. He'd won three NAIA championships, then worked his way up through the college football ecosystem to a head coaching job at the University of Washington. Born and raised in South Dakota, the closest he ever got to the SEC was a flyover.

But DeBoer brought both sideline savvy and industry-wide respect to the table, a combination that was enticing indeed. He wouldn't be Saban 2.0, but then he wouldn't completely spin the program into a clown show, either.

"People have already asked, 'Why would you go to Alabama? Why?'" DeBoer said at his introductory press conference, with Saban and Miss Terry in attendance. "When it comes to tradition and the history of the program, it's second to none. When I look at places that I want to be, it's about winning championships. That's an expectation that I cannot wait and accept as a privilege to try to uphold, winning SEC championships, winning national championships."

As a reminder of just how powerful Saban was, his retirement set off a cascade of job openings as DeBoer handpicked his new staff, plucking head coaches from programs around the country to serve as his assistants. In a matter of hours, Washington went from national title contender to team adrift. In the end, more than 400 coaching jobs would be affected by Saban's retirement, according to an analysis by *The Athletic*. Five more major programs would need a new head coach, and eventually 38 Power 5 schools, 25 Group of 5 schools, 34 other programs, more than a dozen high schools, and 10 NFL programs would be touched in some way by Saban's decision to walk away from Alabama with gas still in the tank.

"Saban's retirement is larger than any other in the history of American team sports because no other sport's modern identity was developed by a single man," Steven Godfrey wrote in *The Washington Post* in 2024. "College football, as we accept and understand its value today, is the result of Nick Saban. Since Saban first overhauled a woefully mismanaged LSU program into a title-winning power in the early 2000s, nothing occurred in this sport that wasn't an attempt to replicate or respond to him."

There will never be another one like Saban, and the T. rex–sized footprint he left on college football's soul certainly won't fill anytime soon.

EPILOGUE

Nick Saban stood on Alabama's Walk of Champions—a path he himself had walked, and enhanced with half a dozen championship plaques, many times over—and looked out over the crowd gathered before Bryant-Denny Stadium. On this warm late-summer day in September 2024, they were here to honor him on a momentous occasion—the field at Bryant-Denny Stadium was being named after him—and he almost, *almost* betrayed a little emotion.

"It's a great honor to have a field named after the legacy that we have been able to create here," Saban said, "but I want this legacy to represent every player who played and worked hard, every coach who helped those players develop, our administration who set a foundation for us to be successful by providing all the resources we needed . . . to have the best program in the country."

He thanked the Tide fans, who finally managed to tie down the famously wandering coach. "You made us part of this community 18 years ago," he said. "It's our home now." And he noted that he won't be going anywhere, but will be keeping watch on the version of the Alabama Crimson Tide that runs onto Nick Saban Field at Bryant-Denny Stadium from here on out.

Given how the 2024 season turned out, you could forgive Alabama for wanting to remain on the friendly grass of Saban Field at Bryant-Denny

Stadium for the foreseeable future. Alabama won all of its games at home, but lost four—four!—games on the road, an execrable record that cost the Tide a slot in the initial 12-team College Football Playoff. For a team that had played in six *championship* games over seven years, 2024 marked a sudden, catastrophic fall from the mountaintop.

Most humiliating of all: in 2024, both Alabama and Auburn lost to, of all teams, Vanderbilt. *Vanderbilt!* The school that Saban had beaten by an aggregate score of 172–13 over the course of his Alabama tenure jumped out to a 13–0 lead over the 2024 Tide *in the first quarter.* Vanderbilt's hyperkinetic quarterback, a six-foot-tall transfer from New Mexico State named Diego Pavia, put Alabama on skates, then did the same thing to Auburn four weeks later, effectively claiming the state of Alabama for himself.

Pavia thus became the symbol of how the transfer portal and NIL have completely upended the old order in college football. Legacy powers like Alabama are realizing just how hard they'll need to work just to keep pace. Programs like Auburn are understanding how much recruiting work and NIL funding it will take every year, for every player, just to climb into the playoff conversation.

The sea changes of 2024 made it clear why Saban walked away when he did. As the 2024 season ended and Saban grew more comfortable in his role as commentator, his critiques of the sport arrived with an extra edge.

"The whole idea of what college used to be is not there anymore," Saban told *The Pivot* podcast early in 2025. "It used to be you went to college to develop value for your future. Now people are going to college to see how much money they can make. And I'm not saying there's anything wrong with that, but you change the whole dynamic of the importance of getting an education, making good decisions and choices about what you do and what you don't do to create value for your future. You changed that whole dynamic."

He wasn't wrong. He also wasn't taking into account the fact that institutions and coaches, himself included, amassed massive revenue and power while denying players their fair share. But his relief at being out of the world of perpetual recruiting was obvious every time he appeared on camera.

His replacement wasn't quite so relaxed. DeBoer posted a 9–4 record in his first year on the Alabama sidelines, still better than Saban's first year on the job in Tuscaloosa... but also the worst record since that debut season. His counterpart over in Auburn, Hugh Freeze, struggled for a second straight year, finishing the season underwater at 5–7.

There's hope for both schools; each ranked in the top 10 in recruiting for the 2025 season, and both still carry war chests and reputations large enough to lure waves of talent onto their rosters. But they're both facing an unexpected and uncharted new reality. Even Bear Bryant and Shug Jordan themselves would have needed time to adjust; Kalen DeBoer and Hugh Freeze don't have that time.

"Whichever coach can get himself established, and in some ways, established over the other guy, that's going to be the battle," Dan Wetzel says, and offers a stark warning for both schools and the conference they've so often dominated.

"I don't expect over the next five years, the SEC to have nearly the might and the institutional strength that they had before, because as much as they care, they just don't have the money that everybody's paying. These Big Ten schools have got a *lot* of money."

Both Auburn and Alabama have spent decades reckoning with their civil rights–era failures and shortcomings, and both are doing what they can to atone for those grim days. One block down from Bryant-Denny Stadium stands Autherine Lucy Hall, home of the university's College of Education, renamed in 2022 in honor of Autherine Lucy, the first Black student to enroll at Alabama.

In 2021, Auburn honored Dr. Harold Franklin, its first Black student, constructing a plaza with a memorial marker near the library where Franklin bravely walked through a phalanx of Alabama law enforcement to register for classes in 1964. The scars of the past remain on both Alabama and Auburn, but the schools now display them as an opportunity to learn from history, rather than hiding them in a vain attempt to conceal sins.

Like Alabama with Saban Field, Auburn is sanctifying its own illustrious football past. In 2021, just before that year's iteration of the Deep South's Oldest Rivalry, the university unveiled statues of three of its greatest legends—Cliff Hare, Shug Jordan, and Pat Dye—which now stand at the south end of Jordan-Hare Stadium. (The field was named after Dye in 2005.) Auburn fans lining up for the Tiger Walk pass these statues, and those of Bo Jackson and Cam Newton, every Auburn home game.

You can find reminders of other Auburn and Alabama football legends around the state, if you look hard enough. Bo Jackson runs an annual Bo Bikes Bama charity cycling event. Cam Newton, now retired from the NFL, is a full-on multimedia celebrity, dispensing truth and hot takes all over social media. Many other former Tiger and Tide stars have retired to The Plains or T-Town, living out their days remembering their heroic moments. You'll spot them around town having coffee, maybe swinging a golf club or a deal, and always in the stands every fall Sunday, remembering the all-too-brief days when they strode that brilliant green turf in front of them like kings.

Children in Alabama grow up imagining themselves playing in the Iron Bowl. A select few get to live out their dreams. For the rest, it's an annual ritual that's as crucial as a birthday, as meaningful as Thanksgiving, and—when the scoreboard tilts your way—as joyful as Christmas morning.

"I went to four or five different pro teams, and I never went into a locker room that I didn't have players come up to me, from Iowa or Michigan or wherever, and say, 'Tell us what it's like to play in that game,'" recalls Auburn's Terry Henley, voicing the thoughts of every player, Tide or Tiger, who's ever played in the Iron Bowl. "And I tell them it's just the greatest feeling in the world. It's an honor, and to this day I treasure that moment every time I think about it."

The roof has collapsed on Shug Jordan's childhood home in Selma. All around it, tiny ranch houses are being bulldozed and replaced by brand-new, 21st-century abodes. There's no historic marker at the home of the man who brought so much joy to so many on The Plains, but there ought to be.

Paul "Bear" Bryant rests at Elmwood Cemetery in Birmingham, just a few miles from Legion Field. He and Mary Harmon lie on a gentle slope, beneath a small granite marker. You can find them by following the crimson stripe on the road that runs through the cemetery. Look for the gravesite that always has a bottle of Coca-Cola beside it.

Not far from Bryant's grave, at the intersection of Clairmont Avenue and 32nd Street South, there's a marker commemorating the first Auburn–Alabama football game. The field is long gone now, buried beneath office parks and apartments and restaurants.

The 5,000 delirious fans who cheered on their patchwork teams that day in 1893 couldn't have imagined they were at the dawn of one of the greatest rivalries in American sports history. But the feverish spark they lit that day still burns, and the reckless and joyous spirit that first animated that game still persists in the heart of every Tide and Tigers fan, every Saturday in autumn.

Roll Tide. War Eagle. Forever.

BIBLIOGRAPHY

The author wishes to express his appreciation for the invaluable archives of the *Birmingham News, Montgomery Advertiser, Tuscaloosa News, Auburn Plainsman, Crimson and White, War Eagle Reader, Auburn Observer,* and newspapers.com. In addition, the archives of Yahoo Sports, ESPN, CBS Sports, Fox Sports, the *New York Times*/The Athletic, College Football Reference, and Winsipedia were useful in verifying facts and scores.

Additional specific sources referenced or cited in the text are noted below.

CHAPTER 1: THE WEST POINT OF THE SOUTH

Bridges, Edwin C. *Alabama: The Making of An American State.* University of Alabama Press, 2016.

Doyle, Andrew. "Turning the Tide: College Football and Southern Progressivism," *Southern Cultures* 3, no. 3, 1997.

Flynt, J. Wayne. *Alabama in the Twentieth Century.* University of Alabama Press, 2006.

Groom, Winston. *The Crimson Tide: The Official Illustrated History of Alabama Football.* University of Alabama Press, 2010.

Hamilton, Virginia Van der Veer. *Alabama: A History.* W. W. Norton & Co., 1977.

Lidz, Franz. "The Greatest Story Ever Told," *Sports Illustrated*, August 30, 2006.

Mellown, Robert. "Tuscaloosa During the Civil War," Tuscaloosa County Preservation Society, historictuscaloosa.org.

Reinhardt, Kellee, ed. *Tuscaloosa: Centennial Progress, Millennial Hopes.* Community Communications, 2000.

Tullos, Allen. *Alabama Getaway: The Political Imaginary and the Heart of Dixie.* University of Georgia Press, 2011.

Weinreb, Michael. "As mass plays threatened the future of football in the 1890s, a fluke pass showed a path forward," The Athletic, February 25, 2019, www.nytimes.com/athletic/834435/2019/02/25/1890s-college-football-flying-wedge-mass-momentum-plays-safety-forward-pass/.

CHAPTER 2: BORN FIGHTING

Cox, Dwayne. *The Village on the Plain: Auburn University, 1856–2006.* University of Alabama Press, 2016.

Flynt, *Alabama in the Twentieth Century.*

Hinton, Ed. "Heisman to Shug," *Sports Illustrated*, December 17, 1993.

Hollis, Dan W. *Auburn Football: The Complete History, 1892–1987.* Auburn Sports Publications, 1988.

Tullos, *Alabama Getaway.*

IRON BOWL 1893: THE FIRST ONE

Griffin, John Chandler. *Auburn vs. Alabama: Gridiron Grudge Since 1893.* Hill Street Press, 2001.

Hollis, *Auburn Football.*

Moore, Daniel. *Iron Bowl Gold.* New Life Art, 2005.

CHAPTER 3: SEPARATE WAYS

"Alabama's Eleven Humbles Old Penn," *New York Times*, November 5, 1922, www.nytimes.com/1922/11/05/archives/alabamas-eleven-humbles-old-penn-southerners-underestimated-gain.html.

Bridges, *Alabama.*

Chatham, Josh. "99 years ago, Alabama arrived under Xen C. Scott,"

SBNation.com, May 28, 2021, www.rollbamaroll.com/2021/5/28/22458420/countdown-to-kickoff-99-years-ago-alabama-arrived-under-xen-c-scott.

Cox, *The Village on the Plain*.

Doyle, Andrew. "'Fighting Whiskey and Immorality' at Auburn: The Politics of Southern Football, 1919–1927," *Southern Cultures* 10, no. 3, 2004.

Flynt, *Alabama in the Twentieth Century*.

"Football's Origin at Alabama," RollTide.com, https://rolltide.com/sports/2016/6/10/trads-football-origin-html.

Glier, Ray. *How the SEC Became Goliath: The Making of College Football's Most Dominant Conference*. Howard Books, 2012.

Groom, *The Crimson Tide*.

Hinton, "Heisman to Shug."

Hollis, *Auburn Football*.

Kazek, Kelly. *Hidden History of Auburn*. The History Press, 2011.

Lidz, "The Greatest Story Ever Told."

"Pennsy Beaten by Alabama in Spirited Game," *Brooklyn Daily Eagle*, November 5, 1922.

Schexnayder, C. J. "Alabama vs. Penn State: A Historical Retrospective," SBNation.com, September 7, 2010, https://www.rollbamaroll.com/2010/9/7/1593198/alabama-vs-penn-state-a-historical.

Tullos, *Alabama Getaway*.

CHAPTER 4: THE GAME THAT CHANGED SOUTHERN FOOTBALL

"Alabama Practice Curtailed by Heat," *Elmira Star-Gazette*, December 29, 1925.

Anderson, Dave. "A Bunch of Farmers Upset Football Tradition," *Sports Illustrated*, December 24, 1962, https://vault.si.com/vault/1962/12/24/a-bunch-of-farmers-upset-football-tradition.

Doyle, "Turning the Tide."

Flynt, *Alabama in the Twentieth Century*.

Gold, Eli. *Crimson Nation: The Shaping of the South's Most Dominant Football Team.* Rutledge Hill Press, 2005.
Groom, *The Crimson Tide.*
Roberts, Diane. *Tribal: College Football and the Secret Heart of America.* HarperCollins, 2015.
Schexnayder, C. J. "The 1926 Rose Bowl: Alabama vs. Washington," SBNation.com, December 21, 2009, www.rollbamaroll.com/2009/12/21/1197952/the-1926-rose-bowl-alabama-vs.
"Stanford Eleven Adjudged Best: Navy Ranks Second Under Dickinson System of Rating Teams," *Morning Post*, December 17, 1926.
Stephenson, Creg. "Remember the Rose Bowl: Alabama's 1926 win vs. Washington put Southern football on national map," AL.com, December 28, 2016, www.al.com/sports/2016/12/remember_the_rose_bowl_1926_wi.html.
Tracy, Marc. "Alabama Win in 1926 Rose Bowl Put Southern Stamp on College Football," *New York Times*, December 27, 2016, www.nytimes.com/2016/12/27/sports/ncaafootball/alabama-crimson-tide-washington-huskies.html#:~:text=The%201926%20game%20put%20Southern,claim%20to%2016%20national%20titles.

TIMEOUT: "YEA ALABAMA" AND "RAMMER JAMMER"
Al-Khateeb, Zac. "Alabama's 'Rammer Jammer' chant, explained," *The Sporting News*, March 24, 2023, www.sportingnews.com/us/ncaa-basketball/news/alabama-rammer-jammer-chant-lyrics-tide-fight-song/xdhlx1tcuffk6uasokgevjpu.
Butler-Burnette, Cathy. "How a Football Championship Gave Us 'Yea, Alabama!'" University of Alabama News Center, September 4, 2018, news.ua.edu/2018/09/how-a-football-championship-gave-us-yea-alabama/.

CHAPTER 5: THE TIDE RISES
Gold, *Crimson Nation.*
Groom, *The Crimson Tide.*

Hicks, Tommy. *Game of My Life: Alabama Crimson Tide*. Sports Publishing, 2006.
Kirk, Jason. "Based on the standards of Alabama's silliest title claim, these 78 teams can award themselves national championships," SBNation.com, May 11, 2018, www.sbnation.com/college-football/2018/5/11/17339224/alabama-1941-national-championship-claim.
Marshall, Benny. *All-Time Greatest Alabama Sports Stories*. University of Alabama Press, 2003.

IRON BOWL 1948: A RESUMPTION OF HOSTILITIES
Griffin, *Auburn vs. Alabama*.
Keith, Walling. "Will the Tide wash The Plains, or The Plains stem the Tide? Let us know when you decide," *Birmingham News*, December 2, 1948.
Walsh, Christopher. "The Iron Feud Between Alabama and Auburn," SI.com, May 5, 2020.

CHAPTER 6: IT'S PRONOUNCED "JERR-DN"
Benn, Alvin. "No coach helped gain bigger victory than 'Shug' Jordan," *Montgomery Advertiser*, June 6, 2014, www.montgomeryadvertiser.com/story/news/local/alabama/2014/06/06/coach-helped-gain-bigger-victory-shug-jordan/10052535/.
Beck, Alfred M., Abe Bortz, Charles W. Lynch et al. *The Corps of Engineers: The War Against Germany*. University Press of the Pacific, 2002.
Cox, *The Village on the Plain*.
Donnell, Rich. *Shug: The Life and Times of Auburn's Ralph 'Shug' Jordan*. Owl Bay Publishers, 1993.
"I Don't Know If I'd Gotten Any Further," YouTube, posted by War Eagle Reader, June 6, 2012, www.youtube.com/watch?v=7LrGmFrZhxg.
Jernigan, Mike. "API Plays Roll in the Statewide Cotton Crisis," Auburn Agriculture Department, 2023.

"September 25: Shug Jordan," Today in Auburn History, undated, https://auburnhistorytoday.com/people/shug-jordan/.

CHAPTER 7: A STARR FALLS ON T-TOWN

Bridges, *Alabama*.

Clark, E. Culpepper. *The Schoolhouse Door: Segregation's Last Stand at the University of Alabama*. Oxford University Press, 1993.

Dunnavant, Keith. *America's Quarterback: Bart Starr*. Thomas Dunne Books, 2011.

Goodman, Joseph. "NFL legend Bart Starr was victim of 'brutal' secret Alabama hazing," AL.com, February 29, 2016, www.al.com/sports/2016/02/nfl_legend_bart_starr_was_vict.html.

Groom, *The Crimson Tide*.

King Jr., Dr. Martin Luther. "When Peace Becomes Obnoxious," The Martin Luther King Jr. Research and Education Institute at Stanford University, March 18, 1956.

Lidz, "The Greatest Story Ever Told."

Raines, Howell. *My Soul Is Rested: The Story of the Civil Rights Movement in the Deep South*. G. P. Putnam's Sons, 1977.

CHAPTER 8: A GRAVEYARD FOR COACHES

Associated Press. "College Football in for Big Reorganization with Return of One-Platoon System," January 15, 1953, www.newspapers.com/article/progress-bulletin-college-football-in-fo/138404527/.

Donnell, *Shug*.

Hinton, "Heisman to Shug."

Hollis, *Auburn Football*.

Housel, David. *Saturdays to Remember*. The Village Press, 1973.

CHAPTER 9: THE MAN FROM MORO BOTTOM

"A Guide to the USS *Uruguay*," Online Archive of California, undated, https://oac.cdlib.org/findaid/ark:/13030/c8dv1kns/entire_text/.

Anderson, Lars. *Chasing the Bear: How Bear Bryant and Nick Saban Made Alabama the Greatest College Football Program of All Time*. Grand Central Publishing, 2019.

Barra, Allen. *The Last Coach: A Life of Paul "Bear" Bryant*. W. W. Norton & Company, 2005.

"Bear Bryant in Chapel Hill," University of North Carolina University Libraries, undated, https://blogs.lib.unc.edu/ncm/2009/10/21/bear-bryant-in-chapel-hill/.

Bryant, Paul and John Underwood. *Bear: The Hard Life and Good Times of Alabama's Coach Bryant*. Triumph Books, 2007.

Dunnavant, Keith. *Coach: The Life of Paul "Bear" Bryant*. Simon & Schuster, 1996.

Dent, Jim. *The Junction Boys: How Ten Days in Hell with Bear Bryant Forged a Championship Team*. Thomas Dunne Books, 1999.

Herskowitz, Mickey. *The Legend of Bear Bryant*. McGraw-Hill, 1987.

Keefe, Carey Henry. *A Tide of Dreams: The Untold Backstory of Coaches Paul "Bear" Bryant, Carney Laslie and Frank Moseley*. Koehler Books, 2022.

Kurchak, Sarah. "The Twisted and Terrible History of Men Fighting Bears," Vice, October 17, 2017, www.vice.com/en/article/the-twisted-and-terrible-history-of-men-fighting-bears/.

Whitley, David. "Hutson was first modern receiver," ESPN.com, undated, www.espn.com/sportscentury/features/00014269.html.

CHAPTER 10: CHAMPION TIGERS

Associated Press. "API Facing Probation for Three Years," *Montgomery Advertiser*, May 3, 1956, www.newspapers.com/image/262370085/

Donnell, *Shug*.

Hinton, "Heisman to Shug."

Hollis, *Auburn Football*.

Housel, *Saturdays to Remember*.

Inabinett, Mark. "Auburn's 1957 national-championship team: 'There wasn't a lot of hoopla about it,'" AL.com, November 23, 2017, www

.al.com/sports/2017/11/auburns_1957_national-champion.html#:~:text=%22There%20wasn't%20a%20lot,Associated%20Press%20national%2Dchampionship%20trophy.

Phillips, Bob. "Additional 3-Year Probation by NCAA Stuns Auburn," *Birmingham Post-Herald*, April 22, 1958, www.newspapers.com/image/792945439/.

Van Hoose, Alf. "Football (SEC brand) makes news any time," *Birmingham News*, January 30, 1956, www.newspapers.com/image/574543529.

CHAPTER 11: FAITH REWARDED

"A Bear at 'Bama," *Time*, November 17, 1961, https://time.com/archive/6872417/sport-a-bear-at-bama/.

Anderson, *Chasing the Bear*.

Barra, *The Last Coach*.

Bryant, *Bear*.

Bone, Andrew J. with Tom VanHaaren. *The Road to Bama: Incredible Twists and Improbable Turns Along the Crimson Tide Recruiting Trail*. Triumph Books, 2020.

Dunnavant, *Coach*.

Gold, *Crimson Nation*.

Groom, *The Crimson Tide*.

Herskowitz, *The Legend of Bear Bryant*.

Hicks, *Game of My Life*.

Keefe, *A Tide of Dreams*.

Stoddard, Tom. *Turnaround: Paul "Bear" Bryant's First Year at Alabama*. Black Belt Press, 2000.

CHAPTER 12: WHEN THE CHAIN HIT THE PIPE

Anderson, Dave. "When the Chain Hit the Pipe," *New York Times*, December 28, 1982 www.nytimes.com/1982/12/28/sports/sports-of-the-times-when-the-chain-hit-the-pipe.html.

Anderson, Lars. *Chasing the Bear*.

Barra, *The Last Coach*.
Brown, Tim. "A Tall Tale About Coaching Towers," Football Archaeology, January 29, 2023, www.footballarchaeology.com/p/todays-tidbit-tall-tales-about-coaching.
Bryant, *Bear*.
Dunnavant, *Coach*.
Gold, *Crimson Nation*.
Groom, *The Crimson Tide*.
Herskowitz, *The Legend of Bear Bryant*.
Keefe, *A Tide of Dreams*.
Matthews, Jay. "Memories of Coach Bryant—Free to Practice." Bear Bryant Memories, June 5, 2013, https://bearbryantmemories.wordpress.com/2013/06/05/memories-of-coach-bryant-free-to-practice/.

TIMEOUT: WAR EAGLE

"Auburn's War Eagle," Auburn University, https://auburn.edu/about/traditions/wareagle.php.
Kazek, *Hidden History of Auburn*.
Liles, Lindsey. "College Football Decoded: War Eagle," *Garden & Gun*, September 24, 2021, https://gardenandgun.com/articles/college-football-decoded-war-eagle/.

CHAPTER 13: THE TARNISHED CROWN

Anderson, *Chasing the Bear*.
Barra, *The Last Coach*.
Bisher, Furman. *Furman Bisher: Face to Face*. Sports Publishing, 2005.
Bryant, *Bear*.
Dunnavant, *Coach*.
Emerson, Seth. "A college football mystery: What did Georgia's Wally Butts say to Alabama's Bear Bryant?" The Athletic, October 23, 2023, www.nytimes.com/athletic/4974333/2023/10/23/georgia-alabama-football-saturday-evening-post/.

Gaillard, Frye. *Cradle of Freedom: Alabama and the Movement That Changed America*. University of Alabama Press, 2004.
Groom, *The Crimson Tide*.
Herskowitz, *The Legend of Bear Bryant*.
Johnson, Richard. "This National Championship isn't even the most controversial game in Alabama–Georgia history," SBNation.com, January 6, 2018, www.sbnation.com/college-football/2018/1/6/16848592/georgia-alabama-1962-bear-bryant-george-burnett-saturday-evening-posst#:~:text=This%20National%20Championship%20isn't,a%20game%2C%20leading%20to%20lawsuits.
Kirby, James. *Fumble: Bear Bryant, Wally Butts, and the Great College Football Scandal*. Harcourt, 1986.
Roberts, Randy and Ed Krzemienski. *Rising Tide: Bear Bryant, Joe Namath & Dixie's Last Quarter*. Twelve, 2013.
Stephenson, Greg. "Darwin Holt, Alabama linebacker involved in infamous 1961 play vs. Georgia Tech, has died," AL.com, September 9, 2023, https://www.al.com/alabamafootball/2023/09/darwin-holt-alabama-linebacker-involved-in-controversial-1961-play-vs-georgia-tech-dies-at-84.html#:~:text=Darwin%20Holt%2C%20an%20undersized%20but,Alabama's%20A%2DClub%20Alumni%20Association.
Tilford, Earl H. *Turning the Tide: The University of Alabama in the 1960s*. University of Alabama Press, 2014.

CHAPTER 14: BIGGER THAN BALL

Anderson, *Chasing the Bear*.
Barra, *The Last Coach*.
Branch, Taylor. *Parting the Waters: America in the King Years, 1954–63*. Touchstone, 1988.
Bryant, *Bear*.
Clark, *The Schoolhouse Door*.

Dunnavant, *Coach*.

Gaillard, *Cradle of Freedom*.

Herskowitz, *The Legend of Bear Bryant*.

Namath, Joe with Sean Mortimer and Don Yaeger. *All the Way: My Life in Four Quarters*. Little, Brown and Company, 2019.

Raines, *My Soul Is Rested*.

Roberts, *Rising Tide*.

Tilford, *Turning the Tide*.

Tullos, *Alabama Getaway*.

CHAPTER 15: FALLING OFF THE PACE

Deusner, Stephen. *Where the Devil Don't Stay: Traveling the South with the Drive-By Truckers*. University of Texas Press, 2021.

Donnell, *Shug*.

Gossom, Thom. *Walk-On: My Reluctant Journey to Integration at Auburn University*. Best Gurl, Inc., 2008.

Hollis, *Auburn Football*.

Kazek, *Hidden History of Auburn*.

Kirshner, Alex. "Why Alabama–Auburn is called the Iron Bowl," SBNation.com, November 25, 2017, www.sbnation.com/college-football/2017/11/25/16694498/iron-bowl-name-why-history-meaning-auburn-alabama.

Scarbinsky, Kevin. "Walk-ons played a role, too, in integrating Alabama and Auburn football," AL.com, October 20, 2013, www.al.com/sports/2013/10/walk-ons_played_a_role_in_inte.html.

Schmidt, William E. "Auburn, Target of Court Wrath, Says It's Trying to Desegregate," *New York Times*, December 13, 1985, www.nytimes.com/1985/12/13/us/auburn-target-of-court-wrath-says-it-s-trying-to-desegregate.html.

White, Marjorie Longenecker. *The Birmingham District: An Industrial History and Guide*. Birmingham Historical Society, 1981.

CHAPTER 16: THE BEAR VS. THE SNAKE
Anderson, *Chasing the Bear.*
Barra, *The Last Coach.*
Bryant, *Bear.*
Dunnavant, *Coach.*
Dunnavant, Keith. *The Missing Ring: How Bear Bryant and the 1966 Alabama Crimson Tide Were Denied College Football's Most Elusive Prize.* St. Martin's Press, 2006.
Freeman, Mike. *Snake: The Legendary Life of Ken Stabler.* HarperCollins, 2016.
Gold, *Crimson Nation.*
Groom, *The Crimson Tide.*
Herskowitz, *The Legend of Bear Bryant.*
Hicks, *Game of My Life.*
Raines, *My Soul Is Rested.*
Stabler, Ken and Berry Stainback. *Snake: The Candid Autobiography of Football's Most Outrageous Renegade.* Doubleday, 1986.
Tilford, *Turning the Tide.*

IRON BOWL 1967: THE RUN IN THE MUD
Bryan, Jimmy. "Tide Played Close for One Big Play," *Birmingham News*, December 3, 1967, reprinted in *Iron Bowl Gold.*
Moore, *Iron Bowl Gold.*
Spotswood, James. "Gallant Tide, Tigers Vie in Stinging Rain," *Birmingham News*, December 3, 1967, reprinted in *Iron Bowl Gold.*

CHAPTER 17: THE PAT SULLIVAN EXPERIENCE
Donnell, *Shug.*
Gold, *Crimson Nation.*
Henderson, Jeremy. "Auburn won the huge 1971 Georgia game because 'the night before kind of ticked everybody off,'" War Eagle Reader, June 30, 2021, www.thewareaglereader.com/2021/06/auburn

BIBLIOGRAPHY

-won-the-huge-1971-georgia-game-because-the-night-before-kind-of-ticked-everybody-off/.

Hollis, *Auburn Football*.

Housel, David. *From the Desk of David Housel: A Collection of Auburn Stories*. Auburn Network, 1991.

Housel, *Saturdays to Remember*.

Murphy, Mark. *Game of My Life: Memorable Stories of Tigers Football*. Sports Publishing, 2007.

Putnam, Pat. "He's Down. He's Out. He's Back. He Wins!" *Sports Illustrated*, October 4, 1971, https://vault.si.com/vault/1971/10/04/hes-down-hes-out-hes-back-he-wins.

"Rare footage of Auburn's Shug Jordan and Pat Sullivan," YouTube, posted by War Eagle Reader, July 23, 2019.

Reed, William F. "Best in the Land," *Sports Illustrated*, December 17, 1993, https://vault.si.com/vault/1993/12/17/best-in-the-land-pat-sullivan-and-bo-jackson-each-won-a-heisman-trophy-but-by-vastly-different-routes.

TIMEOUT: ROLL TIDE

Clements, Caroline Sanders. "College Football Decoded: Roll Tide," *Garden & Gun*, September 2, 2021, https://gardenandgun.com/articles/college-football-decoded-roll-tide/.

CHAPTER 18: THE GAME THAT CHANGED THE SOUTH

Anderson, *Chasing the Bear*.

Barra, *The Last Coach*.

Busbee, Jay. "Documentary tells story of Alabama's most important game," Yahoo Sports, November 15, 2013, www.yahoo.com/news/documentary-tells-story-of-alabama-s-most-important-game-235339493.html.

Bryant, *Bear*.

Dunnavant, *Coach*.

Herskowitz, *The Legend of Bear Bryant*.

Gold, *Crimson Nation.*
Groom, *The Crimson Tide.*
Weinreb, Michael. *Season of Saturdays: A History of College Football in 14 Games.* Scribner, 2014.
Yaeger, Don. *Turning of the Tide: How One Game Changed the South.* Center Street, 2006.

IRON BOWL 1972: PUNT BAMA PUNT
Griffin, *Auburn vs. Alabama.*
Hollis, *Auburn Football.*
Moore, *Iron Bowl Gold.*

CHAPTER 19: THE LAST DAYS OF SHUG JORDAN
Bolton, Clyde. "'Couldn't Buy a Base Hit,' Says Wishing-It-Wasn't-Over Jordan," *Birmingham News,* November 30, 1975, reprinted in *Iron Bowl Gold.*
Donnell, *Shug.*
Hollis, *Auburn Football.*
Housel, *From the Desk of David Housel.*
"Shug's Final Auburn Football Review," YouTube, posted by Dreamweaver Productions, November 29, 2018.

CHAPTER 20: THE SIGN OF THE WOLF
Dye, Pat and John Logue. *In the Arena.* River City Publishers, 1992.
Hollis, *Auburn Football.*
Housel, *From the Desk of David Housel.*
Plexico, Van Allen and John Ringer. *We Believed: A Lifetime of Auburn Football, Volume I: 1975-1998.* White Rocket Books, 2021.

IRON BOWL 1981: THE RECORD
Brown, Scott and Will Collier. *The Uncivil War: Alabama vs. Auburn, 1981–1994.* Rutledge Hill Press, 1995.
Dye, *In the Arena.*

Griffin, *Auburn vs. Alabama*.
Herskowitz, *The Legend of Bear Bryant*.
Moore, *Iron Bowl Gold*.

CHAPTER 21: BO
Dye, *In the Arena*.
Hollis, *Auburn Football*.
Housel, *From the Desk of David Housel*.
Jackson, Bo and Dick Schaap. *Bo Knows Bo*. Doubleday, 1990.
Pearlman, Jeff. *The Last Folk Hero: The Life and Myth of Bo Jackson*. Mariner Books, 2022.
Plexico, *We Believed*.
Reed, "Best in the Land."

IRON BOWL 1982: BO OVER THE TOP
Brown, *The Uncivil War*.
Griffin, *Auburn vs. Alabama*.
Jackson, *Bo Knows Bo*.
Moore, *Iron Bowl Gold*.
Pearlman, *The Last Folk Hero*.

CHAPTER 22: THE LORD GETS HIS FOOTBALL COACH
Anderson, *Chasing the Bear*.
Barra, *The Last Coach*.
Brown, *The Uncivil War*.
Bryant, *Bear*.
Dent, *The Junction Boys*.
Dunnavant, *Coach*.
Gaillard, *Cradle of Freedom*.
Gold, *Crimson Nation*.
Groom, *The Crimson Tide*.
Herskowitz, *The Legend of Bear Bryant*.

Hicks, *Game of My Life*.

Rawls Jr., Wendell. "Bryant's Doctor Tells of Lengthy Illness," *The New York Times*, January 28, 1983, www.nytimes.com/1983/01/28/sports/bryant-s-doctor-tells-of-lengthy-illness.html.

CHAPTER 23: BO DOES ANYTHING, NOT EVERYTHING

Brown, *The Uncivil War*.

Dye, *In the Arena*.

Herndon, Mike. "Wrong Way Bo: Remembering the 1984 Iron Bowl 30 years later," AL.com, November 28, 2014, www.al.com/sports/2014/11/wrong_way_bo_remembering_the_1.html.

Hollis, *Auburn Football*.

Housel, *From the Desk of David Housel*.

Jackson, *Bo Knows Bo*.

Kausler Jr., Don. "Jackson's First TD Run Starts Storm Warnings," *Birmingham News*, December 4, 1983, reprinted in *Iron Bowl Gold*.

Norman, Geoffrey. *Alabama Showdown: The Football Rivalry Between Auburn and Alabama*. Henry Holt & Company, 1986.

Pearlman, *The Last Folk Hero*.

Plexico, *We Believed*.

Sims, Neal. ". . . But It Couldn't Happen Without Bo," *Birmingham News*, December 4, 1983, reprinted in *Iron Bowl Gold*.

Underwood, John. "The Dawning of a New Day," *Sports Illustrated*, September 19, 1983, https://vault.si.com/vault/1983/09/19/the-dawning-of-a-new-day.

IRON BOWL 1985: THE KICK

Brown, *The Uncivil War*.

Carlton, Bob. "Remembering the 1985 Iron Bowl: The Drive that led to The Kick by Van Tiffin," AL.com, November 22, 2016, www.al.com/sports/2016/11/remembering_the_1985_iron_bowl.html.

Dye, *In the Arena.*
Griffin, *Auburn vs. Alabama.*
Hicks, *Game of My Life.*
Moore, *Iron Bowl Gold.*

IRON BOWL 1989: THE FINAL BRICK
Brown, *The Uncivil War.*
Dye, *In the Arena.*
Griffin, *Auburn vs. Alabama.*
Plexico, Van Allen and John Ringer. *First Time Ever: The Untold Story of How Auburn First Brought Undefeated Alabama to Jordan-Hare Stadium—and Beat Them.* White Rocket Books, 2023.

CHAPTER 24: THE SUN SETS ON THE PLAINS
Blinder, Alan. "Pat Dye, Football Coach Who Elevated Auburn, Dies at 80," *New York Times*, June 1, 2020, www.nytimes.com/2020/06/01/obituaries/pat-dye-auburn.html.
Brown, *The Uncivil War.*
Dye, *In the Arena.*
Flynt, *Alabama in the Twentieth Century.*
Looney, Douglas S. "Triumphs and Trials," *Sports Illustrated*, December 17, 1993.
Plexico, *We Believed.*
Rhoden, William C. "A Hard-to-Forget Voice from Auburn's Haunted Past," *New York Times*, November 24, 2010, www.nytimes.com/2010/11/25/sports/ncaafootball/25rhoden.html.

TIMEOUT: AUBIE, BIG AL, AND THE BANDS
Tilford, *Turning the Tide.*
Woodbery, Evan. *100 Things Auburn Fans Should Know & Do Before They Die.* Triumph Books, 2009.

CHAPTER 25: JUNCTION BOY MADE GOOD

Bone, *The Road to Bama*.

Brown, *The Uncivil War*.

Gold, *Crimson Nation*.

Heim, Mark. "Gene Stallings reminisces about 1996 Iron Bowl, reason for resigning," AL.com, November 23, 2018, www.al.com/alabamafootball/2018/11/gene-stallings-reminisces-about-1996-iron-bowl-reason-for-resigning.html.

Hersch, Hank. "The Turning of the Tide," *Sports Illustrated*, November 15, 1993, https://vault.si.com/vault/1993/11/15/the-turning-of-the-tide-in-the-seasons-biggest-upset-lsu-ended-alabamas-31-game-unbeaten-streak-and-saved-coach-curley-hallmans-job.

Hicks, *Game of My Life*.

Jenkins, Sally. "Red Storm Rising," *Sports Illustrated*, December 7, 1992, https://vault.si.com/vault/1992/12/07/red-storm-rising-alabamas-impenetrable-defense-has-the-crimson-tide-on-the-brink-of-a-title.

Karle, Rick. "At 89, Gene Stallings finds every new day is 'the best present I could get,'" AL.com, May 5, 2024, www.al.com/news/2024/05/at-89-gene-stallings-finds-every-new-day-is-the-best-present-i-could-get.html.

Looney, Douglas S. "Loaded for Bear," *Sports Illustrated*, September 24, 1990.

Murphy, Austin. "The End of the Run," *Sports Illustrated*, January 11, 1993, https://vault.si.com/vault/1993/01/11/the-end-of-the-run-with-a-resounding-34-13-sugar-bowl-victory-alabama-put-a-stop-to-miamis-29-game-winning-streak-and-won-its-first-national-title-since-1979.

Stallings, Gene and Sally Cook. *Another Season: A Coach's Story of Raising an Exceptional Son*. Little, Brown and Company, 1997.

CHAPTER 26: THE MOST AUBURN YEAR EVER

Associated Press. "De-clawed Tigers: Terry Bowden resigns as Auburn coach after 1–5 start," CNN/SI, October 24, 1998, https://web

.archive.org/web/20081028114314/http://sportsillustrated.cnn.com/football/college/news/1998/10/23/bowden_out/.

Blaudschun, Mark. "Bowden's Resignation a Slimy Affair," *The Oklahoman*, October 31, 1998, www.oklahoman.com/story/news/1998/10/31/bowdens-resignation-a-slimy-affair/62264011007/.

Burton, Larry. "Auburn's Bobby Lowder: Coming to the End of the Road," Bleacher Report, June 14, 2009, https://bleacherreport.com/articles/198840-auburns-bobby-lowder-is-coming-to-the-end-of-the-road-at-auburn.

Ernsberger Jr., Richard. *Bragging Rights: A Season Inside the SEC, College Football's Toughest Conference*. M. Evans & Co., 2000.

Finebaum, Paul. "When Bobby Lowder exits the Auburn scene, his presence will be sorely missed," AL.com, June 2, 2009, www.al.com/press-register-sports/2009/06/finebaum_when_bobby_lowde_exi.html.

Fish, Mike. "A Tiger of a trustee," ESPN.com, January 9, 2006, www.espn.com/college-football/news/story?id=2285976.

Griffith, Noah. "When silence spoke 'Lowder' than words," *Auburn Plainsman*, November 16, 2023, www.theplainsman.com/article/2023/11/when-silence-spoke-lowder-than-words.

Guest, Larry. "Sources Say Oliver Was In On Ouster," *Orlando Sentinel*, November 11, 1998, www.orlandosentinel.com/1998/11/11/sources-say-oliver-was-in-on-ouster/.

Looney, Douglas S. "Born to Coach," *Sports Illustrated*, December 17, 1993.

Marshall, Phillip. "1998: The real story of Terry Bowden's departure from Auburn," 24/7 Sports, April 23, 2020, https://247sports.com/college/auburn/article/1998-the-real-story-of-terry-bowdens-departure-from-auburn-146388451/.

O'Keefe, Brian. "The man behind 2009's biggest bank bust," CNN, October 12, 2009, https://web.archive.org/web/20091015085855/http://money.cnn.com/2009/10/09/news/companies/bobby_lowder.fortune/index.htm.

Plexico, *We Believed*.
Price, S. L. "Bear Tracks," *Sports Illustrated*, November 21, 1994, https://vault.si.com/vault/1994/11/21/bear-tracks-sure-auburn-is-unbeaten-but-terry-bowdens-sights-are-set-on-bigger-game.

CHAPTER 27: THE TIDE RECEDES

Ernsberger Jr., *Bragging Rights*.
Layden, Tim. "The Loneliest Losers," *Sports Illustrated*, November 18, 2002, https://vault.si.com/vault/2002/11/18/the-loneliest-losers-fifteen-years-ago-smus-powerhouse-football-program-was-obliterated-by-a-pay-for-play-scandal-and-the-ncaas-first-quotdeath-penaltyquot-since-then-20-other-college-programs-including-alabama-football-this-y.
Maisel, Ivan and Kelly Whiteside. *A War in Dixie: Alabama v. Auburn*. HarperCollins, 2001.
Moore, Mal with Steve Townsend. "Crimson Heart: Let Me Tell You My Story." Crimson Heart Foundation, 2016.
Orr, Rodney and Ray Melick. *Bigger Than Bama: The Inside Story of Tider Insider*. Crest Publishers, 2023.
Price, S. L. "Trading Places," *Sports Illustrated*, August 14, 1995.
St. John, Warren. *Rammer Jammer Yellow Hammer: A Road Trip into the Heart of Fan Mania*. Crown Publishing Group, 2004.

CHAPTER 28: THE MAN FROM MONONGAH

Anderson, *Chasing the Bear*.
Anderson, Lars. *The Storm and the Tide: Tragedy, Hope and Triumph in Tuscaloosa*. Sports Illustrated Books, 2014.
Burke, Monte. *Saban: The Making of a Coach*. Simon & Schuster, 2015.
Glier, *How the SEC Became Goliath*.
Moore, *Crimson Heart*.
Saban, Nick and Brian Curtis. *How Good Do You Want to Be? A Champion's Tips on How to Lead and Succeed at Work and in Life*. Ballantine Books, 2005.

Talty, John. *The Leadership Secrets of Nick Saban: How Alabama's Coach Became the Greatest Ever.* Matt Holt, 2022.

CHAPTER 29: FEAR THE THUMB

Bramblett, Rod. *Touchdown Auburn: Carrying on the Tradition of the Auburn Tigers.* Triumph Books, 2016.

Dellenger, Ross. "Ole Miss won't forget old 'pine box' comments," *Decatur Daily*, October 26, 2007, https://web.archive.org/web/20201120154531/http://archive.decaturdaily.com/decaturdaily/sports/columns/071026c.shtml.

Maisel, Ivan. "Rebuilding Auburn needs a lot more than just a touch-up," *Sports Illustrated*, May 17, 1999, https://vault.si.com/vault/1999/05/17/260793/inside-college-football.

Wise, Mike. "Auburn Knows, and Shows, Who's No. 1," *Washington Post*, January 3, 2005.

CHAPTER 30: THE PROCESS COMES TO TUSCALOOSA

Anderson, *Chasing the Bear.*
Anderson, *The Storm and the Tide.*
Bone, *The Road to Bama.*
Burke, *Saban.*
Finebaum, Paul and Gene Wojciechowski. *My Conference Can Beat Your Conference.* HarperCollins, 2014.
Gibbs, Chad. *God and Football: Faith and Fanaticism in the SEC.* Zondervan, 2010.
Glier, *How the SEC Became Goliath.*
Godfrey, Steven. "Nick Saban's shoes won't be easy to fill by Kalen DeBoer or anyone else," *Washington Post*, January 12, 2024, www.washingtonpost.com/sports/2024/01/12/nick-saban-replacements/.
Gold, Eli and M. B. Roberts. *From Peanuts to the Pressbox: Insider Sports Stories from a Life Behind the Mic.* Thomas Nelson, 2009.
Moore, *Crimson Heart.*

Orr, *Bigger Than Bama*.
Saban, *How Good Do You Want to Be?*
Talty, *The Leadership Secrets of Nick Saban*.

CHAPTER 31: SUPERMAN ON THE PLAINS
Bramblett, *Touchdown Auburn!*
Evans, Thayer. "Source: Newton left Florida after cheating scandal," Fox Sports, November 9, 2010.
Guilbeau, Glenn. "A New Cam," Gannett News Service, October 20, 2010, www.newspapers.com/image/220223547.
Newton, Cam. "My Path to the Pros," *ESPN the Magazine*, June 20, 2013, www.espn.com/nfl/story/_/id/9407038/carolina-panthers-cam-newton-path-pros-espn-magazine.
Shpigel, Ben. "At Blinn College, Cam Newton Plotted a Return to the Big Time," *New York Times*, February 2, 2016, www.nytimes.com/2016/02/03/sports/football/super-bowl-50-cam-newton-blinn-college.html.
Zimmermann, Luke. "Cam Newton's forgotten year in junior college," SBNation.com, February 1, 2016.

IRON BOWL 2010: THE CAMBACK
Bramblett, *Touchdown Auburn!*
Rovell, Darren. "Auburn fires Gene Chizik," ESPN.com, November 25, 2012.

CHAPTER 32: THE MAN WITH TOO MUCH BAMA IN HIM
Benedict, Jeff and Armen Keteyian. *The System: The Glory and Scandal of Big-Time College Football*. Doubleday, 2013.
Burke, *Saban*.
Finebaum. *My Conference Can Beat Your Conference*.
McGee, Ryan. "Breakfast with the Bears," ESPN.com, September 19, 2018, www.espn.com/college-football/story/_/id/24730931/the-annual

-paul-william-bear-bryant-namesake-reunion-brings-700-named-alabama-crimson-tide-coach.

Roberts, *Tribal*.

Staples, Andy. "Toomer's Corner poisoning should enrage all college football fans," *Sports Illustrated*, February 17, 2011, www.si.com/more-sports/2011/02/17/toomers-corner.

Sutton, Joe. "Harvey Updyke, who poisoned landmark oak trees at Auburn University, dies at 71." CNN, August 1, 2020, www.cnn.com/2020/07/31/us/harvey-updyke-alabama-auburn-dead/index.html#:~:text=Harvey%20Updyke%2C%20the%20Alabama%20man,He%20was%2071.

Thompson, Wright. "The life and times of Harvey Updyke," ESPN.com, May 22, 2011, www.espn.com/college-football/columns/story?id=6575499.

Tomlinson, Tommy. "Something went very wrong at Toomer's Corner," Sports Illustrated, August 15, 2011, https://vault.si.com/vault/2011/08/15/something-went-very-wrong-at-toomers-corner.

CHAPTER 33: TRAGEDY AND HEALING

Anderson, *The Storm and the Tide*.
Burke, *Saban*.
Cross, Kim. *What Stands in a Storm: A True Story of Love and Resilience in the Worst Superstorm in History*. Atria Books, 2015.
Finebaum, *My Conference Can Beat Your Conference*.
Southern, Ed. *Fight Songs: A Story of Love and Sports in a Complicated South*. Blair, 2021.

IRON BOWL 2013: KICK SIX

Bramblett, *Touchdown Auburn!*
Burke, *Saban*.
Finebaum. *My Conference Can Beat Your Conference*.
Henderson, Jeremy. "Iron Bowl Earthquake? 'Suspicious' seismic activity

registered Saturday as far away as Huntsville correlates to Auburn's last-second Iron Bowl touchdown," War Eagle Reader, December 4, 2013, www.thewareaglereader.com/2013/12/iron-bowl-earthquake-suspicious-seismic-activity-registered-saturday-as-far-away-as-huntsville-correlates-to-auburns-last-second-touchdown-to-beat-alabama/.

Weinreb, *Season of Saturdays.*

CHAPTER 34: JOYLESS MURDERBALL

Bone, *The Road to Bama.*

Burke, *Saban.*

Orr, *Bigger Than Bama.*

Sherman, Rodger. "How Alabama exploited a tiny Clemson error into the Championship's deciding play," SBNation.com, January 14, 2016, www.sbnation.com/college-football/2016/1/14/10763992/alabama-onside-kick-clemson-national-championship-nick-saban-adam-griffiths-marlon-humphrey.

Suttles, Aaron. *The Program: Alabama, A Curated History of the Crimson Tide.* Triumph Books, 2022.

Talty, *The Leadership Secrets of Nick Saban.*

CHAPTER 35: CHAOS ON THE PLAINS

Bonagura, Kyle. "Review shows Hugh Freeze made at least 12 calls to escort services," ESPN.com, August 22, 2017, www.espn.com/college-football/story/_/id/20421042/review-shows-former-ole-miss-coach-hugh-freeze-made-least-12-calls-escort-services.

Dodd, Dennis. "Bo Nix's unforeseen revival at Oregon is proving doubters wrong, awakening Ducks' playoff hopes," CBS Sports, October 28, 2022, www.cbssports.com/college-football/news/bo-nixs-unforeseen-revival-at-oregon-is-proving-doubters-wrong-awakening-ducks-playoff-hopes/.

Green, Tom. "Auburn hires Hugh Freeze as next head coach." AL.com,

November 29, 2022, www.al.com/auburnfootball/2022/11/auburn-expected-to-hire-hugh-freeze-as-next-head-coach.html.

Green, Tom. "Gus Malzahn fired as Auburn head coach," AL.com, December 13, 2020, www.al.com/auburnfootball/2020/12/gus-malzahn-fired-as-auburn-head-coach.html.

Hall, Spencer. "The Auburn Tigers, college football's greatest ruiner of things," Banner Society, November 13, 2019, www.bannersociety.com/2019/11/13/20926835/auburn-football-upsets-collapses-and-other-mayhem.

Low, Chris and Pete Thamel. "Auburn Tigers football coach Bryan Harsin 'not planning on going anywhere' amid program's volatility," ESPN.com, February 4, 2022, www.espn.com/college-football/story/_/id/33216111/auburn-tigers-football-coach-bryan-harsin-not-planning-going-anywhere-amid-program-volatility.

Peter, Josh. "Who is Hugh Freeze? Conflicting views of former Ole Miss coach emerge," *USA Today*, July 29, 2017, www.usatoday.com/story/sports/ncaaf/2017/07/29/who-hugh-freeze-conflicting-views-former-ole-miss-coach-emerge/522705001/.

Scarborough, Alex. "Auburn Tigers fire football coach Gus Malzahn after eight seasons," ESPN.com, December 13, 2020, www.espn.com/college-football/story/_/id/30512340/auburn-tigers-fire-coach-gus-malzahn-eight-seasons.

Scarborough, Alex. "Why Lane Kiffin chose to stay at Ole Miss and didn't take the Auburn job," ESPN.com, April 11, 2023, www.espn.com/college-football/story/_/id/36091229/why-lane-kiffin-chose-stay-ole-miss-take-auburn-job.

Schlabach, Mark. "NCAA hits Ole Miss with additional year of bowl ban, scholarship restrictions," ESPN.com, December 1, 2017, www.espn.com/college-football/story/_/id/21629060/ole-miss-rebels-get-two-year-bowl-ban-scholarship-reductions-ncaa.

Waters, Jacob. "Auburn football players voice their opinions of Bryan Harsin on social media," *Auburn Plainsman*, February 4, 2022,

www.theplainsman.com/article/2022/02/auburn-football-players
-voice-their-opinions-of-bryan-harsin-on-social-media.

CHAPTER 36: MAKE BAMA GREAT AGAIN

Boren, Cindy. "Alabama mayor resigns after comments on Crimson Tide's Black Lives Matter video," *Washington Post*, June 30, 2020, www.washingtonpost.com/sports/2020/06/30/alabama-mayor-resigns-after-comments-crimson-tides-black-lives-matter-video/.

Collins, Kaitlan. "Trump repeatedly calls famed Alabama football coach by the wrong name on the eve of Senate race," CNN.com, July 14, 2020, www.cnn.com/2020/07/14/politics/trump-lou-saban-nick-saban-alabama-senate/index.html.

Goodman, Joseph. *We Want Bama: A Season of Hope and the Making of Nick Saban's Ultimate Team*. Grand Central Publishing, 2021.

Southern, *Fight Songs*.

Talty, *The Leadership Secrets of Nick Saban*.

Trump, Donald J. "Remarks by President Trump on Safely Reopening America's Schools." Trumpwhitehouse.archives.gov, July 7, 2020, https://trumpwhitehouse.archives.gov/briefings-statements/remarks-president-trump-safely-reopening-americas-schools/.

CHAPTER 37: SENATOR COACH TUBERVILLE

Heim, Mark. "Tommy Tuberville on Bobby Petrino, JetGate, pine box quote and leaving recruits at a restaurant," AL.com, May 23, 2019, www.al.com/auburnfootball/2019/05/tommy-tuberville-on-bobby-petrino-jetgate-pine-box-quote-and-leaving-recruits-at-a-restaurant.html.

Maisel, *A War in Dixie*.

Myerberg, Paul. "Tommy Tuberville left recruits at dinner to take Cincinnati job," *USA Today*, December 12, 2012, www.usatoday.com/story/gameon/2012/12/12/tommy-tuberville-texas-tech-cincinnati/1763615/.

Thornton, William. "'Anti–Tommy Tuberville' Tim Walz an embarrassment to coaching, Alabama senator says," AL.com, August 15, 2024, www.al.com/news/2024/08/anti-tommy-tuberville-tim-walz-an-embarrassment-to-coaching-alabama-senator-says.html.

IRON BOWL 2023: GRAVEDIGGER

Busbee, Jay. "Alabama spring football: The next Bryce Young hasn't emerged yet as Tide QBs struggle," Yahoo Sports, April 22, 2023, https://sports.yahoo.com/alabama-spring-football-the-next-bryce-young-hasnt-emerged-yet-as-tide-qbs-struggle-000223900.html.

Busbee, Jay. "Fourth-and-31! Alabama yanks miracle victory away from Auburn," Yahoo Sports, November 25, 2023, https://sports.yahoo.com/fourth-and-31-alabama-yanks-miracle-victory-away-from-auburn-000442305.html.

Dellenger, Ross. "With 'Gravedigger,' Isaiah Bond and Alabama deliver fourth-and-31 miracle that will live on forever in Iron Bowl lore," Yahoo Sports, November 25, 2023, https://sports.yahoo.com/with-gravedigger-isaiah-bond-and-alabama-deliver-fourth-and-31-miracle-that-will-live-on-forever-in-iron-bowl-lore-024621100.html.

Kelly, Nick. "Inside fourth-and-31: How Alabama football buried Auburn with 'Grave Digger,'" *Tuscaloosa News*, November 25, 2023.

Smith III, Kennington. "How Alabama beat Auburn on fourth-and-31: Add 'Gravedigger' to Iron Bowl lore," The Athletic, November 25, 2023, www.nytimes.com/athletic/5089285/2023/11/25/alabama-auburn-iron-bowl-jalen-milroe-gravedigger/.

CHAPTER 38: THE END OF AN ERA

Davis, Rece. "Exclusive Nick Saban interview after his Alabama retirement," YouTube, January 11, 2024, www.youtube.com/watch?v=m-NTaEbfAtg.

Gibson, Mathey. "Everything Kalen DeBoer Said At Introductory Press

Conference," *Sports Illustrated*, January 13, 2024, www.si.com/college/alabama/football/live-updates-kalen-deboer-introductory-press-conference.

Godfrey, Steven. "Nick Saban's shoes won't be easy to fill by Kalen DeBoer or anyone else," *Washington Post*, January 12, 2024, www.washingtonpost.com/sports/2024/01/12/nick-saban-replacements/.

Kelly, Nick. "Nick Saban retired same day he interviewed Alabama football staff candidates," *Tuscaloosa News*, January 10, 2024, www.tuscaloosanews.com/story/sports/college/football/2024/01/10/nick-saban-retires-alabama-football-coach-hire-national-championship/72182493007/.

Olson, Max, Bruce Feldman and Sam Khan, "Exploring the Nick Saban butterfly effect, 400-plus job changes later: 'You better be prepared,'" The Athletic, July 12, 2024, www.nytimes.com/athletic/5631427/2024/07/12/nick-saban-retirement-kalen-deboer-jedd-fisch/.

Smith III, Kennington. "Why did Nick Saban retire? 'Age started to become an issue': Inside his final hours at Alabama." The Athletic, January 11, 2024, www.nytimes.com/athletic/5196874/2024/01/11/nick-saban-retirement-alabama-football/.

EPILOGUE

Florio, Mike. "Nick Saban would coach in the NFL before taking another college job," Pro Football Talk, January 21, 2025, www.nbcsports.com/nfl/profootballtalk/rumor-mill/news/nick-saban-would-coach-in-the-nfl-before-taking-another-college-job.

ADDITIONAL SOURCES CONSULTED

Browning, Al. *Crimson Coronation*. Five Points South, 1999.

Housel, David. *Auburn University Football Vault: The Story of the Auburn Tigers, 1892–2007*. Whitman Publishing, LLC, 2007.

Housel, David and Tommy Ford. *Alabama–Auburn Rivalry Vault*. Whitman Publishing, LLC, 2009.

Smith, Alex Martin. *SEC Football's Greatest Games: The Legendary Players, Last-Minute Prayers and Championship Moments.* Lyons Press, 2018.
Walsh, Christopher. *100 Things Crimson Tide Fans Should Know & Do Before They Die.* Triumph Books, 2008.
Watson, Taylor. *Inside the Vault: The Paul W. Bryant Collection.* Paul W. Bryant Museum, 2013.

PODCASTS:

College Football Enquirer, Bammers, Beat Everyone, Until Saturday, Andy & Ari On3, ESPN College Football, Marty & McGee, The Auburn Undercover, The Auburn Observer, Shutdown Fullcast, Locked On Bama, NFL Players: Second Acts.

DOCUMENTARIES:

Roses of Crimson, Roll Tide/War Eagle, A Football Life: Nick Saban, Training Days: Rolling with the Tide, Against the Tide, Three Days at Foster

ACKNOWLEDGMENTS

Put this on your bucket list, right now:
Attend football games at Jordan-Hare Stadium and Bryant-Denny Stadium.

Sip a Toomer's lemonade. Listen to the Million Dollar Band. Take in the Tiger Walk and the Walk of Champions. Revel in everything that Auburn University and the University of Alabama have to offer on a fall afternoon, because college football Saturdays are some of the most glorious days you'll spend on earth.

I'm grateful to have spent so much time at these fine institutions, and even more grateful that I got the opportunity to write about them and share so many of their stories with you. Now, a moment for some thank-yous.

First, thanks to my agent, Joseph Perry, who eclipsed the Aerosmith dude as the best Joe Perry when he secured this book deal back in 2023.

Big ol' thanks to the fine folks at BenBella Books, starting with Matt Holt. His cheerful, author-friendly approach to publishing has made this entire experience a true delight, and I'm proud to have this book in the Matt Holt stable. Lydia Choi's keen eye for edits, Brigid Pearson's exceptional work on the cover, Kim Broderick's work on the interior design, Kelly Brillhart's incisive eye for detail, Kerri Stebbins's marketing

ACKNOWLEDGMENTS

acumen . . . so many fine people are doing such great work at BenBella, and it's an honor to publish with them.

An enormous thank-you to all the people who spoke to me for this project, both on the record and on background. My only regret is that I didn't have 10 times the amount of space to tell all the stories I heard, and even that probably wouldn't have been enough. Deep gratitude to the many fine libraries in Alabama: the Alabama Department of Archives and History in Montgomery, the Special Collections Room at the Ralph Brown Draughon Library at Auburn University, the University of Alabama Libraries Special Collections, and the Paul W. Bryant Museum. Thanks also to the sports information staffs at both universities, including Kirk Sampson and the Auburn University team, and Aaron Jordan and the University of Alabama crew.

My appreciation is limitless for all the authors, journalists, artists, podcasters, and commentators who have tilled parts of this ground before me. There's a vast selection of magnificent books on every element of the Alabama and Auburn experiences; check this book's bibliography and dive down some rabbit holes next offseason.

I'm grateful to my bosses and colleagues at Yahoo Sports for all their support, advice, and good cheer. To my Augusta brothers, Jay Hart and Dan Wetzel, a million thanks. Next beer at the Rhinoceros is on me. Also a deep thanks to my many Yahoo colleagues, including Johnny Ludden, Al Toby, Cody Brunner, Joey Gulino, Henry Bushnell, Jeff Eisenberg, and Nick Bromberg, among so many others.

I'm fortunate enough to work in an industry where many of the smartest voices are also the finest people, and I thank them for their insight and perspective. People like Ryan McGee, Ross Dellenger, Pat Forde, Jason Kirk, Spencer Hall, Nubyjas Wilborn, Steven Godfrey, Tommy Tomlinson, John Talty, Paul Finebaum, and Lars Anderson are the very best, and you should consume their content wherever possible.

A few more shoutouts to deeply supportive friends, if I may. Thanks to early readers, including Jay Hart, Nick Bromberg, Rodney Orr, Justin Ferguson, and Beth Wyner, and to the Vogel armada for their Day One support

ACKNOWLEDGMENTS

and love. To Frank Schwab, Eric Edholm, Kevin Kaduk, and Pat Whiting: next, an SEC game. To the Low Rollers . . . now, finally, I can come play some Friday golf. To Team Africa: here's what I was working on by the Limpopo; somebody pour me a Castle Light. To Tom Madison, Lynn Lane, and Rachel Monroe, thanks for the right conversations at the right times. To John T. Edge, Wright Thompson, and Tim Horgan: let's ride.

A special tip of the ball cap to the beers of Virginia Beer Company, Pontoon Brewing, and Wild Leap Brewing, as well as the music of Sturgill Simpson, Zach Bryan, Jason Isbell, and the Drive-By Truckers, all of which powered me through this writing.

Finally, my family, my ever-solid rock. Love to my mother, the toughest and most cheerful person I know. Raise a glass of Wild Turkey to the memory of my dad, who was so excited to hear about this project, and with whom I shouted myself hoarse while we watched Kick Six unfold.

Love to my extended family: Stephen and Valynnda, Andrew and Ann, Brian and Shannon, and Stacey and Toby Summerfield. Love to all my nieces and nephews: Vendela, Cadence, Whitt, David, James, Cohen, Hadley, HG, and Watson, who have their marching orders for publicizing this book. Love to Toby the beagle, who cheerfully chilled in my office during much of the writing of this book and kept a watchful eye on me. And, of course, to Annarita McGovern, who saw the light and ditched the Virginia Cavaliers for the Crimson Tide.

So much love to my children, Riley and Logan, who supported me through the entire process. They're last here because they're first in my heart . . . and also because I know they're looking for their names, and I wanted to make them wait.

Finally, a tip of the red Solo cup to you, my readers. Hope you've enjoyed this ride as much as I have. Whether you're Roll Tide or War Eagle, you're a friend, and I thank you. See you at the tailgate!

Jay Busbee
January 2025

ABOUT THE AUTHOR

Jay Busbee is a senior writer for Yahoo Sports, where he's covered the Super Bowl, the Olympics, the World Series, the Masters, the Daytona 500, the Indy 500, the Kentucky Derby, and the national championships of college football and basketball. His work has been honored by the Associated Press Sports Editors and Best American Sports Writing. He's the author of *Earnhardt Nation*, a biography of NASCAR's Earnhardt family, and he writes a weekly Southern newsletter, *Flashlight & A Biscuit*. He lives in Atlanta with his family and worships at the church of SEC football.

Find Jay at @jaybusbee on all social media platforms, or online at www.jaybusbee.com.

KEEP THE TAILGATE GOING!

For more of Jay Busbee's writing on Auburn, Alabama, and all of Southern culture, including top-shelf music, remarkable food, and great books, check out Jay's weekly newsletter *Flashlight & A Biscuit.*, available free on Substack and at jaybusbee.com. From cultural commentary to beer and barbecue recommendations to playlists for your next road trip, it's a fine place to hang out. Join us!

Follow Jay on social media:

Instagram / Facebook / X / TikTok: @jaybusbee

Website: jaybusbee.com

Email: jay.busbee@yahoo.com